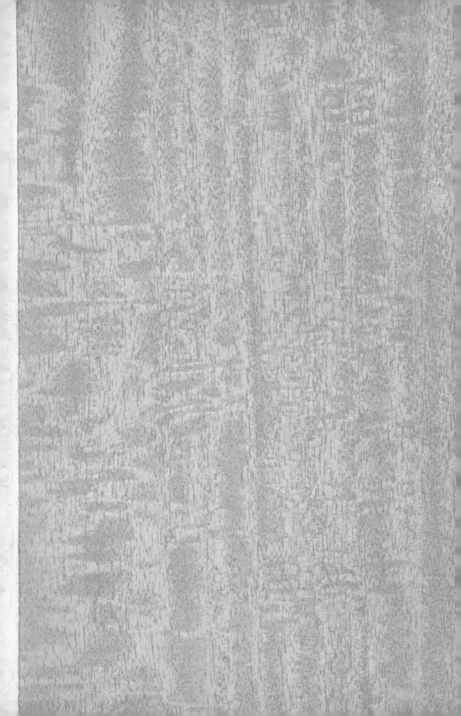

FAMOUS AMERICAN ATHLETES
OF TODAY

FAMOUS LEADERS SERIES

Each, one volume, cloth decorative, illustrated

BY CHARLES H. L. JOHNSTON $2.00

Famous Cavalry Leaders
Famous Indian Chiefs
Famous Scouts
Famous Privateersmen and Adventurers of the Sea
Famous Frontiersmen and Heroes of the Border
Famous Discoverers and Explorers of America
Famous Generals of the Great War

BY CHARLES H. L. JOHNSTON $2.50

Famous American Athletes of Today, First Series
Famous American Athletes of Today, Second Series

BY LEROY ATKINSON AND AUSTEN LAKE $2.50

Famous American Athletes of Today, Third Series

BY CHARLES H. L. JOHNSTON $2.50

Famous American Athletes of Today, Fourth Series

BY LEROY ATKINSON AND OTHER
SPORTS WRITERS $2.50

Famous American Athletes of Today, Fifth Series

BY HAROLD KAESE AND OTHER
SPORTS WRITERS $2.50

Famous American Athletes of Today, Sixth Series

BY JERRY NASON AND OTHER
SPORTS WRITERS $2.50

Famous American Athletes of Today, Seventh Series

BY EDWIN WILDMAN $2.00

Famous Leaders of Industry, First Series (Revised Edition)
Famous Leaders of Industry, Second Series

BY TRENTWELL M. WHITE $2.50

Famous Leaders of Industry, Third Series

BY HARRY IRVING SHUMWAY $2.50

Famous Leaders of Industry, Fourth Series

BY EDWIN WILDMAN $2.00

The Founders of America
The Builders of America
Famous Leaders of Character (Revised Edition)

BY CHARLES LEE LEWIS $2.00

Famous American Naval Officers

GAME BETWEEN GEORGIA TECH AND UNIVERSITY OF MISSOURI
MIAMI ORANGE BOWL, NEW YEAR'S DAY, 1940

FAMOUS AMERICAN ATHLETES OF TODAY

I-4

Seventh Series

By

JERRY NASON
AND OTHER SPORTS WRITERS

Foreword by
EDWARD S. PARSONS
Professor of Physical Education
Northeastern University

L. C. PAGE & COMPANY
BOSTON ❦ PUBLISHERS

920
Nason

920
Nason

920

Copyright, 1940, by
L. C. PAGE & COMPANY
(INCORPORATED)

———

Made in U. S. A.

First Impression, January, 1940

Gift (pnb) 2.50 list

PRINTED BY THE COLONIAL PRESS INC.
CLINTON, MASS., U. S. A.

FOREWORD

THE famous athletes who perform in the principal athletic competitions of the nation are frequently, or perhaps usually, known to us only as stars in a particular event or sport. We recognize them because we see their pictures repeatedly on the sports pages of our daily newspapers, and occasionally we learn a little more about their daily lives from short feature stories which touch briefly upon their background. As a rule, however, they exist in our minds primarily as almost legendary figures—as Babe Ruth, the Big Bam; Glenn Cunningham, the King of Milers; Eddie Shore, the Edmonton Express.

All too frequently our mental picture of some great athlete is drawn from an isolated incident. On one extreme is the athlete who is the victim of some unfortunate circumstance that is interesting to the public and naturally results in a deluge of publicity. He lives in the public eye not as the good, conscientious athlete, but rather as "the man who ran the wrong way." The one mistake in his career is the one by which he is judged. On the other extreme is the mediocre athlete who just once in his career gives a brilliant performance. On the basis of that one play, he may be held up as an athletic ideal, the paragon of all sports virtues. Thus, at either extreme, the picture is not com-

plete or perhaps even truthful, and we cannot truly do the athlete full justice because we do not have a sufficient body of facts concerning his life by which to judge him.

From this book we will receive a more balanced presentation of the life and achievements of each of the athletes included. We shall, I believe, reach the happy conclusion that our champions in sports are fully entitled to the acclaim they receive, and to the respect and affection in which we hold them.

It is on the playgrounds and athletic fields of this great nation that the sturdy bodies of our youth are in a large measure developed. It is here that the spirit of fair play is learned. It is here that many other characteristics included in our ideal of American manhood and womanhood are developed.

The splendid example of our athletic "greats" has a profound influence on the many thousands of the youth of our nation who daily tax to the limit our playground and athletic facilities. It is fitting that we should be able, as we lay aside our copy of FAMOUS AMERICAN ATHLETES OF TODAY to say to ourselves, "These young Americans truly live up to our ideal."

Edward S. Parsons
Professor of Physical Education
Northeastern University

CONTENTS

vii

CONTENTS

LIST OF ILLUSTRATIONS

ix

PATTY BERG

PATRICIA "PATTY" BERG

also played baseball. As a hockey player she was a constant scoring threat once she got hold of the puck. Hers was a vitality that could be loosed only by participation in the rough-and-tumble games played by the boys of the neighborhood.

Not that Patty didn't have girls to chum around with at this time. Her two sisters, Helen and Mary, are only a couple of years older than she. But Patty had a brother too, and it was to him that she turned for companionship in her sorties of rough-and-ready play. Herman Berg is three years younger than Patty, but they have always had a lot in common. Only last year he won the prep-school golf championship of Minneapolis.

When Herman and his pals decided to play football on the vacant lot near the Berg homestead, it was only natural that Patty, their companion in all things, should be included in the lineup. By the time she reached the age of twelve, however, her mother had put her foot down and won her point; that football was no game for a growing girl. But not before effecting a compromise with her daughter that allowed her to remain as the coach.

While divorced from actual participation in the rougher sports, Patty continued to be the pal of her brother. They still put their heads together on intricate football plays. Just when Mrs. Berg thought that the practical side of the game had ceased to fascinate Patty, she looked out of the window one evening in 1938 and there was her husky daughter illustrating to her son Herman how Harold Van Every of her beloved Minnesota football team had faded back to decoy the Michigan U linemen out of position and then either passed or ran them dizzy as the Gophers won 7-6. Of course, Mrs. Berg didn't realize what was going on when she looked out of the window and saw the National Woman's Golf Champion romping around, but that is the explanation she got from her daughter.

Dad Berg, who refuses to get excited about his daughter's golfing ability, albeit he is quite proud of her competitive record, attributes her success to her early associations with boys and her enthusiasm for their type of athletics.

"Frankly," he says, "I don't think Patty is one bit better than most of the golfers she competes against, but I do know this; that because she was brought up among the boys in the neighborhood, she has attained the vigor, the stamina, and the energy so necessary to a winner."

Patty herself attributes her success to exceptional golfing luck. On her way to her fourth straight victory in the 1939 Miami-Biltmore tournament at Coral Gables, Florida, she defeated Laddie Irwin of Glen Ridge, New Jersey, 7-5 in the semi-final round. "Gee, Laddie," she said to the girl who was her roommate, "you had all the tough luck. I had all the good luck!"

Laddie, and Patty's other opponents who have bowed to her on the links, however, have a different story to tell. They are loud and unanimous in their praise of her golf game and approach to a sport which is apt to rasp the nerves of the emotional or unsettled.

Not that Patty didn't have her own period of being unsettled, of being troubled by nerves. When she went to England as a member of the Curtis Cup team she was not at her best. Dispatches said she was jittery. In fact, these dispatches brought on a family council when Patty returned.

"I came mighty near making Patty stop playing golf for good after that summer," Mr. Berg reveals. "I didn't mind her getting beat, but some of the stories in the papers said she was so jittery that she had to be carried around by her partner in the doubles. I thought if she was taking the game so much to heart, it was time for her to quit.

"I told her that if the game was bothering her or making her nervous, she had better quit when she came back to this country, but she convinced me that there was nothing to those stories, so I let her go on playing. Since then she hasn't shown any sign of being under a severe mental strain that I could see while she was playing, but she still retains her competitive approach."

Which sums up in some degree Miss Patty's mental approach to the game of which she is so much a part. I have had an opportunity of watching her in action under pressure several times. No matter how tense or charged with suppressed excitement the gallery is, Miss Berg steps up to the ball as loose as she can be. With the typical waggle to her hips which golf galleries have come to recognize, with a stance that reminds one of the stance Hack Wilson took at the plate when he was hammering home runs for the Chicago Cubs, the Minneapolis mistress of the mashie outdrives her opponents enough to shatter their confidence in themselves.

Her exceptional ability to concentrate when

under fire and to take only as long to make a shot as is absolutely necessary, makes her a feminine counterpart of Ralph Guldahl on the links. No matter what the score, she is out there shooting against par in an attempt to squeeze her score down to the most minute total possible. When she turns in her card she is usually at the top of the list or thereabouts. Having been weaned on the rough-and-tumble give-and-take of boys' sports, the pressure of tournament golf which has driven many high-strung girls almost to nervous distraction, holds no hidden terrors for this miss whose rolling gait over the fairways is as distinguishing in golf as that of Babe Ruth's was in baseball.

"Patty doesn't always win," says her father. "Most of these girls she beats in a tournament have taken her out with them in friendly games and have beaten the tar out of her. That's why I say that, aside from stamina and that incentive to win that a tournament gives her, she is no better golfer than many of them."

Cool and painstakingly careful, Patty is all business in a tournament. She never becomes ruffled and seldom allows a poor shot to upset her game. "This shows," Dad Berg says, "her *guts!*" Certainly an inelegant word, but none more expressive has been coined to label that indefinable something which distinguishes the champion from the run-of-the-mill player.

According to her intimates, Patty never second guesses herself after a tournament in which she loses, never alibis. Consequently she does not suffer the torment that comes with contemplating what might have been.

"I did the best I could," is her stock statement when someone tries to alibi a poor showing of hers. Then she changes the subject and promptly proceeds to shunt into the back of her mind the tournament that is over.

Doing the best she can is her credo, her mental badge to be worn foremost in the mind.

Now a sophomore at the University of Minnesota, where she is taking a business course, Patty is the football fan of fans. She firmly believes that no football team is comparable to Bernie Bierman's Minnesota Gophers. She rejoices in their victories and is downcast when they meet defeat.

Naturally, tournament golf interferes with her studies during the winter. During the winter of 1939, for example, she played in several matches down South. She missed the second quarter of the school term, but she worked so hard before going south that she managed to chalk up three B's and a C before she left.

A normal, healthy girl with an intense affection for sports in general and golf in particular, Patty has her dates. Most of them with the leading athletes of the University of Minnesota. She's their pal. Her knowledge of sports provides common ground upon which they meet. She devours the sports pages daily and quotes readily from the batting and fielding averages of the major leagues.

Considering Patty Berg as a national champion, the hardest thing to realize about her record is that her golfing career didn't begin until 1932. Patty's father was the first in the family to get a golf bug. Being a family man he subscribed to a family membership in the Interlachen Country Club in Minneapolis, hoping, he freely admits, that Herman Jr. would join him on the links and provide him with companionship.

Herman did eventually, but for a long time, his father relates, he was more interested in looking for lost golf balls which he could convert into cash with which to go to the movies than he was in his golf game. But that was to be expected of a boy of nine.

Patty, naturally, demanded the same attention

as her brother, so her dad took her out on the course six or eight times during that 1932 season in which she was introduced to the game as a girl of thirteen.

No doubt it would make a better story to say that Patty started playing as smooth and finished a game as she plays now—a born golfer—but truth compels us to relate that she actually had a rough time of it, slamming the ball into the rough, into traps, and losing her patience. Nevertheless, in spite of her discouragement, there was something about the game that was fascinating to Patty. Not that she was ready to admit that she liked it as well as she did football, but she did admit its appeal.

Not until the latter part of that season—1932— did Patty actually display anything more than a casual interest in the game. Then Dad Berg began to find her on the links more often; squinting her eyes, gritting her teeth, and leaning on the ball for distance. Her tenacity and enthusiasm attracted the attention of the club professionals, Will Kidd and Jim Pringle, and they began to give her hints on how to improve her game.

Always willing to learn, Patty made the most of this instruction, proving an apt pupil. Kidd and Pringle worked on her stance, her form, and other technical details. Naturally, her golf game improved by leaps and bounds.

Toward the close of the season interest ran high in the approaching Minneapolis City tournament that was to be staged at what is now the Minnesota Valley Club, but was then known as the Bloomington course. The Interlachen Club, to which the Bergs belonged, wanted to send a large delegation to this tournament and make a good showing.

Patty was urged to enter by Patricia Stephenson, then one of the leading players in the section. Because she was such a ranking player, Miss Stephenson was Patty's idol. As the champion explains it today, "I really didn't want to let her down; she was so anxious to have Interlachen make a good showing."

None of the folks at home knew of Patty's decision to enter the tournament until she stopped her father on his way to work one morning and informed him that she needed the necessary caddy and entrance fees. She came running out to the car to see him, having almost forgotten the fees.

"What are you going to do for clubs?" asked her dad as he dug down into the family treasury.

"Oh," said Patty quite casually, "I've got one of your old brassies, three irons, and a putter."

She had no bag to put her implements of warfare into, however, so Mr. Berg contacted a friend of his who kindly loaned one. Off to the city tournament Patty went with borrowed clubs, borrowed bag, and her own courage.

While she had hit a golf ball around in friendly matches, Patty was not fully conversant with all the rules. Finding herself in a trap on the thirteenth hole she confidently built a little mound for the ball and teed off on it. This unintentional error cost her two shots. Later in the same round she hit the ball into a puddle of water. Thinking herself rather clumsy and the course architect rather stupid for leaving such a hazard in that particular spot, she picked up her ball and threw it into the fairway. Penalty: two more strokes!

After she had hacked and hoed her way over the course she added up her score and found that it had taken her 112 strokes to get the ball into the final pot. That was her score in her first tournament, but in 1938 she returned to the home course and scored a seventy from the men's tees. Some improvement, what?

Improvement which, of course, wasn't realized overnight. Day in and day out, from that time on, redheaded Patty Berg was on the links at Interlachen. Rambling over the course with her space-eating, rolling gait, she would stop, squint her eyes at the ball, grit her teeth, and lean on her drive for distance. By that time she could afford to lean on it, because she had a good idea where it was going.

Having enjoyed her first taste of tournament competition in the city tournament the previous year, Patty now entered the Minnesota State tournament. She qualified for the championship flight with a 101, thereby inaugurating a record, for ever since, she has qualified for every tournament she has entered.

The following summer she went to her usual retreat, a summer camp in the upper part of Minnesota, without realizing how large golf loomed in her life. Surrounded with plenty of opportunities for play in every sport but the one which she had come to like best, Patty became restless with a longing for her daily game.

As she now puts it she "made a deal" with the family to take her out of camp. The arrangement was, that the money set aside for the term at camp should be utilized to send her to two tournaments a year.

She had definitely crossed the Rubicon to become a tournament golfer. There was no trouble in closing this deal with the family because Mother Berg was just as intensely interested in her husky, healthy daughter as Dad Berg, and was just as much her pal.

The same Minnesota State tournament was her first objective after retirement from camp life. Whereas she had qualified in 1933 with a 101 she cut down her qualifying score to a 90. A defeat at the hands of the same Patty Stephenson who had introduced her to tournament play in Minneapolis two seasons before, eliminated her in the third round.

But Patty was gaining confidence in herself in every tournament, and back she went to the city title-play at Interlachen, and with all the savoir-faire and sang-froid of a tournament golfer rich in experience, Patty annexed her first title.

Kansas City for the Trans-Mississippi tournament was the next stop on her itinerary. Qualifying with an eighty-seven, she was eliminated in the second round by Mrs. Opal S. Hill, a capable woman golfer with plenty of tournament experience who is still good enough to be ranked tenth on the same rating list of women golfers led by Patty.

Shooting a 353 to finish sixth in the seventy-two-hole medal play of the Women's Western Derby at the Beverly Country Club in Chicago, Patty convinced her Dad that she was definitely ready for a more extensive tournament program the following year and he decided to take her to Florida for the winter play.

Starting her 1935 program in the Miami-Biltmore tournament, Patty was eliminated in the first round by Lillian Zech, but not before she forced her opponent to the nineteenth hole for the decision. After that start she went to the Palm Beach Country Club and shot a brilliant seventy-six to be the tournament medalist, but again she dropped a decision on the nineteenth hole in match play.

This time it was Marian Miley of Lexington, Kentucky who upset her hopes. It was her first meeting with the girl from the Blue Grass State, but a significant one because Marian and Patty are still hot rivals whenever they meet.

For the third successive year Patty entered the Minnesota State tournament. In typical form she shot an eighty to be the tournament medalist, but for a change that distinction did not jinx her. Beatrice Barrett bowed to the magic of the Berg girl's clubs, seven and six in the finals and Patty had won her first tournament of national importance. Her cup of joy was not complete, however, for on her way to the crown she had to defeat her old idol, Patty Stephenson.

It so happened that the National Women's Championship that year was to be played at Patty's home club, Interlachen. Naturally enough, the Minneapolis girl carried the hopes of her home city into that affair. Qualifying with an eighty-five she beat her way into the finals by shooting the quality of golf which attracted the attention of the critics.

Opposing her in the finals was Mrs. Glenna Collett Vare, seven times a national champion and the feminine counterpart of Bobby Jones in golf. Nobody gave Patty a chance in the match. She had her own doubts, but in the same manner as she had played football back on the corner of 50th block on Colfax Avenue, she threw herself wholeheartedly into the task ahead of her without considering her inexperience. She was doing the best she could in typical Patty Berg fashion.

She didn't win, but neither did she meet with the rout that a girl of her corresponding experience, but not as good a competitor, might have been expected to meet with. The final score was three and two in favor of the many times national champion, but Patty emerged from the match with an even

greater confidence in herself. She had met probably the best woman golfer in the world of the
period and but for a few slips here and there might
have emerged the victor.

From that match Mrs. Vare and Patty developed a warm friendship. They played on the
Curtis Cup team together. Mrs. Vare has taken
a particular interest in Patty and has poured
many words of golfing wisdom into her ears during their association.

The final tournament of the 1935 season found
Patty again a medalist. Playing in the Women's
Western Derby at the Northmoor Country Club in
Chicago, Patty shot a seventy-seven in the opening round of the seventy-two-hole medal play, but
her 327 total was only good enough to enable her
to finish second to Marian Miley.

The year 1936 was not as spectacular as it was
progressive for Patty. She won five of twelve
tournaments after opening her program with a victory in the Miami-Biltmore tournament, the first
of four in this winter fixture. In annexing the
crown under the palms of the Coral Gables course
she defeated her old nemesis, Marian Miley, but
Marian was still two matches up on her.

She ran her string to two straight when she de-

feated the famous Maureen Orcutt in the finals of
the Championship of Champions at Punta Gorda,
the same course where the Ryder Cup matches
were played in 1938. To pin defeat on Miss Orcutt,
however, Patty had to come back and win two and
one after being five down at the end of the first
eighteen holes of the thirty-six-hole finale.

That tournament was the first in which Patty
made one of her sensational comebacks to win after
a poor showing. It was the first indication of the
competitive approach which was to inspire the admiration of the golf critics later.

Her tournament program was far from a parade
of triumphs that year, however, as Maureen
avenged the Punta Gorda defeat in the Palm
Beach finals, four and three. Medalist at Ormond
Beach, Patty shot a brilliant seventy-three, but
dropped the final match to Lucille Robinson on the
third extra hole. Again the medalist, this time at
St. Augustine, Patty was eliminated in the semi-
finals by Mrs. Opal S. Hill, one up.

However, she had shown enough in tournament
competition to be chosen to make the trip to England as a member of the Curtis Cup team. During
the play on the other side of the water against the
best of the women golfers in England, she was

teamed with Mrs. Glenna Collett Vare as the United States doubles team. The greatest woman golfer in the history of the game in this country and the freckle-faced lass who was being mentioned as her successor tied their British rivals, but Patty was not at her best.

In her singles match against Mrs. Andrew Holm, Patty went down to defeat. This was the match in which the sports writers cabled home that Patty was jittery and also pointed to her poor form in the doubles match to substantiate their opinions, making the statement that Patty had been carried by her more experienced partner.

That comment, regardless of whether or not it was true, did not disturb Patty as much as it did her father. When she returned to America she promptly took up where she had left off before leaving for England. The Minnesota State Championship, the Mason-Dixon Championship, and a Women's Invitation tournament were captured by Miss Berg in succession. Proving that to her, at least, golf was just another game. After that brilliant showing, Dad Berg was forced to abandon all discussions as to whether or not Patricia Jane was taking the game too seriously, to the detriment of her nerves.

Her defeats in 1936 after returning from New England included the Trans-Mississippi at Denver where she bowed to Beatrice Barrett, two up in the third round; the Women's Western Closed Championship at South Bend, Indiana, where Beatrice again defeated her by the score of two up, this time in the semi-finals; the Women's National Championship where Mrs. Hill took her measure in the third round, four and three; and the Women's Western Derby at Chicago where she was topped by her old rival, Marian Miley. Patty scored a 324 while finishing as a runner-up to the Kentucky girl.

The following year, 1937, Patty went into one of those slumps which plague all athletes. She competed in thirteen major tournaments, but won only four while always threatening to crash through. Had her game been away off she would have known what to do, but she was shooting good golf, only not quite good enough. Not easy to discourage, she worked all the harder to improve her game.

Her victories were scored in the Women's Title Holder's Championship at Augusta, Georgia, in fifty-four-hole medal play. Medalist with a seventy-three, Patty shot a 240 to annex the title.

It was in the Miami-Biltmore tournament that

she was at her best, however. Scoring her second straight victory in this tournament, Miss Berg had to defeat Jean Bauer of Providence, Rhode Island in the finals. She overpowered that New England miss, ten and nine.

Helen Dettweiler was next to bow to the Minneapolis girl, four and three, in the Palm Beach Country Club tournament. Her final victory of the year was collected in the Women's Invitation tournament at Aiken. Qualifying with a seventy-six, she defeated Barbara Bourne in the finals, five and four.

The toughest defeat for her to swallow that year was in the Women's Western Derby at the Onwentsia Country in Chicago when she forced Marian Miley to break the tournament record to beat her 318 score after being medalist with a seventy-four. She thought she had that one won until Marian turned in her score.

Where a girl of less competitive courage than Patty might have been discouraged by the fact that she was so often close to her objectives without actually gaining them, Patty's setbacks only stiffened her resolve, inspired her to spend more time on polishing up her game and ironing out the minor faults which were tripping her up. Patty

Berg was of championship caliber. If an astrologer could have gazed at her stars, consulted her charts, he would have said, "1938 will be your year, young lady!"

Sweeping all classes of competition before her, Patricia hung up the remarkable tournament record of ten victories in the thirteen tournaments she played. Definitely her best record in competition and one of the most remarkable in golf annals when it is considered that she was only nineteen and had only started to play golf six years before.

She launched her remarkable record at Augusta, Georgia when she took the Women's Title Holder's Championship, seventy-two-hole medal play, with a 311 after shooting a seventy-seven to capture medal honors. Following this achievement she defeated Jean Bauer in the finals of the Women's Championship of Champions at Punta Gorda, ten and eight.

For the third year in succession she won the Miami-Biltmore crown when she defeated Jane Cothran, four and three, after shooting an eighty to win the medal. A seventy-four at Ormond Beach gave her another medal and she went on to win the tournament. Four straight tournament victories were hers before she bowed to Miss Cothran at St.

Augustine, two up. She was also the medalist in
that tournament, so she had some degree of consolation in defeat.

Her second of three defeats for the year came
immediately afterwards when she bowed to her
old nemesis, Marian Miley, in the Belleair finals,
two up. She returned to form again in the Wom-
en's Mid South tournament at Southern Pines,
North Carolina. Here she shot a seventy-three to
be medalist and her 224 score for the fifty-four-
hole medal play was good enough to break the
record.

Mrs. Opal S. Hill fell before her powerful
mashie in the Trans-Mississippi tournament at
Tulsa, Oklahoma, six and five. From then until
she lost to Mrs. Hill in the quarter finals of the
Women's Western Open, one up on the nineteenth
hole, after shooting a seventy-nine for the medal,
Patty was at her best.

She reached her peak in the National tournament at Westmoreland. For the second year in a
row she swept through the tournament with ease
and faced Mrs. Estelle Lawson Page in the final.
It was the first time in the history of the game in
this country that the same finalists had opposed
each other for the second consecutive year, but this

time Patty avenged her seven and six defeat at the hands of Mrs. Page in the finals of the 1937 tournament, by defeating her six and five to reach the pinnacle of women's golf while still in her teens.

Naturally enough she again made the Curtis Cup team for the matches played at the Essex Country Club in Manchester, Massachusetts. Once again she was teamed with Mrs. Glenna Collett Vare in the doubles, but they lost to their British rivals. But Patty was more than satisfied with the tournament for she was able to defeat Jessie Anderson, the 1937 British champion, one up, in the singles match. It repaid her in immeasurable self-satisfaction for her defeat in the singles of the Curtis Cup play in 1936 in England.

Her crowning achievement, however, was in being chosen the outstanding woman athlete of 1938.

The year 1939 started off auspiciously enough for Patty when she won her fourth Miami-Biltmore Invitation tournament title by defeating Dorothy Kirby of Atlanta, Georgia, but when she looks back on it she will remember it only with sadness. On the eve of defending her national title Patty was stricken with appendicitis and had to let her title go by default. Just prior to the Christmas holidays, when she was preparing for her annual campaign on southern links, the greatest tragedy that could enter any young girl's life threw its shadow over hers when her mother and constant companion passed away.

However, in characteristic fashion, Patty, while grieving deeply over the loss of her mother, started her campaign to regain her title by heading south with her dad, with the thought in mind that her mother would most certainly have preferred that she pursue this course had she been able to express the wish before her death.

Still in the prime of her young and athletic life, Patty Berg is too fine a golfer, too game a sportswoman, to have her career blasted by the shadows which enveloped her during 1939.

PATRICIA JANE BERG

Born Minneapolis, Minnesota, 1919.

1933

Minnesota State Championship; qualified with 101, defeated in first round.

1934

Minnesota State Tournament; qualified with 90, defeated in third round by Patty Stephenson.

Minneapolis City Championship; won.

Trans-Mississippi Tournament, Kansas City; qualified with 87, lost in second round to Mrs. Hill.

Women's Western Derby at Beverly C. C., Chicago, 72-hole medal play; shot 353 to finish sixth.

1935

Miami-Biltmore; defeated in first round by Lillian Zech on 19th hole. 88 qualified.

Palm Beach Tourney; medalist with 76, defeated in third round by Marian Miley on 19th hole.

Trans-Mississippi, Omaha, defeated by Marian Miley in finals.

Minnesota State Championship at Duluth; medalist with 80, defeated Beatrice Barrett in finals, 7-6.

National Women's Tournament at Interlachen C. C., Minneapolis; qualified with 85, defeated by Mrs. Vare in finals, 3-2.

Women's Western Derby, Northmoor C. C., Chicago; 72-hole medal play; medalist with 77, second with 327. Won by Marian Miley.

1936

Miami-Biltmore; medalist with 80, defeated Marian Miley in finals, 413.

Women's Championship of Champions, Punta

Gorda, Florida; defeated Maureen Orcutt, 2-1, in final 36 holes after being five down at end of first 18.

Palm Beach C. C.; defeated by Maureen Orcutt in finals, 4-3.

Ormond Beach; medalist with 73; defeated in finals by Lucille Robinson on third extra hole.

St. Augustine; medalist with 74, defeated in semi-final round by Mrs. Hill, one up.

Curtis Cup Team at England; with Mrs. Vare as partner, tied in doubles. Miss Berg defeated in singles by Mrs. Andrew Holm.

Trans-Mississippi, Denver; medalist with 74, lost to Beatrice Barrett in third round, two up.

Minnesota State Championship; medalist with 79, won in finals from Ann Haroldson, 5-4.

Women's Western Championship (closed), South Bend, Indiana; defeated in semi-final round by Beatrice Barrett, two up.

Mason-Dixon Championship, White Sulphur C. C., West Virginia; medalist with 78, defeated Virginia Guilfoul in finals, 12-11.

Women's Invitation Tournament, 54-hole medal, Eqwanock C. C., Manchester, Vermont; medalist with 72, won shooting 229.

Women's National Championship; qualified second with 80, defeated in third round by Mrs. Hill, 4-3.

Women's Western Derby, Midlothian C. C., Chicago; second with 324. Won by Marian Miley.

1937

Women's Title Holder's Championship, Augusta (Georgia) C. C., 54-hole medal; medalist with 73, won with 240.

Women's Championship of Champions, Punta Gorda, Florida; defeated in finals by Katherine Hemphill, 3-2.

Miami-Biltmore; medalist with 80, defeated Jean Bauer in finals, 10-9.

Palm Beach C. C.; defeated Helen Dettweiler in finals, 4-3.

Ormond Beach; medalist with 74, defeated in second round by Dorothy Traung, two up.

St. Augustine; medalist with 74, defeated in finals by Katherine Hemphill on second extra hole.

Belleair; defeated in first round by Jean Bauer, one up.

Women's Invitation Tournament, Aiken, South Carolina; qualified with 76, defeated Barbara Bourne in finals, 5-4.

Trans-Mississippi, San Antonio, Texas; co-medalist with 78, defeated in finals by Betty Jamieson, 4-3.

Women's Western Championship, Town & Country Club, St. Paul; defeated in third round by Marian MacDougall on 18th hole, one up.

Minnesota State Championship, Interlachen C. C.; medalist with 77; defeated in finals by Beatrice Barrett, 5-4.

Women's Western Derby, Onwientsia C. C., Chicago; medalist with 74, second with 318. Marian Miley broke tourney record to win, 309.

Women's National Championship, Memphis; defeated in finals by Mrs. Estelle Page, 7-6.

1938

Women's Title Holder's Championship, 72-hole medal, Augusta (Georgia) C. C.; medalist with 77, won with 311.

Women's Championship of Champions, Punta Gorda, Florida; defeated Jean Bauer, 10-8.

Miami-Biltmore; medalist with 80, defeated Jane Cothran, 4-3.

Ormond Beach; medalist with 74, defeated Mrs. Helen Hockenjos, one up.

St. Augustine; medalist, 76; defeated on first round by Jane Cothran, two up.

Belleair; defeated in finals by Marian Miley, two up.

Women's Mid-South Tournament, 54-hole medal, Southern Pines, North Carolina; medalist with 73, won with 224 to break record.

Trans-Mississippi, Tulsa, Oklahoma; defeated Mrs. Hill, 6-5.

Minnesota State Championship, Rochester; medalist with 76, defeated Beatrice Barrett in finals, 10-9.

Women's Western Championship (open); medalist with 79, lost to Mrs. Hill in quarter finals one up on 19th hole.

Women's Western Championship (closed), Olympia Field, Chicago; defeated Edith Estabrook in finals, 4-3.

Women's Western Derby, 72-hole medal, Butterfield C. C., Chicago; medalist with 73, won with 308, breaking record.

Women's National Tournament, Westmoreland C. C., Chicago; defeated Estelle Page in finals, 6-5.

Curtis Cup Competition at England; played No. 2 post; with Mrs. Vare lost, one up, in doubles; in singles Miss Berg defeated Jessie Anderson, 1937 British champion, one up.

1939

Women's Title Holder's Championship, Augusta (Georgia) C. C., 72-hole medal; won with 319.

Miami-Biltmore, defeated Dorothy Kirby of Atlanta, Georgia, 3 and 1.

Florida East Coast Championship, defeated Betty Jamieson of San Antonio, Texas, 3 and 2.

Belleair (Florida) Women's Championship, lost to Dorothy Kirby in semi-finals, 3 and 2.

Trans-Mississippi Tournament, defeated Marian Miley of Lexington, Kentucky, 1 up after 19 holes.

DOUGLAS G. CORRIGAN: WRONG WAY FLIER

DOUGLAS "WRONG WAY" CORRIGAN

CHAPTER II

By Harold Kaese, Sports Writer, *Boston Evening
Transcript*

WINGS over the Atlantic! No longer does the
heart leap as it did only a few years ago at the
vision of a slender, sharp-nosed monoplane ghost-
ing its way in and out of cloud banks, now casting
its swift shadow on a placid sea, now flying blind
in the blackness of the storm above the tossing
waves. Many, many times since the great ocean
was first spanned by airplane in 1919 when John
Alcock and A. W. Brown completed the transatlantic hop, wings have been over the Atlantic.
With the establishment of commercial air traffic
from Europe to America, another romantic fron-
tier vanishes. What was once an adventure now
becomes a commonplace.

Flying some 3600 miles over the Atlantic Ocean
was an adventure in May, 1927, when Captain

37

Charles A. Lindbergh flew alone from New York to Paris. So favorable were the circumstances then that Lindbergh became the world's most famous aviator. He was the first to solo the hazardous route, a route on which there could be no safe landing, and while others have followed, it will never be forgotten that it was he who set the pace. *The Spirit of St. Louis* and the Lone Eagle rest secure in the highest niche of aviation's Hall of Fame, although there have been more than 125 successful and unsuccessful expeditions over the Atlantic since 1918.

Among those who followed Lindbergh successfully across the great body of water on solo flights were the late Amelia Earhart, who in 1932 flew from Harbor Grace, Newfoundland, to Londonderry, Ireland; James Mattern, who in 1933 flew from New York to Norway; Wiley Post, who completed a voyage from New York to Berlin in 1933, as part of his round-the-world flight; and Felix Waitkus, who on a trip from New York to Lithuania in 1935 was forced down at Ballinrobe, Ireland. Howard Hughes created flying's proudest record in July, 1938, when he circled the world in three days, nineteen hours, eight minutes, and ten seconds, yet even he failed to threaten the position held by the silent, intrepid flier who soloed from New York to Paris when marathon flying was in its infancy. The climax of all transatlantic flights, perhaps, was in 1933, when General Italo Balbo led twenty-four Italian planes in formation on a round-trip journey between Rome and New York.

A great variety of records have been made since Lindy set his monoplane down in Paris. In Augsburg, Germany, a twenty-four-year-old pilot, Fritz Wendel, flew a test course at a speed of 469.2 miles an hour on April 26, 1939. Commandant Yuso Fujito and Fukujiro Tukahasni of Japan in May, 1938, set a long-distance, non-stop mark of 7239 miles. Flight Lieutenant Maurice J. Adams of Great Britain on June 30, 1937, climbed to an altitude of 53,936 feet. Howard R. Hughes, of round-the-world fame, set an East-West record from California to New York in 1937 of seven hours, twenty-eight minutes, twenty-five seconds for 2445 miles. Include the names of Ellsworth, Byrd, Post, Wilkins, Earhart, Stephens. They are aviation's royalty; Lindbergh is their king.

Only one aviator has come close to matching Lindy in popular appeal, only one has been taken into the public's heart as Lindy was. He is Douglas G. Corrigan—Wrong Way Corrigan, who won quick fame when he flew from New York to Dublin, Ireland, in July, 1938, after announcing his destination as San Diego when he left Floyd Bennett Field early on the morning of July 17, 1938.

"I'm Douglas Corrigan. Just got in from New York. Where am I? I intended to fly to California," said the young man who stepped out of a $900 crate to gaping attendants at Baldonnel Airfield, Dublin, at 2:20 P.M. on July 18.

He started for California, he landed in Ireland! The public could not restrain its laughter—and admiration. Corrigan was instantly famous: his fortune was made. He had hit the world on its crazy bone, and now all he had to do was maintain his natural modesty and his contagious Irish grin to capitalize on the strangest wrong-way run since Roy Riegels, University of California center, ran sixty yards the wrong way with the ball in the Rose Bowl football game against Georgia Tech, January 1, 1929.

A week earlier Corrigan had crashed the headlines by flying non-stop from San Diego to Roosevelt Field, N.Y., 2700 miles, in twenty-seven hours and fifty minutes, in a nine-year-old plane that had cost him only $900 when bought second hand. Originally built to hold a pilot and two passengers in 1929, Corrigan had converted it into a single seater with fuel tanks that would hold 325 gallons. When his flight from California ended at 7:50 o'clock Saturday evening, July 9, he was almost unnoticed, because of exciting preparations for the world flight by Hughes. When reporters, finally struck by the cheapness of the plane, caught up with Corrigan, he said modestly, "I had a nice time. I ran into dust storms in New Mexico. Not much trouble, though."

"He told us he was going for a little jaunt to San Diego and the next we heard from him he was in New York City," said his uncle, Reverend Fraser Langford, pastor of the First Baptist Church of Santa Monica. The week before, Reverend Langford had talked Corrigan out of a trip to Hawaii.

Ostensibly Corrigan was heading for home when his plane was wheeled onto the Floyd Bennett Field runway early on the morning of July 17, a week after he had landed on his flight from California. He had made overtures on the possibility of obtaining a permit from the Air Commerce Bureau for a flight across the Atlantic but had not applied formally when officials let him know they would not give him permission to fly such a flimsy and dangerous craft as the Corrigan Clipper across the broad Atlantic.

Thus, there were few people present when Corrigan climbed into his plane at 5:15 A.M. on July 17, and tied the door shut with a piece of wire, because he had lost the handle to the latch. He had attracted some attention by his unexpected flight from California, for which he had received official permission, but now the public, still excited over Hughes's record-breaking round-the-world flight which had ended only six days earlier, was ready to forget him. Kenneth Behr, airport manager, was there, and so too were Neal Grignon, Dock Department inspector; Rudy Arnold, field photographer; an ambulance surgeon, policemen, and firemen.

During the week between the time he landed on his flight from California and his take-off on July 17, Corrigan lived at the Hempstead, Long Island, home of an old friend and associate of his, Steve Reich. The night of the flight he slept in the hangar with his plane. Corrigan asked permission of Behr to take off in the moonlight at 2 o'clock in the morning, "so I can fly across the desert when it's cool." Behr refused permission and told him to wait for dawn.

A newsreel company had asked Corrigan to delay his departure so they could photograph his take-off, but he refused, saying he was not interested in publicity. He pinned two pages from an old atlas on the barren instrument board of his plane, which he called *Sunshine,* when he rolled out of the hangar at four o'clock in the morning. A mechanic could not start the engine by spinning the propeller, so Corrigan got out and spun it himself.

Corrigan's plane was filled with 325 gallons of gasoline. After the flight from California, he bought 218 gallons of 73 octane gasoline at 28 cents a gallon. He paid $61.04 for the gasoline, plus $1.22 in the city sales tax, in cash. The fuel supply had not been screened through chamois, as it usually is for transatlantic flights. With the heavy load, Corrigan had to run his ship nearly 3000 feet along the 4000-foot runway before he could lift it. As he vanished into the northeast without banking, Behr, the field manager, said softly, "I have a hunch this fellow is on his way to Europe."

Behr was right. Corrigan did head for Europe. From the time he left Floyd Bennett Field at 5:15 A.M. until he was sighted over Belfast Harbor at

1:08 o'clock the next afternoon, no one knew where Corrigan was, although several people guessed correctly when he did not show up in California. At 2:20 P.M. he landed at Dublin, asked his amazing question of officials at Baldonnel Field— "Where am I? Is this California?"—and a few minutes later the blackest and largest headlines on English and American newspapers were proclaiming his wrong-way masterpiece.

What happened from 5:15 A.M. on July 17 to 2:20 P.M. on July 18? Let Corrigan himself account for the hiatus:

"I left the flying field in New York at 5:15 yesterday morning. The machine was heavy and I had to run about 2500 feet to take off. It was slow business but I got off without a hitch. Then, flying by compass, I headed, as I thought, for California.

"I had no intention of flying to Ireland, although I had thought of a flight to this country and had studied maps. When up about five thousand feet I came into a bank of clouds. For about twenty-six hours I was in the clouds all the time at an altitude of five to six thousand feet and reckoned I must be well on the way to California.

"It was impossible to try and get my bearings

from anything around me, so I just flew by compass and only came down to fifteen hundred feet when I ran into rain. I caught a glimpse of the water then, but I rose again to five thousand feet.

"The light was good when I came down again, and the first things I saw were fishing boats, but even then I thought I was off the Pacific Coast. About a half hour later I sighted the first land.

"Then, when I saw the layout of the country and the little white houses dotted here and there, I realized it did not look like what it should look like to me. I kept on over the land and hit water again.

"Then I decided to hug the coast line until I struck some big town. The old bus was running fine and I had no worries, although I was feeling just a little sleepy and I was deaf in both ears from the noise of the engine. Along the coast I sighted several small towns, but I kept on until I came over the city.

"It took me some time coasting around to find the airfield. The ship came down nicely, and here I am in Dublin, far away from Los Angeles, to which I wanted to go."

Of the scanty food supplies with him, Corrigan ate only one box of fig biscuits and drank about a glass of water. When he landed he had $15 in money on him. He emerged from the cockpit of his plane with a light gray waterproof coat over his arm. He was dressed in oil-stained gray pants, a leather jacket, and an open-neck gray shirt. He did not appear weary, and when asked if he had taken ammonia tablets, he answered, "No, when I felt tired I stuck my head out the window."

He had 30 gallons of gasoline left in his tanks when he landed. One tank had leaked and flooded the cockpit. Corrigan's flight of 3150 miles required 28 hours 13 minutes. He averaged a little over 110 miles an hour on his hazardous journey.

Corrigan's plane, valued at $900, had no maps, radio, or fancy instruments. A Curtiss Robin built in 1929, it had a wing span of 41 feet, was 26½ feet long, had a wing area of 224 square feet, a normal speed of 118 miles an hour, a cruising speed of between 90 and 100 miles an hour. It was powered by a Wright Whirlwind motor, 165 horse-power, five cylinders, and air cooled. He left without a weather report on the North Atlantic; his flight was unsponsored; he depended on an old spirit compass; his only instruments were bank and turn indicators, fuel and motor gauges, and an inclinometer.

Hughes, on his round-the-world flight finished only a few days earlier, had taken advantage of every scientific development for airplanes. Lindbergh made his flight eleven years earlier than Corrigan, but his *Spirit of St. Louis* was a better equipped plane than the *Sunshine*. Lindbergh's plane cost $13,000; Corrigan's cost him about $900. Lindbergh was competing for the Orteig Prize of $25,000 for the first flight to Paris. Corrigan was gambling on public reaction to his daring stunt.

Asked if he was ever in danger during his flight, Corrigan answered, "Why, no, I was just up there above the clouds in nice clear air, and there is no danger in clouds; you can go through them if there is nothing behind them."

He landed without a passport or a permit. When officials asked him for landing papers, Corrigan grinned and replied, "Forget it! I thought I was on the way to California." Offered a drink, he said, "Naw, I'm not a drinking man."

When news of Corrigan's arrival was delivered, the United States legation sent an automobile for him. United States Minister John Cudahy had just got back from a horseback ride and was in time to welcome his unexpected guest. Corrigan had dinner at the legation, talked with writers and posed for photographers, and then spoke over the radio from a Dublin broadcasting station to his brother Harry in Baltimore, and his Uncle Langford in Los Angeles. For this appearance, his first after the sensational flight, Corrigan received $2000. It was a taste of what was coming.

Corrigan was figuratively swamped by offers. So many were his opportunities to "cash in" on his stunt that he was urged to accept some of them immediately by Minister Cudahy, but Corrigan refused to rush into any commitments. Examples of the offers he was receiving before he had been on Irish soil for twenty-four hours:

The Advertising Club of New York—to pay the transportation of the flier and his plane back to the United States.

The United States Steamship Line—free transportation home.

An Amusement Park—$25,000 to name the plane for the park.

Texas Banker—to pay his fine, if he were fined by the Department of Commerce.

New York tug boat fleet owner—to send a tug to Ireland to bring the plane home.

Three moving picture companies immediately began bidding for a contract. The first price offered was $5000, the last price was $50,000. He was offered $25,000 to appear at a night club. There were vaudeville offers. Several publishers wanted to print his life story.

Many of the offers were made for mere publicity's sake; they were not real. In the first few weeks Corrigan rejected opportunities that would have brought him $200,000, if they were sound. But Corrigan bided his time, selected the offers with the most appeal, and made $75,000 the first three months after his flight. He wrote his biography, a 55,000-word article he scribbled in long hand when his "ghost writer" insisted on including imaginary romances. When RKO-Radio starred him in the moving picture, *The Flying Irishman,* he refused to allow the inclusion of "mushy" scenes. "I can't get over the number of girls who seem to think because I flew the Atlantic I would make a perfect husband. I am not having any feminine entanglements in my young life yet, however," he said.

Used to small funds, Corrigan exasperated some people when he lived in Hollywood because of his rigid economy. One gossip monger wrote that while he was making thousands of dollars a week, he lived in a low-price room, relined the brake bands on his ten-year-old automobile, rode to the studio on a bus, lunched on nickel bars of ice cream, and refused to give a percentage of his salary to a relief fund for actors, saying, "I'm not an actor. I don't believe in asking for charity or giving it."

Hard to deal with, Corrigan was accused of becoming selfish and conceited. Yet there is much to be said for this intrepid young aviator who won his triumph the hard way, who punished his stomach so he could feed the motor of his plane, who worked for many years as a mechanic, pilot, and instructor at less than fifty dollars a week. Shrewd, and a hard bargainer, he was not an easy mark for either sharpers or trained business men. One associate said of him, "He's got a way of doing things his own way and you've got to give him credit for having the courage to say no."

Corrigan's flight was illegal. That is the main reason why he would not admit he had flown purposely to Ireland, yet it was the palpable fib of this charming young Californian with the incorrigible Irish grin and the sharp Irish wit that most caught the fancy of laymen. During the many receptions given him throughout the country on his return to the United States, he was often given compasses plainly marked East and West. It was the wrong way angle that tickled folks; fancy a man heading for California and winding up in Ireland. He was given a life membership by the well-known Burlington Liars' Club of Burlington, Wisconsin. Indeed, when he submitted to a lie-detector test in Boston, he was found to have lied when he said he did not know he was flying to Ireland.

Air Commerce Bureau officials were flabbergasted when news came that Corrigan had landed in Ireland. "It ain't right," said one. Regulations provided for fine and revocation of his license, but Dennis P. Mulligan, chief of the Bureau, said, "It's a great day for the Irish. Instead of worrying about the punishment, right now I want to stop him from flying back." They suspended his license.

"I'm sure ashamed of that navigation, all right," admitted Corrigan, when told that his license had been suspended. "I don't use any light maps, so I fly across the right number of hours, then look and see if I'm there. . . . It was just dumb luck."

On July 30, however, the Department of Commerce announced that Corrigan would receive only a "nominal" penalty. His commercial pilot's license would be suspended for five days, because of the "world-wide sentiments of good will" which were accorded the trip. It was on July 30 that Corrigan sailed for home from Queenstown, Ireland, after spending nearly two weeks in the British Isles, where he was handsomely treated. He was complimented in person by President Douglas Hyde of the Irish Free State; by Joseph P. Kennedy, United States ambassador to England; and by Prime Minister Eamon de Valera of Ireland, who told him his arrival undoubtedly was the result of a homing instinct. When Corrigan sailed, he bore under his arm a silver cup given him by Dublin citizens.

His reception in Ireland was a pink tea compared with what was in store for him when he reached New York. On the United States liner *Manhattan*, he sailed up New York Harbor early on the evening of August 4, after eighteen days spent off American soil. It was a spectacular harbor welcome he had, with two hundred Corrigans from Brooklyn among the first to greet him. He had one day of rest before spending the biggest day of his life being fêted by New York and Brooklyn.

Through the deep, man-made canyons of Manhattan, Corrigan led a triumphal procession on the morning of August 5, a grinning, bare-headed, boyish young hero who weathered the midsummer blizzard of ticker tape and confetti clad in his old leather windbreaker. Thirty miles Corrigan paraded that day. It was estimated that 1,500,000 people saw him. A force of 1470 policemen guarded the route of his parade. Irish officials said 200 tons more of confetti were showered on him than on Lindbergh in 1927 or on Hughes a few weeks before.

"You may be from California, but henceforth you are one of ours," said Mayor LaGuardia of New York.

"I'm an All-American," answered Corrigan, correcting the mayor good-naturedly.

At noon there was luncheon at the Advertising Club; in the afternoon he paraded in Brooklyn; in the evening there was a private dinner given by Mayor Adrian F. Levy of Galveston, Texas, city of Corrigan's birth, attendance at a huge rally in Yankee Stadium, and a visit to Lewisohn Stadium to hear his first symphony concert, which he found "interesting and educational." When the day was over, the five-foot-five, 135-pound hero was exhausted; he had lost weight; his right hand was swollen from constant hand-shaking; a cartilage was displaced in his chest when someone had thumped him with too much gusto.

In all, Corrigan visited forty-four cities before he finished his nation-wide tour in Los Angeles. "He looked as modest as Lindbergh as he stepped out of his little ship at the Glendale Airport," wrote an observer. From Dublin had come the observation the day after Corrigan completed his flight: "Not since Lindbergh has any young airman so unspoilt, so unselfish, and so filled with the true spirit of the American pioneers hit these shores."

Corrigan's first two ventures when he reached home were writing his autobiography, *That's My Story,* and acting in the moving picture of his flight, *The Flying Irishman.* His autobiography is not a notable addition to American literature, being poorly written and hastily assembled. Of his acting, the magazine *Newsweek* says in its March 27, 1939 issue: "As a single concession to screen glamour, Corrigan allowed his gold tooth to be painted white. Otherwise, wearing his famous leather jacket, he makes no attempt to do more than walk through his part—an awkward, wistful little fellow with a high nasal voice and more than his share of courage."

Corrigan's flight raised him from obscurity. Reporters found it difficult to learn facts about his life while he was in Ireland because his background was not well known. Friends knew a few things to be sure: He had worked on Lindbergh's plane while it was being built in 1927; he had flown about fifteen hundred hours; he was thirty-one years old and had reddish-brown hair; one called him a "depressed aviator, who put every dime into his plane"; he was exceptionally quiet, a light eater, an early riser. Later other facts were learned.

His early life was one of struggle, toil, and misfortune. He was born January 22, 1907, at Galveston, Texas, the son of a construction engineer and a school teacher. He had a brother, Harry, one year younger than himself, and a sister, Evelyn, four years younger. From 1909 to 1913 the Corrigans lived at Aransas Pass, Texas, where the father worked on a causeway being built by the Southern Pacific Railroad.

In 1913 the family moved to San Antonio. Corrigan's father built houses and sold them, for a short time, then he bought a store that sold candy, ice cream, soda, and bakery goods. The family prospered until 1916, when a business depression made it necessary for the father to mortgage his property. A few months later he ran away from his family, and in July, 1919, he was divorced by his wife. Named for his father, Douglas had his name changed from Clyde to Douglas at this time.

From 1913 to 1919 Corrigan lived in San Antonio. He went to school, he sold newspapers and was happy if he made as much as twenty-five cents a day, he suffered a broken leg while playing in the school yard when only eight years old, he started to run away when only ten years old but returned home when he thought of his mother's sorrow. His boyhood ambitions were to be a baseball pitcher, a locomotive engineer, a banker, and a movie actor. One of the proud moments of his childhood was when he sold a newspaper to Douglas Fairbanks.

For three years his mother rented rooms in San Antonio. In 1919, however, she gathered her three children and moved to Los Angeles, where she started another rooming house. The Corrigan boys went to Virgil Intermediate School, and Douglas says, "I was fair in arithmetic, poor in geography, poor in English, and good in history." His idol as a boy was Abraham Lincoln.

In 1920 Douglas got a job washing apricots and

beans in a canning factory. Sometimes he earned eighteen dollars a week and the family lived well. But in the fall of 1920, it was learned that his mother had cancer and required an operation, so the rooming house was sold and the family left for the East. While his mother was being treated at her old home in Tarentum, Pennsylvania, Douglas and Harry lived with their father, who in the meantime had married again. Douglas thus went through the ninth grade of public school in New York City, giving more attention, he admits, to the school paper than to his studies.

In June, 1921, he and Harry rejoined their mother and sister at Pittsburgh, and together they traveled to Los Angeles, where another rooming house was opened. Now fourteen years old, Douglas worked in a soda-water plant for ten dollars a week. He learned to drive a Model T Ford and made deliveries. Soon he changed to another bottling company and had his salary raised to twenty-five dollars a week.

But his happiness vanished this very same year when his mother was taken to the County Hospital, where she died a few weeks after admission. "One noon I went to work and the foreman told me to go to the hospital, for my mother was dying," recalls Corrigan. "When I got there, she was dead. I had saved a hundred dollars and used it to buy a lot and pay for the funeral."

Sister Evelyn went to live with an aunt and uncle in Vallejo, California, while Douglas and Harry lived together. Douglas worked on a sanding machine in a lumber yard, and then, ambitious now to be an architect, got a place keeping charts for a house-building company. It was while riding to work on a bicycle one day that he had a collision and lost the tooth which was replaced with a gold imitation.

In 1925 Corrigan became interested in aviation. On his way to work, he passed a new flying field, and one Sunday he bought his first ride for two dollars and fifty cents. A few weeks later, October 25, he paid five dollars for a fifteen-minute lesson from George W. Allen, and was thrilled by his first tail spin. For five months he took weekly lessons, and his ambition to be an architect faded away.

It was on March 25, 1926, that he made his first solo flight, and his passion to fly overwhelming him, he joined the California National Guard, 115th Observation Squadron, where he increased his knowledge of planes and motors. In the Fall of

1926 he was ready to open a flying field of his own
with a friend, Donald Rossiter, but the latter was
killed in a mail-plane crash and Corrigan had lost
his closest friend.

In January, 1927, Corrigan quit his job with the
house-building company to become a mechanic at
a field in San Diego, working for B. F. Mahoney
on Dutch Flats. In February, a tall slender chap
came to the field and stunted a new ship, the M1.
He liked it so well that he ordered a ship built on
the same lines that would fly from New York to
Paris. This was Captain Charles A. Lindbergh.

Corrigan was transferred from the field to the
factory to work on Lindbergh's plane, known as
the N.Y.P.—NX211. He spent two months making
wing ribs, assembling wings, installing gas tanks
and gas lines, sewing fabric and covering it with
dope. Lindbergh was there, supervising the construction, and Corrigan found him to be an inspiration. Two months after it was started, on April
28, 1927, Lindbergh's plane was completed. Less
than a month later Lindbergh made his flight to
Paris and there was a wild, noisy celebration back
in San Diego, in which Corrigan took part.

As a result of Lindbergh's successful flight, the
Mahoney plant prospered. Corrigan became a

welder and at this time started to save for his own plane, oftentimes going without lunch and always going without breakfast. He continued to fly steadily, buying his time in the air, and in December, 1927, he passed his Airplane and Engine Mechanics' Test given by the Department of Commerce.

On June 3, 1928, Corrigan was working in the factory when Lindbergh suddenly appeared. He recognized the young mechanic who had helped build the *Spirit of St. Louis,* and Corrigan later wrote, ''That handshake was my inspiration to keep trying, because in my estimation, Lindbergh was, and still is, the greatest character in the history of the world.''

In October, 1928, the Mahoney factory was moved to St. Louis, but Corrigan did not go along. He worked as a mechanic with the San Diego Air Service and with the Airtech, a flying school. In 1929 he got his pilot's license, and a little later passed his transport test with a high rating. For a few months he was stationed at Palm Springs as assistant pilot and chief mechanic. Then for four months he was pilot-mechanic of the Southern California Flying Club at Los Angeles.

In June, 1930, he drove to New York City in a Model T Ford, there to settle his father's estate.

His father had been killed a few years earlier working as a switchman for the New York Central. Corrigan was not able to collect a penny for the accident, and he became a mechanic at Roosevelt Field, where he worked on a number of famous planes. In May, 1931, he left Roosevelt Field and began barnstorming with Steve Reich, whose planes he flew at Norfolk, Glenrock, and Virginia Beach. His job was to fly passengers whenever any appeared, for Reich did not have a pilot's license.

Corrigan bought his first plane, a Hisso Eaglerock, in the winter of 1931 for $240. It had been cracked up and stowed away. He and his brother, Harry, who had now completed his engineering course at the University of California, reconditioned the plane and barnstormed with it in Maryland, Virginia, and North Carolina until it was cracked up during a storm in June, 1933, and was a total loss.

He wanted to return to California after the accident, in which Harry had sustained a broken wrist, so he bought an OX5 Robin from Frank Cordova for $325. It took him eighteen days to fly the craft to California, in such poor condition was the engine, but he reached home October 19, 1933.

After working at a private field for four months, Corrigan became a mechanic at the Northrop and Douglas Aircraft plants in Los Angeles. To save money, he slept in the little hangar he rented for his plane.

In January, 1935, he went to work in the Ryan Factory in San Diego and brought his Robin with him. Not until October, 1935, did the thought of a Newfoundland-Ireland flight enter his head, and when it did, it prompted him to buy a used Wright J6-5 motor from Felix Blum at Roosevelt Field, New York. In the spring of 1936, having overhauled the motor, he began installing gasoline and oil tanks. The plane was licensed for cross-country flights, but when he flew to Roosevelt Field in August, he found that he could not get permission for a flight to Ireland.

He flew back to California, testing the plane with a 1900-mile non-stop flight from Roosevelt Field to San Antonio by way of Jacksonville, Florida. After his return to San Diego he worked for Ryan once more, then gave up his mechanics job to become an instructor at Chula Vista.

In 1937 Corrigan applied for permission to fly from New York to London, but found that long solos were being discouraged because Amelia Earhart Putnam had recently been lost in the Pacific. With the intention of making a secret flight across the Atlantic, the young flier flew across the continent in August, but failed to find a satisfactory airfield in Maine for his take-off, so he "sneaked" back, as he puts it, to Chula Vista.

An ocean flight had become a passion with Corrigan by this time, so in October, 1937, he flew East again, only to find the weather too cold for a transatlantic flight. He loaded up on 290 gallons of gasoline, although his plane was unlicensed, and flew back to the Coast, making 2100 miles on the first hop to Texas. When he reached San Diego, he was forbidden to fly in the winter of 1937-38. Financially flat after his two transcontinental trips, he was willing to leave his plane in a hangar for six months.

Corrigan went to work welding tanks at the Northrop factory. He lived at the home of his Uncle Langford. During the winter he overhauled his engine again and installed more gasoline tanks. In the spring he asked for permission to fly to New York and back and was given an experimental license in June, 1938.

Thus, on July 8, 1938, he left Long Beach, California, destined to make only one more stop before he landed at Dublin, Ireland, a world-famous young aviator. He landed at Roosevelt Field at sundown, July 9, with only four gallons of the gasoline he started with left in his tanks. Living with Steve Reich the next week, Corrigan worked on his plane and studied weather maps and information for his flight back to California. Ruth Nichols, internationally known aviatrix, offered him her parachute for his journey, but he refused it, saying that he did not have room.

Then came his take-off at dawn July 17 before a handful of spectators, his long run down the fairway, his disappearance into the northeast, and Behr's whisper: "I've a hunch this fellow is on his way to Europe."

In his book Corrigan explains that he found the upper compass not to be working properly. Some liquid had leaked out. He flew by the lower compass. "I looked down at the compass, and now that there was more light I noticed I had been following the wrong end of the magnetic needle on the whole flight. As the opposite of west is east, I realized that I was over the Atlantic Ocean somewhere. But where!"

That's Corrigan's story and he sticks to it! Whatever it was that led him to Dublin, homing instinct, a broken compass, a compass misread, or good marksmanship, it led him also to the Hall of Fame and the Gallery of Gold. Lowell Thomas summarized Corrigan's wrong-way flight with these kind words:

"He illustrated with graphic and unmistakable clarity the capacity and resourcefulness of the mechanical mind. He became the latest personification of the type of mentality that has lifted mankind within three centuries from a race of crawlers to a generation of fliers, the kind of mind which has given us modern surgery, modern plumbing, and the ability to talk to one another though separated by thousands of miles of space."

FRANK (PAT) DENGIS: THE MIGHTY MAN OF MARATHON

FRANK "PAT" DENGIS

CHAPTER III

FRANK (PAT) DENGIS : THE MIGHTY MAN OF MARATHON

By Jerry Nason, Sports Writer, *Boston Globe*

In their untiring search for athletic characters with that elusive and undefinable something known as "color," the sports authors of the nation's journals have managed to ignore at some length the very personification of what they seek to brighten their daily literary output.

To our way of thinking, Frank Dengis, who will hereafter be known as Pat, which would be his wish, is deserving of a place among any biographical collection of great athletes such as this book aspires to be. And the garrulous, lovable, competent Welsh immigrant would not assume such a position under false pretenses or by virtue of his never-failing, salty wit.

The fact of the matter is that Pat has by right of conquest risen to the pinnacle of that tedious 26 mile, 385 yards event—the Marathon race. So, then, there is no need to explain Dengis' presence among his athletic contemporaries between these covers. Suffice to say that among modern American Marathon runners at least, he knows no equal, either as a distance runner or as a prince of wit.

From June, 1937, to November, 1938, Pat Dengis competed in thirteen Marathon races, won eleven of them and placed second in the two he failed to win.

This seventeen-month Marathon record is believed to be without parallel in the annals of American athletics, because Dengis defeated every top-notch Marathon runner of United States, Canada, Greece, and the Argentine in the process.

Although he was thirty-nine years old on July 18, 1939, the gifted aeronautical tool-maker and mechanical expert from Baltimore knocked lustily upon the portals of sports fame and was admitted at an age when the average man is selecting for himself a comfortable rocking chair. But measured by any yardstick, Pat Dengis is no average mortal.

He was thirty-two years old before he ever entertained ambitions in the field of distance running. At thirty-two, the boxing champion has disappeared down the sunset slopes of his career, the major league ball player is congratulating himself for wise investments with his heyday salaries, the champion of the cinder paths has put his spikes away forever and is basking in the glories of the past.

But at thirty-two Pat Dengis was bitten, as he expresses it, by the Marathon bug, bitten so badly that in the course of seven ensuing years he was to win three national championships and be honored four times with selection for the All-American track and field team by Mr. Dan Ferris of the Amateur Athletic Union.

This, mind you, was after a patchwork-quilt career that started in the Welsh coal fields and embraced such fascinating incidents en route as torpedoings by German "U" boats off the coast of Wales, blood-and-thunder soccer games among the miners of the Rhondda Valley, voyages on tramp steamers to ports in all corners of the globe, three shipwrecks, and virtual starvation on the desolate pampas of the Argentine.

The truth of it is that Dengis has led a life that almost defies telling, and one attempting to tell it is torn between the desire to concentrate on his athletic prowess and the temptation to relate experiences that would make a grand tale.

So we will endeavor to blend together the two chapters of Pat Dengis' life, since one supersedes the other and at no time do the two entwine.

First, let us inspect the gentleman himself: He is thirty-nine years old, as previously stated, yet not a thread of silver gleams in that raven's-wing shock of curly hair. He emigrated to the United States in September, 1926, the day Tunney beat Dempsey for the heavyweight boxing championship at Philadelphia. Dengis weighed 192 pounds, all salt and sinew, as the expression goes, when he saluted the Statue of Liberty from the deck of the *S.S. Majestic.*

Today Pat weighs 137 pounds, when groomed for one of his inimitable terrific rushes into the lead in the late miles of a Marathon race.

"When I landed in New York," says Pat, by way of explaining this fifty-five-pound difference in weight, "I heard that many Welshmen were working in the steel mills at Baltimore, so I headed there and took a job as machinist. A few weeks later I transferred to the rolling mill department. Weighing 192 pounds, and as strong as an ox, I possessed, and still do, an uncanny ability to withstand the terrific heat of the white-hot bars, even on a midsummer's day.

"I was making a fine salary, but one winter's day I came to the realization that I was working myself to death, for I no longer weighed 192 pounds, but only 140. Everyone was burnt out physically at the age of thirty or thirty-five at this job. In one mad fit I packed my duds, and in six hours was working my passage back across the Atlantic on a Swedish tramp steamer."

After creating such a surprise by his unexpected return to the family hearth in South Wales that his mother, two sisters, and his brother's wife fainted away when he walked unannounced across the threshold, Pat subsequently returned to America. He went into the steel mills again, lured by the fat wages.

Then came the financial letdown of 1929. Wages dropped at the mills, so Pat returned to his first love, the machinist's trade. And he has advanced. Today he holds a foreman's position in one of America's biggest airplane factories.

"I guess I'm holder of at least one distinction as a Marathon runner," he grins. "I am probably the only one who isn't hoping to win some big race and get a job as a result!"

Back in Swansea, South Wales, where he was born in 1900, Dengis was an unusual product of those hard-working sons of the coal fields. He was a child prodigy. He entered the public school situated across from the modest Dengis home at the tender age of two. He was through the grades and given a special high school scholarship before he was ten years old. Here his classmates were rough-and-ready boys of sixteen to nineteen years.

In three-quarters of the usual period of high schooling Pat had completed the four years at the school and had won a scholarship to an engineering school, having an undeniable genius for things mechanical.

"Like all 'prodigies' I was true to the type," confesses Pat, "in that I was pale, sickly and very much unlike my parents. My father was the John L. Sullivan type, about five feet, eight inches tall, with a forty-eight-inch chest and a ferocious handle-bar mustache. At eleven he had run away to sea and he followed the ocean for twenty-five years. I still remember the stories he told of far-away places—Frisco, the Barbary Coast, Rio and the Klondike when they were wild and woolly."

But young Pat never did complete his course at engineering college. When he was sixteen his father died of lead poisoning as a result of an accident at the zinc refinery in which he worked. Pat had three years of college, and a runaway record of his own, having thrice during the year between his fourteenth and fifteenth birthdays shipped off to sea (men were scarce in war days, informed Pat) and been torpedoed by the German "U" boats lurking off the coast.

"Twice we were twenty miles out of port when we got it," reminisces Dengis. "So I was back home again the same day and received a sound thrashing. The third time we were two days out of port and in a convoy of one hundred vessels. But being the slowest we fell behind and were easy pickings for the German subs that trailed us. It took ten days to get home that time, but I received the business end of a leather belt, just the same!"

When Pat's father died the future American Marathon champion's schooling was over. But his escapades at sea were not. The tales his father had told before the flickering hearth on many a damp Welsh evening in the Rhondda Valley were lodged in a fertile imagination.

"It is not surprising that after I had finished my trade schooling I should go off to sea for upwards of nine years, off and on," remarks Pat.

But somewhere back in the days following the World War the pale, sickly lad who entered high school before his tenth birthday had grown into hardy Welsh manhood. Presumably sports had an influence.

"That's so," relates Dengis. "In the long evenings—and there is twilight in Wales till eleven at night for five or six months of the year—we played the maddest hell-for-leather kind of soccer for four or five hours at a stretch on the bare, stony field on a hillside, shod in heavy, hob-nailed working boots. You get toughened up at that. After awhile I became the wild man who tore around after the ball, smashing men down like ten-pins.

"I also played Rugby football on week-ends. And I may say that Rugby in the Welsh valleys is legalized murder compared to American football, for we wore no protective suits of armor at it. To this day my legs are a mass of scars and weals from my football days."

Not only scars and weals, for Dengis' unusual flat-footed style of running that defies the critics of Marathon form, is a result of those ferocious soccer and Rugby skirmishes back in Swansea, Wales. Over the second knuckle of the big toe is a knot the size of a baby's fist. He is unable to bend that foot up or down except from the ankle itself. The cartilage was removed from his right knee as a result of still another soccer game played with wild abandon in 1919.

Meantime the wild young Welsh soccer player was making his trips to sea, as had his father before him. He apparently thrived on the salt air and the coarse but healthy fare, for he was soon a rugged physical specimen of 190 pounds and happily conscious of a size seventeen collar.

Shipping as a hand on tramp steamers of every nationality, Dengis called at the ports of the world his father had long before told of, and some he hadn't. Cape Town, Durban, Santos, Genoa, Calcutta, Singapore, Rio de Janeiro, Melbourne, Shanghai, Hong Kong, New York, Karachi, all the ports of the French and Spanish coasts—these passed in an endless procession before the keen brown eyes of the young Welshman.

He'd been up the Riga in Russia following the Revolution, and had seen humans starving, so he knew what starvation was like. Indeed, he was later to experience the unpleasant feeling of his stomach shriveling into a kernel for lack of food. That was up the River Plate (Rio de la Plata) in 1924, while loading wheat at the South American port of Rosario.

"I had money on me," he recollects with some evidence of distaste. "One night on shore somebody slipped a powder into my wine and when I regained consciousness I was hundreds of miles up in the pampas, picked clean, barefooted, clad only in a shirt and denim pants, and bouncing merrily along in a freight car."

Dengis nearly starved in his bare-footed march of more than three hundred miles back to civilization. He was in rags and on the verge of utter exhaustion when a month later he finally tramped over the last rows of railroad ties into Buenos Aires, there to be fed and clothed at Canon Brady's justly famous "Seaman's Mission."

Dengis worked fifteen months in Buenos Aires as a refrigerating engineer for an American meat-packing firm. He loved the city as he has loved no other before or since. His job was good and the life gay, but the wanderlust claimed him again in 1925. He shipped on a cattle boat bound for Rotterdam, getting his passage and five dollars in return for giving the beasts feed.

But Pat and his new pets parted company at the first port of call, which was St. Vincent, a coaling station in the Cape Verde Islands off the west coast of Africa. "The cattle ship was nothing but a Greek 'coffin' tub and between the bad weather and the ship's crazy antics I decided to leave her," reviews Dengis today.

He subsequently returned to Wales via London on a more sea-worthy craft and almost immediately shipped for New York, which particular voyage all but cut short the career of the present American Marathon champion. For ten days out to sea the stodgy tramp steamer had her rudder beaten away in a terrific storm and was almost reduced to salvage when a sister ship happened along and towed the craft to Fayal, Azores Islands, for repairs.

This was eventually to be Pat's most significant voyage, for before its conclusion he was to shovel snow on the streets of New York, an experience that, strangely enough, had as much to do with his future American citizenship as any other.

Three days out of Fayal, headed for New York, a volcano erupted at the former port, spreading disaster which Dengis fortunately escaped. New York was reached thirty-five days after leaving Liverpool. It was snowing. The crew was forced to spend a day on shore while their vessel underwent the process of fumigating, as all must that come in from Fayal.

"Signs were placed in the piles of snow along Broadway, I recall," he says. "They read: 'Men Wanted. $1 per hour.' Soon all of us were at it, and we shoveled snow for ten hours. Yes sir, ten easy dollars, and it took a week and a half to make that much on board ship. Later, when I got back to South Wales, I never could get out of my mind that dollar an hour for shoveling snow. The sidewalks of New York were not paved with gold, but dollar bills certainly grew in snow piles!"

But before Dengis was to return to New York the second time destiny beckoned him on to South American grain ports again, where he was to nearly lose his life in the swift, ugly current of the Parana River when a speedboat swept him from the staging while painting the vessel.

It was after experiencing his fifth shipwreck that Pat once and for all decided to leave the sea. It was his last voyage, from South America bound for Rotterdam, that decided him. Hear Pat tell it:

"We were but a few hours out of San Nicholas when we came to a fork in the Parana River and another ship tried to cut across our bows. Being the loaded ship, and headed downstream, we had the right of way. As plain as a move on the checkerboard a collision was inevitable.

"The river pilot we had aboard gave the order
. . . 'Hard-a-starboard' and I threw the wheel
over to the last spin and cocked one eye to see how
far it was to the nearest shore when I heard the
pilot making gurgling noises in his throat. Sure,
the crash came, and we ripped a hole forty feet
long in the other ship's engine room. She struggled on to the river banks a mile away and
grounded. We followed suit and soon stopped with
twenty feet of water in the forepeak and Number
1 hold. Both anchors were driven back into the
ship's forepeak and were useless.

"Well, a salvage tug came up from Buenos
Aires and slapped a wooden patch over the bow,
then towed us 150 miles down the river, bumping
the bottom all the way for ten days. It took us a
month to get patched up, then we sailed for Rotterdam, 6,500 miles away, with the bows smashed
back flat so that it looked like we were carrying a
billboard in front of us. The forepeak and Number 1 hold had been packed with cement to stop
leaks. That journey took fifty-two days. We
landed at Rotterdam on my twenty-sixth birthday
and I swore an oath to quit the water then and
there. I'd had five shipwrecks and sooner or later
my luck would fail me."

And Pat Dengis has never been to sea since in other than a traveler's role.

It was in September, 1931, that Dengis first ran a foot race. This was after his second return to the United States, and his decision to leave the Baltimore steel mills for the machinist's trade.

Dengis' associates were holding their annual work picnic and the Welshman was somewhat surprised to learn that his name was among the entries in the mile run, one of the athletic events. He protested immediately.

"Listen, Dengis, you're the youngest man in my gang," his foreman informed him, "and every department is expected to put an entry in every event, so it's you for the mile run!"

Pat of the toothsome smile gleefully recollects the day and deed. "I'd been told that milers wore spiked shoes so I bought a pair. My training consisted of a parade once around the track to officially start the meet."

Victory did not crown Pat's baptismal race, unfortunately. He was twenty-fifth among twenty-six starters after three-quarters of a mile and taking a loud round of ridicule from his shop mates as he trudged past. Suddenly, quite as much to his own surprise as theirs, Dengis bounded madly around the track with a mad sprint, passing runners in droves, and plunged across the line in second place, only a yard behind the winner.

"Glenn Cunningham couldn't have worried much at the time," remarked Dengis. "The time was something like 5 minutes, 27 seconds."

The fact that Pat almost passed out upon finishing his violent mile effort, temporarily blighted his running career. He who had just run himself dizzy in a mile race wasn't then thinking in terms of twenty-six miles, the Marathon distance.

About four months later Pat made the acquaintance of an elderly gentleman named "Pop" Hertz, who completely amazed the young Welshman by his ability to jog around a track lap after lap with no apparent disaster.

It was "Pop" Hertz, recalling Dengis' one and only foot race, who gave Dengis the distance running "germ." "Pop" forwarded the opinion that Dengis was cut out for distance running, even went so far as to get him an A.A.U. registration card and enter him in the South Atlantic ten-mile championship at Richmond, Virginia. That was on Feb. 22, 1932.

Pat made very unorthodox preparations for his initial road race, training on a local cinder track in Baltimore by means of a self-devised program that involved running one lap the first night of training, two the second, three the third, etc.

Despite all, Dengis stunned the one hundred contestants in the championship race by running third behind Billy Agee, then the national fifteen-miles and Marathon champion. His time was more or less phenomenal, being fifty-nine minutes.

The fact that this black-haired, grinning neophyte outran a dozen famous distance runners in his first race led to a prominent display on the sports pages. Being human, Pat enjoyed it immensely and decided right away that he'd go up to Boston on the 19th of April, and compete in the famous Boston A.A. Marathon race.

It is a whimsical coincidence that this venerable race, oldest of all Marathon runs barring the Olympic event, should be the agency through which Pat launched his Marathon career. The records show that it is the only Marathon race of any significance on the North American continent he has failed to win at least once.

He'd give a year of his life to win it, because no Marathon run is more famous, more publicized or more colorful than the forty-four-year-old Boston race.

The Marathon critics, the curbstone critics, he calls them, claim Pat will never win at Boston on account of a leering ''jinx'' that awaits him there. Pat doesn't subscribe to the ''jinx'' theory, despite the persistence with which the fates conspire to thwart his efforts on the long, winding, Marathon course at Boston.

He has raced on this course eight times in vain. In the races of 1935 and 1938 he finished second. In 1939 he was fourth, a valiant effort considering the conditions under which the race was held, it being a cold, rainy day and Dengis shackled from the beginning with a heavy cold. In 1932 he finished twenty-eighth, it being his first Marathon, and a year later he was fourteenth.

Of his first Boston Marathon start Dengis recalls: ''A stranger in Boston, I arrived at the club house at nine-thirty in the morning and was told the race started in Hopkinton, twenty-six miles away. So I thumbed a ride out there, roasted a ham bone over a fire made by some nature-food expert of newspapers, then started the race.

''I ran at a fair clip and was told I was seven minutes behind the leaders somewhere on the hills at eighteen miles. But I was utterly spent in the last three miles and sat on a curbing to rest. Everyone shouted "The finish is just around the corner," and I yelled back, "So is recovery!" But they were right. I sat there and let seven or eight runners go by, then got up to find the finish really was just around the corner."

In the 1934, 1936 and 1937 Marathons at Boston, Dengis failed to finish, three of the four times in his career that he has been unable to run the full 26 miles, 385 yards.

His effort at Boston in 1936, an Olympic trial, almost tolled the knell of his Marathon running. Although he was in fine condition, Pat ran twenty-one miles that day and almost collapsed from an affliction known to men of medicine as paroxysmal hemoglobinuria, an internal weakness of a dangerous nature.

Four years before he'd been stricken similarly and was told by a specialist that he had but six months to live.

The following year, when Pat and a company of friends were celebrating his victory in the national Marathon championship, the specialist was the guest of honor! But until his breakdown at Boston in 1936 the durable Dengis had suffered only occasionally. Now he was really troubled. He lost fourteen pounds in the race, in addition to bringing on the old ailment. His burning ambition to represent his adopted land in the Olympic Marathon at Berlin alone kept him going for twenty miles.

But there was another tryout race at Washington, five weeks later. Dengis was determined to run, despite his physical condition and his failure to gain back more than six of the pounds he lost in Boston. He planned to put all his eggs in one basket so to speak. "My only chance under the circumstances is to go out with all the speed I've got from the very start and hope to last the distance," he plotted.

For eighteen miles this man who should have been under a doctor's care broke all course records in Washington. Then exhaustion in the guise of paroxysmal hemoglobinuria overtook him and with it, Billy McMahon and Johnny Kelley, the ultimate first- and second-place winners. Pat, wan, weary and disconsolate, finished eighth after walking six of the twenty-six miles.

Again in 1937 the Boston "jinx" stopped him, although he felt mostly fatigue, rather than the ravages of paroxysmal hemoglobinuria, this time. So Pat stalked into Johns Hopkins Hospital, Baltimore, three days later, for a thorough physical checkup, with the threat of dropping Marathon running completely if he wasn't fit.

"A week of intense examinations had all of them puzzled," says Pat of that episode. "Finally, as a test, I got out of bed, ran twenty-five miles and lost seven pounds doing it. They couldn't induce a recurrence of my old trouble that was knocking me out in my races, nor could they give a definite answer as to what ailed me. So I decided to have one last fling, in the national championship, and if I didn't finish in the first three I'd drop out of the game."

Training for that particular race was a nightmare, or rather a dawnmare for Pat. He ran into a stretch of over-time work that prevented him from training at night, so that he arose before the sun, put in his mileage before breakfast, then tackled a fourteen-hour working day. He'd also rigged up a pulley device designed to strengthen his back, where the old ailment was wont to strike him down.

The national championship was in Washington, and Pat toed the line in good condition but short of sleep, prepared to drop from the ranks of Marathon if he was badly beaten. He led the field at a hot pace for sixteen miles before weakening and losing his lead to Mel Porter, whom Pat calls the hardest man of all to beat.

"I was groggy and sick of it when the veteran Clarence De Mar passed me too," he says. "Another man was right on my heels. I was ready to chuck it all and let him pass. I started to walk. My wife and loyal friend, Bill Schlobohm, were in a car, looking very glum indeed. Then I started to give myself a good tongue lashing, chiding myself for letting a veteran like De Mar, nearly fifty years old, beat me. Suddenly I started to run again, put on one of my patented finishing drives, and I caught and passed De Mar. But I failed by less than two minutes of catching Porter, who won, although I cut seven minutes from his lead in the last five miles."

That was the turning point in Pat's career. Not since that day has paroxysmal hemoglobinuria bothered him. And from that point on, he launched one of the most remarkable Marathon records here or anywhere. His second place in the national race gave him the long-cherished right to wear a United States track emblem on the breast of his running jersey, for he was selected to represent Uncle Sam in the Pan-American Marathon championship at Dallas, Texas.

Jubilant over the honor, and vowing to be a glorious defender of the star-spangled shield, Pat won the race after a savage battle from the eighteenth to the twenty-first mile with Ribas of the Argentine, holder of the world record for covering the distance in two hours.

Pat remembers that day for other reasons, as well. "It was my thirty-seventh birthday," he says. "We ran the first two miles inside the stadium and I was dead last, with twenty thousand spectators singing 'Happy Birthday, dear Dengis.' The temperature was 103 degrees, and I ran the best-judged, most confident race of my life."

Pressed, he will also tell you how a wayside watermelon dealer on the course promised him a luscious melon if he won. Pat went around later to collect his prize only to find the stand closed. A bronzed sheriff, hearing of the story, personally gained entrance by means of an axe and invited Pat to take his pick saying: "Texas hospitality demands you have your melon!"

Pat, the fair and smiling Mrs. Dengis, and faithful Bill Schlobohm made quite a picture that evening dissecting a forty-pound watermelon on the campus of Southern Methodist University.

The triumph at Dallas was the first by the

United States in an international Marathon in three decades and Dengis automatically became the Marathon man of the hour.

Under the stimulus of that win, which he claims made him a 25% better runner because it gave him the confidence he lacked, Pat went on to clean up the Port Chester and Yonkers Marathons in New York for three straight wins that season.

At the former race he won by the stunning margin of nearly seven minutes, about a mile, from Leslie Pawson, holder of the Boston course record at the time. At Yonkers he was given only a fighting chance, since he had suffered a wrenched knee and several bad gashes prior to the race when he fell over a detour sign while training in the Stygian darkness of the Maryland night. He was in twentieth position at eighteen miles, limping badly, but rallied with a terrific finishing spurt to catch Gerard Cote, Canada, about a mile from the finish.

He went on to win by four hundred yards. He claims it was the greatest finish he ever made in a Marathon race. It had to be to bring home the trophy.

Never had a Marathon runner swept all the major races in one season and that was Pat's ambition when the 1938 rolled around four months after his sensational victory over Cote at Yonkers.

Barring a bad lapse in strategy Dengis would have achieved that ambition, for he was beaten in the Boston race by Leslie Pawson, then won consecutively the Salisbury, Provincial, Port Chester and Yonkers events.

It was the consensus of opinion among the Boston press writers that Dengis virtually handed Pawson the only race he lost. The day was a perfect one for the Baltimore runner to break the Boston "jinx," being exceptionally warm for April in Massachusetts, and a warm day generally found Dengis unbeatable.

But Pat plotted to stay well off the early pace, then come rushing up in the late miles, a formula he had found a winning one. This time he underestimated Pawson's staying powers on a hot day. For Pawson took the lead almost immediately and stretched out a long gap of macadam between himself and Dengis, who was in thirty-second position at five miles.

At ten miles Pat found himself in twentieth position and suddenly realized he would have to start moving fast before it was too late. It was too late. Dengis overpowered runner after runner in a mad rush from the twelfth mile to the finish. He passed them all, but he had granted Pawson too long a lead.

Within a mile of the finish Dengis' dark head could be seen through the blue haze of gas fumes, less than a half mile from the leader and drawing nearer with incredible swiftness. No human could possibly overcome such a tremendous deficit, and Pat knew it. But he tried. He crossed the finish line scarcely a minute after Pawson had fractured the tape.

"With all credit to Les Pawson, a fine fellow and a fine runner," he said, "I honestly feel that this was the one race of my career I tossed away."

He refuses to recognize the presence of the reputed "jinx" that awaits him each April at Boston, even after that and his 1939 appearance, when he came to Boston's cold clime from balmy Baltimore three days before the race, caught a bad cold and ran fourth in a chill rain with his fastest race on that particular course.

But his failure to catch Pawson on the home stretch in 1938 taught Dengis a valuable lesson. He who had been constantly laying back in the early stages of a Marathon and driving up in the closing miles with his inimitable power—well, Pat decided to ever after take charge at the start.

Those were his tactics throughout the season following his defeat by Pawson. At Salisbury Beach he took the lead at ten miles and broke the course record by fifteen minutes. At Montreal he again smashed into the lead early and won in two hours, forty-two minutes over a course that measured nearly twenty-eight miles.

At Port Chester he made an unprecedented move into the lead at eight miles and defeated Mel Porter by nearly ten minutes, an almost unbelievable margin over a top-notch Marathon runner.

Three weeks later found Pat preserving these new tactics in the national championship at Yonkers, New York, a race conducted by his old friend Schlobohm. He was third at five miles and carving out the pace at ten. Cote alone could stay with him and the French Canadian submitted to Pat's furious running over the hills at the twenty-mile mark. So Pat won his fourth race of the season and became crowned the national Marathon champion for the second time in four years.

But two burning desires kept him running. One was to win the famous Boston Marathon, only established race on the continent of North America he had failed to win. The other was to represent

United States in Olympic competition at Helsinki in 1940.

Pat was married in August, 1934, to a blond and lovely descendant of Charles Carroll, a signer of the Declaration of Independence, and—you guessed it—they honeymooned to the national 25-kilometer championship race at Beverly, Massachusetts!

Eve Dengis is Pat's staunchest supporter, attends all his races, and is frequently on hand at the finish to make victory official with an enthusiastic embrace.

"My wife," boasts Pat with pardonable pride, "has witnessed every race I have ever been in since the very start, and is without doubt the greatest Marathon fan in captivity. I am one runner who can honestly say my training takes precedence over social activities, thanks to the cooperation and interest of my wife."

Dengis is otherwise generous with credit for his astounding Marathon successes. The loyalty of Schlobohm, a Marathon runner of much worth in the early 1900's; the kindliness and advice of Albert Monteverde, a venerable gentleman from Mays Landing, New Jersey, now in California, and Pete Gavuzzi, the old Bunion Derby runner, who trained him for his comeback after the Boston breakdown in 1936—these are men to whom Pat says "Thanks!"

Monteverde was sixty-six years old when these two first met, and was still competing in Marathon races, having raced 116 of them in his time. The meeting took place at Los Angeles, 1932, where the Olympic games were held.

Pat and an Olympic 50,000 meters walk aspirant named Newton decided to hitch-hike back to New Jersey, and did. Walking, running and riding they made the journey East.

"One day we walked from Williams to Flagstaff, Arizona, a distance of fifty-four miles," declares Pat. "Another day we walked from Albuquerque to Santa Fe, New Mexico, about forty-five miles, and I noticed I was always forging ahead of Newton, that he was ready to call it a day before I was every time. Yet this man was almost on the Olympic team that year."

Monteverde had asked Pat to look him up back East. Pat was jobless at the time, and since they'd become fast friends, he visited the veteran at Mays Landing and trained seriously under Monteverde's supervision on a small track on the old gentleman's property.

After a brief interlude as a walker, in which he led the national championship field at world-record-breaking time to within a mile of the finish, then literally crawled across in second place, Pat ended six months of idleness by going back to the steel mills and toughening himself up for a determined bid for Marathon fame.

He has always claimed that Monteverde's kindly understanding and advice set him on the right road at a trying time.

The Port Chester Marathon of 1935, in Pat's estimation, was the greatest ever raced anywhere, anytime. Dengis was the loser, being beaten in a sensational finish by Pawson, the New Englander.

"In the first place, I knew the course was long. Instead of being the regulation 26 miles, 385 yards, it measured 27.8 miles. Porter and Pawson had a hot battle for a dozen miles, where I caught Porter. In the next mile I came up with Pawson and we had it out hot and heavy to the finish.

"We passed the twenty-six-mile mark in 2h 27m 30s, almost two minutes under the present Olympic Marathon record, but we still had nearly two miles to go. I hoped the extra distance would stop Pawson, because I was strong as ever, but he held on gamely and with a jack-rabbit sprint in the last fifty yards he beat me by a couple of strides.

"Had the race finished at twenty-six miles there certainly would have been a world record for the Marathon made. In our twenty-two-mile duel never more than a few yards separated us. The lead changed hands at least fifty times. I started the race with a very sore neck. I recall being unable to turn my head. Yet after the race the stiffness was gone and a lump of muscle the size of a pigeon's egg came up on the back of my neck and is there to this day!"

Dengis has no dietary fads, thinks they are all "bunk," as he forcibly puts it. He eats hard boiled eggs for breakfast 365 days of the year and except when in strict training never says "no" to an occasional glass of beer.

And this is Frank (Pat) Dengis, the mighty man of Marathon, our nomination to be listed among the great American athletes of his time.

Certainly any professional boxer with the background of living and learning that is Pat's would have long since been made a million dollar piece of athletic bric-a-brac by the professional tub thumpers of the prize ring.*

* Frank (Pat) Dengis was killed in an airplane crash on December 17, 1939 at Baltimore, Maryland.

FRANK (PAT) DENGIS
Born Swansea, South Wales, July 18, 1900.

1932

South Atlantic A.A.U., 10 miles........	3rd	59m 02s
Boston A.A. Marathon.................	28th	2h 51m
Olympic Tryouts (Salisbury, Maryland).	15th	3h 31m
National 50,000-Meters Walk:.........	4th	5h 40m 36s
Port Chester (New York) Marathon....	7th	2h 59m
Ward Marathon (Montreal)............	8th	2h 58m

1933

Boston A.A. Marathon................	14th	2h 47m 9s
National 50,000-Meters Walk..........	2nd	5h 15m
Port Chester (New York) Marathon....	4th	No Time
National Marathon (Washington).......	Dropped out at 23 miles	

1934

North Medford (Massachusetts) 20-Miles	2nd	2h 1m 59s
Boston A.A. Marathon................	Dropped out at 14 miles	
National Marathon (Washington).......	5th	2h 56m 8s
Washington 10 Miles.................	1st	No Time
National 25-Kilometers (Beverly, Massachusetts)...........................	5th	1h 34m 8s
National 30-Kilometers (Pawtucket, Rhode Island)......................	4th	1h 50m 49s
Richmond (Virginia) 10 Miles..........	1st	54m 30s
Port Chester (New York) Marathon....	1st	2h 31m 30s (Record)
Wilmington (Delaware) Marathon......	3rd	2h 38m 27s

1935

North Medford (Massachusetts) 20-Miles	5th	2h 30m 12s
Boston A.A. Marathon................	2nd	2h 34m 11s
National Marathon (Wilmington, Delaware).............................	1st	2h 53m 53s
Valley Forge Marathon (Philadelphia) ..	1st	2h 38m 24s
National 30-Kilometers................	3rd	1h 36m 57s
Port Chester (New York) Marathon....	2nd	2h 37m 50s
Yonkers (New York) Marathon........	4th	2h 41m 13s

1936

Boston A.A. Marathon................	Dropped out at 21 miles	
National Marathon (Washington).......	8th	2h 52m 15s
British A.A.A. Marathon (London).....	4th	2h 40m 2s
Port Chester (New York) Marathon....	2nd	2h 37m 19s
Yonkers (New York) Marathon........	3rd	2h 41m 17s
National 30-Kilometers (Cincinnati)....	1st	1h 44m 45s
		(Record)

1937

North Medford (Massachusetts) 20-Miles	3rd	2h 00m 36s
Boston A.A. Marathon................	Dropped out at 15 miles	
National Marathon (Washington).......	2nd	2h 46m 36s
Pan-American Marathon (Dallas, Texas)	1st	2h 42m 43s
Port Chester (New York) Marathon....	1st	2h 33m 45s
Yonkers (New York) Marathon........	1st	2h 42m 50s

1938

Boston A.A. Marathon................	2nd	2h 36m 40s
Salisbury (Massachusetts) Marathon....	1st	2h 33m 27s
		(Record)
Provincial (Province Quebec) Marathon.	1st	2h 42m
Port Chester (New York) Marathon....	1st	2h 42m 29s
Yonkers (New York) National Marathon	1st	2h 39m 38s

1939

Boston A.A. Marathon................	4th	2h 33m 22s
Salisbury (Massachusetts) Marathon....	1st	2h 32m 54s
		(Record)
Laurel-Baltimore Marathon............	1st	2h 44m 30s
Waterbury (Connecticut) Marathon.....	1st	2h 42m 11s
Port Chester (New York) Marathon....	1st	2h 45m 2s
Yonkers (New York) National Marathon	1st	2h 33m 45.2s
		(Record)

Recapitulation (Marathon races only): Competed in 36 Marathons, won 15, placed second five times, third twice, fourth four times, and fifth once.

BILL DICKEY: KING OF CATCHERS

WILLIAM B. "BILL" DICKEY

CHAPTER IV

BILL DICKEY: KING OF CATCHERS

By Harold Kaese, Sports Writer, *Boston Evening Transcript*

PERSPIRATION beaded Bill McKechnie's forehead as he watched the Yankees in their hitting practice. It was a hot Sunday in Cincinnati, unusually hot for October 8, and the sun was making an oven of the home team's bench at Crosley Field, where the manager of the Reds sat beside Al Schacht, the clown prince of baseball, who was an outlandish figure as he rested there, a tall silk hat askew on his head and a swallow-tail coat pulled back from the baseball uniform he was wearing.

McKechnie might have been perspiring because of the intense heat, or he might have been perspiring because of the desperate situation of the Reds in this 1939 World Series—they had already lost three games to the mighty Yankees—or he might have been perspiring because of the exhibition of

103

slugging the champions were giving in their batting practice.

"Al," he began, nudging the comedian, "look at that Dickey up there. He's lost a half-dozen balls in practice already. You've seen him play more than I have. What's the best way to pitch to him?"

Schacht thought for a moment before answering. Then he replied, "Bill, the safest way to pitch to Dickey is low and behind him."

McKechnie chuckled. "Behind him, eh," he said, "Well, from what I've seen of him this series that's about the only kind of a pitch he can't hit. Maybe we'll try it."

When it came to the seventh inning of the game, about two hours later, McKechnie wished he had ordered his big pitcher, Paul Derringer, to throw behind Dickey, for the lanky catcher smashed a pitch far into the stands in right center field for a home run. Coming on top of Charlie Keller's homer, it gave the Yankees a 2-0 lead and made it necessary for McKechnie to remove Derringer for a pinch hitter in the next inning. That was the end of the Reds. The Yankees won their fourth consecutive game for their fourth consecutive championship in ten innings by a 7-4 score.

Experts argue about the greatest team of all time. Some take the Philadelphia Athletics of 1910-1914; some choose the Chicago White Sox of 1919; others like the New York Giants of 1921-1924; many pick the New York Yankees of 1926-1928; but most believe the modern Yankees, who won four pennants and four World Series in 1936-1939, to be the greatest of all baseball clubs. What greater honor, then, could there be for Bill Dickey than to be universally acclaimed as the key man on this team, the leader who dictated the strategy on the field and the personality who dominated the spirit of the regulars?

When so many superb players are brought together under one banner, there is bound to be argument as to which one is the best of all. Most critics agree that for sheer ability, Joe DiMaggio is tops, but Charlie Keller, Joe Gordon, Red Ruffing, Red Rolfe and Bill Dickey are in his class. Dickey stands high in value because of the responsibility he bears in filling the catcher's position, probably the most important of the eight fielding positions.

Shortly after Dickey had hit his home run off Derringer that hot afternoon in Cincinnati, and the Yankees had won the championship, the ace pitcher for the Reds was cooling off in the club house.

"Who do you think is the best player on the Yankees?" he asked.

"Joe DiMaggio," was a prompt reply.

"Nope, not for my money," said Derringer. "I'll take Dickey before DiMaggio from what I've seen of him in this series, and I don't say that because he singled to beat me in the first game and then hit that homer off me today."

"Why do you say it then?"

"Because of the way he handles pitchers and because of the way he leads the team. He's something more than a great hitter. He's a great thinker, and mechanically he's just about a perfect catcher."

Bill Werber, Cincinnati's third baseman, chimed in with, "You can give Dickey a lot of credit for the great pitching of the Yankees. Take a flighty fellow like Monte Pearson. He pitches a two-hit game against us only because Dickey's there to steady him down when he starts getting wild. Dickey watches the batter's feet as he stands up at the plate and from that can tell what the batter is looking for. He's really smart."

The catcher has more chance to think and use

his wits than any other player, including the pitcher. After all, he tells the pitcher what to throw and where to throw it. Yankee pitchers rarely disagree with Dickey's judgment in signaling for pitches.

"When they do shake me off," says Dickey in baseball vernacular; "I let them throw what they want to. I don't argue with a pitcher. He's the fellow who's got to throw the ball and it's always better to let him use the curve or fast ball in which he has the most confidence."

Naturally the catcher must study hitters. Some of them keep note books on the strength and weaknesses of all batsmen in their league. Dickey does not; he memorizes their traits. Ask him the way to pitch to Jimmy Foxx and he will tell you:

"In Boston where the left-field fence is close, you've got to keep the ball low and outside, so Foxx can't pull it. In New York, where right field is close, you keep the ball high and inside, hoping he will hit a fly to center or left, where there is a lot of room. Of course, against an exceptional hitter like Foxx, you have to be lucky. You can pitch to him perfectly sometimes and he'll still hit the ball out of the lot."

Before every game, while the rival team is having hitting practice, Dickey can be seen in the Yankee dugout, watching the batters and talking to the teammate who is going to pitch. When new players come up from the minor leagues, the catcher is especially observant, studying such details as these: where he holds the bat, the plane of his swing, the length of his stride and his position in the batter's box.

If the Yankees have trouble getting a new player out, Dickey takes advantage of the grapevine system and discusses the problem with other catchers. Supposing a Detroit rookie by the name of Joe Clout makes a half-dozen hits against the Yankees in three games. Dickey worries over this phenomenon. A few days later, when the Yankees are in Chicago, he asks Mike Tresh, White Sox catcher, "What sort of luck have you had against Clout?"

"Good! He hasn't hurt us a bit," answers Tresh.

"Well, how do you get him out?" Dickey asks.

"Fast balls on the fist," replies Tresh, meaning that Joe Clout does not like speed when it is over the inside of the plate. Dickey stores the hint away in his mental catalogue, and uses it the next time the Yankees play Detroit.

Dickey uses his brain in other ways. He tries to

steal the other team's signals and often succeeds. A favorite offensive device is known as the hit-and-run play: the runner on first base starts for second with the pitch, and the batsman tries to hit the ball, whether it is over the plate or not, through the hole left by the shortstop or second baseman, who is covering second on the play.

If Dickey can catch the hitter giving the hit-and-run signal to the runner, or if he can guess correctly, he calls for a pitch-out from the hurler. Then when the runner starts for second, the pitcher throws the ball so high and wide to Dickey that the batsman cannot possibly hit it, and Dickey throws out the runner. American League players say Dickey is uncanny in his ability to break up hit-and-run plays. Sometimes he detects the signal; sometimes he makes the right guess. And of course he makes some wrong guesses, but the only damage in that case is a ball on the batter.

Dickey tells the pitcher and infielders where to throw when they pick up bunts. He gives signals for attempts to pick runners off base. He tells infielders when to cut off throws from the outfielders, throws that will not cut down an opponent at the plate. He yells out loudly and clearly on infield and foul fly balls. But most of all he talks to and encourages his pitcher. He gives the hurler confidence in himself if he needs it; he tries to remove the pressure of a bad inning; he does not let the hurler work too quickly and he signals Manager Joe McCarthy on the bench if the pitcher tires and loses his stuff.

Frank Frisch, cheering hard for the National League though he was in the 1939 World Series, could not withhold his admiration of Bill Dickey.

"Gee!" exclaimed the former Fordham Flash, "What a catcher that fellow Dickey is! If a fellow couldn't pitch to him, he couldn't pitch to anybody. Watch how he tucks that glove under his arm as though it were a newspaper when he walks out to talk with the pitcher. He's not a bit nervous. He's not shouting and pounding his glove as though he's excited. He makes the game seem easy; there's no effort in his catching."

A calm disposition undoubtedly is one of Dickey's major assets. Rarely does he lose his temper. He questions the judgment of umpires as much as any catcher, but not so boisterously as most. Only a few times has he been banished from games by umpires. He is a Southerner, and some baseball men think Southerners are too lackadaisical to be aggressive players, but Dickey is an alert, quick-acting catcher despite his quiet nature.

He is not nearly as fiery and aggressive as Mickey Cochrane, but he is in the same class with the former Philadelphia star and Detroit manager. A few years from now they will be debating whether or not Cochrane was a better catcher than Dickey. They are different types, but both became wonderfully efficient units in championship organizations. Cochrane was more conspicuous when he was in his prime, but Dickey is no less a grand leader.

Once, however, Bill Dickey lost his temper, and with dire consequences. Like most men who are slow to anger, when he becomes aroused he is a dangerous customer, a man to be avoided. It was in 1932 when the Yankees and Senators were battling for league leadership that the one black mark was set on Dickey's conduct record. The teams were playing in Washington that hot day. The game was a close one, play was hard, and tempers ran short.

Midway through the game there came a spectacular play at the plate. Carl Reynolds, Washington outfielder and a mild-mannered Texan, steamed full speed down the third base line (and Reynolds was one of the fastest men in the league) eager to beat the throw to Dickey. The throw was somewhat up the third base line, in front of the plate, and just as the Yankee catcher caught the ball, Reynolds crashed into him. Both flew sprawling from the terrific collision.

The umpire called Reynolds out, but a Washington teammate shouted to him, ''Get up and touch the plate. He hasn't tagged you yet.''

Reynolds climbed to his feet and ran to where Dickey was standing at home plate. He had no sooner reached the Yankee catcher than he was felled by a fierce right hook to the jaw. He fell senseless and was carried from the field. Dickey was banished from the game, and order was at last restored. A report of the fray was sent to President William Harridge of the American League by the umpires.

In the hospital it was learned that Reynolds' jaw had been broken by Dickey's punch, and that he would be unable to play for several weeks. Harridge dealt severely with Dickey, suspending him for a month and fining him $1000. The Yankees protested, but Dickey was clearly in the wrong and the decision stood. Despite the handicap, the

Yankees went on to win the pennant and with Dickey eligible to play in the World Series, they defeated the Chicago Cubs in four straight games.

Reynolds has never spoken to Dickey since that day in Washington. After all, he argued, he had only been playing the game; he had not challenged Dickey or made any attempt to hit him; he had been struck when he was unprepared.

What was Dickey's reaction? Just this: "I was never so sorry for anything. I'll always regret hitting Reynolds that day. After we collided and he fell to the ground, the Senators started yelling at him. I didn't know they were telling him to tag the plate. When he jumped up and came at me I thought he was going to hit me, so to be safe I got in the first punch. It was entirely a misunderstanding on my part."

The event was quickly forgotten by most baseball fans. Dickey was so obviously not a roustabout or trouble seeker that his explanation of the fray was accepted by the public, although he had to be punished according to League law. It is the only fight on Dickey's playing record as this is written.

Like all catchers, Dickey has taken a lot of physical abuse. Before his bout with Reynolds, for example, he had been shaken up by hard slides and bruised on the arms and legs by foul tips. Add such injuries to a catcher's weariness from catching day after day in hot weather, and you have the answer to why Dickey was so quick with his punch that afternoon in Washington.

A few years later in Boston there was a similar play at the plate. Eric McNair was the runner and he crashed into Dickey while trying to score. Both men were hurt, and Dickey had to be taken to a hospital. It was reported at first that he had a ruptured spleen. Then it was said a kidney had been injured so severely that it would have to be removed. Dickey's big league career hung in the balance for a few days, and then he began to improve rapidly. No operation was needed and although Dickey played in only 104 games, the fewest for him until then, when the Yankees opposed the Giants in the 1936 World Series, there he was behind the plate once more.

Split and broken fingers from foul tips handicapped the lanky receiver in his early years with the Yankees. It was these, and a .279 batting average in 1935, that made him change his style in 1936.

"I made myself over both as a hitter and as a

catcher," he explains. "In hitting I started to pull the ball more, so I could hit more home runs in Yankee Stadium. And in catching I moved up closer to the plate. I'm so tall I can't get under the hitter like most catchers, but I got so I could keep pretty close. The closer you are the less danger there is in being hit by tips. I haven't been hurt by foul balls nearly so much since 1936 as I was before then."

Dickey stands six feet one and one-half inches tall, and because he weighs only 185 pounds, he looks even taller. Although not brawny like Gabby Hartnett and Ernie Lombardi, he ranks as a better hitter than either of them. Indeed, no modern catcher at the close of the 1939 season could match Dickey's lifetime batting average of .320. He seems certain to be the first catcher to attain 2000 hits. Starting the 1940 season, his twelfth in the American League, he needs 421 more bingles, and since he is only thirty-two years old, he appears good for four or five more full campaigns.

When he fell below .300 for the first time in 1935, batting .279, he experimented with his style and had excellent results, for in the next four seasons he hit .362, .332, .313, and .302, and in these seasons he knocked in 107, 133, 115, and 105 runs. He also totaled 102 home runs. Joe McCarthy placed him fifth in the New York batting order, and the winning of the Yankees' four consecutive championships was largely through his timely stickwork. Dickey in these years has acquired the reputation of being a "clutch" hitter—a man who produces in the pinch.

"If I were a pitcher there are two men I'd hate to see come up to the plate with men on the bases," said outfielder Mel Almada of the Browns one day. "They are Joe Cronin of the Red Sox and Bill Dickey of the Yankees. They are more dangerous in the pinch than any other hitters in the League."

A perfect example of Dickey's coolness in a crisis occurred in the first game of the 1939 World Series, between the Yankees and Reds in New York. Paul Derringer and Red Ruffing were locked in a brilliant pitching duel that day, and as the Yankees entered the last of the ninth inning, the score was tied 1-1.

The first New York hitter was retired, but the next one, Charlie Keller, tripled off Ival Goodman's glove in deep right center. Now a long fly, a base hit, or a hard infield chance would win the game for the champions. Joe DiMaggio was intentionally passed, bringing up Dickey.

"They'll pass Dickey, too," said American Leaguers; "bringing up Selkirk with bases full."

But, no, the Reds elected to pitch up to the New York catcher, who had not made a safe hit all afternoon. Derringer's first pitch was wide of the plate; a ball. The next cut a corner; a strike. The third pitch never crossed the plate, for Dickey swung and the ball went on a line to land in center field for a hit. Keller trotted home from third with the winning run.

"Gosh, Bill, why did you pitch to Dickey?" McKechnie, manager of the Reds, was asked. "He's one of the best men alive in a clutch."

"We knew that," replied McKechnie, "but with Dickey being a slower runner than Selkirk, we thought we had a better chance to get a double play by pitching to him. We took a chance and lost."

What is it that makes some players more dangerous when there are men on bases than when the paths are empty? Courage, of course, is the chief ingredient. Other essentials are concentration, coolness, and relaxation. Dickey has all of these, particularly relaxation. He does not "tighten up" or "choke up," as athletes say. Underneath he may be nervous, but it does not upset his timing or throw him off form. His heart does not leap into his mouth even though victory and defeat rest squarely on his shoulders.

You would appreciate Dickey's coolness if you went quail shooting with him some chilly morning in the Arkansas countryside he loves so well. He takes two beautiful bird dogs with him. He has trained them himself. When they point, you shiver in anticipation. Then, from the cover about fifteen yards ahead, there comes a drumming of wings and more than a dozen birds explode into the air.

You shoot into the flock—it seems impossible to miss—but nothing happens. No bird falls. Then Dickey shoots. Down plops a bird. He shoots again, and another bird falls.

"How could I miss?" you ask.

"Never shoot at a covey," advises your comrade. "Pick out the bird you want and get him."

Dickey is a masterful field shot, perhaps as good as there is. Quail shooting is his favorite sport, baseball being his favorite business, of course. Each winter Dickey roams over the Arkansas hills bird hunting. Friends who accompany him marvel at his marksmanship. He rarely misses. He says it is because he does not become nervous. He is as relaxed when pointing a gun at a bird as he is when pointing a stick at a star in the sky.

William Balcom Dickey was born in Bastrop, Louisiana, June 6, 1907, the son of John Dickey and his wife, Laura May Dickey. He has two brothers: Gus, who is a railroad man, and George, who is also a professional baseball player. His two sisters, who are married, were named Johnny and Leo, which causes confusion now and then, as when one of Bill Dickey's brothers-in-law says, "Yes, I married Leo Dickey."

John Dickey is a railroad man, a conductor, who is now retired. One of his big thrills was serving as conductor on a special train the Yankees used in traveling through the South in 1936. That was one trip which was a smooth ride for the Yanks.

The Dickeys moved about considerably while they were raising their family. When Bill was two years old, they moved to Kensett, Arkansas. He played baseball and basketball there in grammar school. He went to high school at Searcy, Arkansas, where he was a third baseman. Finally the family moved to Little Rock, and at Little Rock College, Bill was a pitcher and a catcher.

"I wasn't much of a pitcher," Dickey recalls.

"I remember that I used to alternate—three innings of catching and then three innings of pitching. But when I was only eighteen and still in school, I got a job catching for a semi-pro nine in Hot Springs, not very far from home."

It was at Hot Springs that he was discovered by Bob Allen, owner of the Little Rock team of the Southern Association, and Lena Blackburne, then Little Rock manager. The 1925 season was nearly over and the young catcher did not get into a single league game. Blackburne attempted to smooth off irregularities in the form of the awkward youngster during pre-game practice.

"Bill was a pretty crude catcher when I first saw him," recalls Blackburne, now coach for the Athletics. "I remember the day I saw him play for the Hot Springs team. I went there to look over a third baseman, but signed Dickey instead, even though he threw a ball against the right field fence trying to pick a man off first. I could see that he had a strong arm."

Dickey started the 1926 season with Muskogee in the Western Association, after failing to win a job with the faster Little Rock team. He was getting the experience he needed by catching for

Muskogee every day, but in mid-season the club failed financially and dropped out of the league. Instead of taking Dickey back, Little Rock sent the young catcher to Minneapolis of the American Association, one of the best minor leagues in the country.

The competition there was too fast for him and he sat on the bench day after day, apparently forgotten, and when he was returned to Little Rock late in the season, it was with a record of not having played a game for Minneapolis. Little Rock used him in twenty-one games before the season closed and he batted .375.

In 1927 Little Rock had a working agreement with the Chicago White Sox, whereby the latter club was to have its pick of any Little Rock player it wanted at the close of the season for $10,000. It was clear to Little Rock officials that Dickey was the outstanding man on their squad, so when Johnny Nee, Yankee scout, offered them $15,000 for the young catcher, they were chagrined not to be able to accept it.

But they had an idea. Instead of keeping Dickey, they farmed him out to Jackson in the Cotton States League. Then, when the White Sox looked over the players on the Little Rock team, there was no Dickey. Indeed, one Chicago official asked, "You don't seem to have anyone we could use. Where is this fellow Dickey we've heard of?"

"Oh, Dickey?" said Bob Allen. "Why, we sent him to Jackson in the Cotton States League."

"Humph! Well, if he isn't good enough for you, he isn't good enough for us," and the Chicago official hung up the telephone receiver. A few days later Little Rock sold Dickey to the Yankees for $15,000.

Dickey trained with the Yankees in 1928 and made an impression on Miller Huggins, a famous manager and leader of the Yankees when Babe Ruth was their star. The Yankees had two experienced receivers in Benny Bengough and John Grabowski, so they sent Dickey to Buffalo of the International League. He played only three games with the Bisons before Little Rock reminded the Yankees of the conditions of Dickey's sale: if the Yankees released the young catcher on option, it would be to Little Rock. And thus Dickey returned to his home town, where he hit .300 in sixty games before being recalled by the Yankees.

The Yanks won the pennant that season and

went on to overpower the St. Louis Cardinals in four straight games. Bill Dickey caught in ten games near the end of the campaign, after the pennant was clinched, and he sat on the bench, eligible to compete, during the World Series. He did not take part in a fall classic, however, until 1932, the next time the Yankees were pennant winners, but only the following year, in 1929, he established himself as regular catcher for the Yanks, ahead of Bengough and Grabowski, and played 130 games.

"Gosh, I sure was scared when I was sold to the Yankees for $15,000 in 1927," Dickey now recalls. "I didn't think I was worth so much money. And then to be on the same team with Babe Ruth, Tony Lazzeri, Lou Gehrig, Joe Dugan, Herb Pennock, and Earl Combs sure was enough to frighten a green kid. But they were good fellows and they made it easy for me to break in."

Like all the men who played for him, Dickey had great admiration for little Miller Huggins. Indeed, Dickey has played for only two managers in the big leagues, Huggins and Joe McCarthy. To him they seem alike in methods and results. Huggins was unusually sympathetic towards rookie players. So, too, is McCarthy, who never played a game in the major leagues. Both are sticklers for detail; both are fine organizers. Dickey does not believe that every manager could have led the powerful Yankee teams to pennants as did Huggins and McCarthy.

During the 1939 World Series, Dickey was asked to pick an All-Star team from players he has played with and against. For his pitchers he named Lefty Grove, Lefty Gomez, and Red Ruffing. His first baseman was Lou Gehrig, his roommate and closest friend on the Yankees until a spinal disorder forced Gehrig to retire from baseball in 1939, after having played in 2,130 consecutive American League games.

Charlie Gehringer was his selection at second base, the Detroit star ranking just a little better than Tony Lazzeri and the youthful Joe Gordon. At shortstop he named Joe Cronin of the Red Sox, and at third base Joe Dugan of the old Yankees. His outfielders were Joe DiMaggio, Babe Ruth, and Al Simmons, and Dickey's idea of the best catcher he had ever seen was Mickey Cochrane.

"I tried to copy Cochrane," admits Dickey, "but I was so much taller that I couldn't get my right leg back the way he did. When I made myself over in 1936, I started using a lighter, smaller glove, and I learned the trick of catching many pitches with one hand. This saved my right hand from foul tips.''

Catching pitches with one hand is a trick for the veteran. For young catchers, Dickey thinks this advice is suitable:

1—Like your job. Make up your mind that it is the best position on the team. Never regret becoming a catcher.

2—Don't give in to weariness and injuries. A catcher must expect to be bruised by foul tips and shaken up by rough slides. Learn to take it.

3—Practice catching low balls. Anyone can catch high balls, but the pitches that are in the dirt or at the ankle tops are the ones that test a catcher.

4—Make throwing automatic. A catcher should be able to throw accurately to every base mechanically. He should get rid of the ball quickly. He shouldn't worry about his throwing.

5—Make the pitcher glad you are catching him. Give him a feeling of confidence in you and in himself. Make him produce his best, which means that you must study hitters and take advantage of their weaknesses.

The scarcity of capable catchers in recent years

has not puzzled Bill Dickey. "When I was a boy, everyone wanted to be a pitcher," he says. "Then a few years later when Babe Ruth was breaking records, everyone wanted to be a slugger. The emphasis is still on hitting. Catching is a hard, disagreeable job, but it has its rewards. For example, it gives an opportunity to heavy men who are slow runners. Then, too, good catchers are well paid. If I had my choice to make over again, I'd still be a catcher."

Dickey worked his way up the wage scale until he was receiving $20,000 for playing the 1939 season. He is married and the father of a girl. During the off-season he makes his home in Little Rock, where his father and mother also live. Besides hunting, Dickey enjoys fishing. He is a keen checker player and takes delight in mastering his younger brother, George (who is nicknamed Skeets) at this indoor pastime. He is an amateur prestidigitator, specializing in card tricks.

The hardest pitchers to catch, says Dickey, are left-handers, who are often wild, and knuckle-ball hurlers. He says he can tell when Jimmy Foxx socks a home run merely by the sound of the bat meeting the ball. He thinks the 1936 Yankees the best club he ever played with. He learned the fundamentals of baseball from his father, who was a minor league player at one time. To improve his speed of foot, he learned to run on his toes, but he never became a speedster.

Bill Dickey has won no great batting titles, but one of his big thrills came in 1937, when he hit home runs with bases filled in two consecutive games, something only Babe Ruth had ever accomplished before. Dickey holds several brilliant catching records, however: highest American League percentage (.996 in 1931); most assists in an inning (three in a 1929 game); fewest passed balls in a season (none in 125 games in 1929).

In 1932, 1933, 1936, 1938, and 1939, Dickey was voted by experts to be the best catcher in baseball. By some he is already being called the best catcher the grand old game has ever had. But such honors and tributes do not upset the equanimity of this mild and modest Southerner. "My biggest thrill in baseball," he says, "has come from winning and from playing with a winning team like the Yankees. It's a privilege to be a member of a championship club. Baseball has been a lot of fun. It has been productive, well-paid work. I have

made a lot of friends. I think I've been lucky,
don't you?''

Lucky, Bill, and good, too!

WILLIAM B. DICKEY

Born, Bastrop, Louisiana, June 6, 1907
Bats Left. Throws Right. Height, 6 feet, 1½ inches.
Weight, 190 pounds.

YEAR	CLUB	LEA.	POS.	G.	R.	H.	T.B.	R.B.I.	S.B.	AVG.
1925	Little Rock a	S. A.		...	..	...	..	..	..	...
1926	Muskogee b	W. A.	C	61	27	60	91	..	1	.283
1926	Minneapolis c	A. A.		...	..	...	...	..	..	...
1926	Little Rock	S. A.	C	21	6	18	29	8	0	.375
1927	Jackson d	C. S. L.	C	101	46	108	154	..	6	.297
1927	New York e	A. L.		...	..	...	...	..	..	...
1928	Buffalo	I. L.	C	3	0	1	...	..	0	.125
1928	Little Rock	S. A.	C	60	22	61	97	32	1	.300
1928	New York	A. L.	C	10	1	3	6	2	0	.200
1929	New York	A. L.	C	130	60	145	217	65	4	.324
1930	New York	A. L.	C	109	55	124	178	65	7	.339
1931	New York	A. L.	C	130	65	156	211	78	2	.327
1932	New York	A. L.	C	108	66	131	204	84	2	.310
1933	New York	A. L.	C	130	58	152	234	97	3	.318
1934	New York	A. L.	C	104	56	127	195	72	0	.322
1935	New York	A. L.	C	120	54	125	205	81	1	.279
1936	New York	A. L.	C	112	99	153	261	107	0	.362
1937	New York	A. L.	C	140	87	176	302	133	3	.332
1938	New York	A. L.	C	132	84	142	258	115	3	.313
1939	New York	A. L.	C	128	103	145	246	105	5	.302

	YRS.	G.	R.	H.	T.B.	R.B.I.	S.B.	AVG.
Major League Totals	12	1353	788	1659	1517	1033	30	.310

World's Series Record

				G.	R.	H.	T.B.	R.B.I.	S.B.	AVG.
1932	New York	A. L.	C	4	2	7	7	4	0	.438
1936	New York	A. L.	C	6	5	3	6	5	0	.120

1937 New York...A. L.	C	5	3	4	6	3	0	.211
1938 New York...A. L.	C	4	2	6	9	2	1	.400
1939 New York...A. L.	C	4	2	4	10	5	0	.267
World Series Totals		23	14	24	38	19	1	.287

a Optioned by Little Rock to Muskogee for 1926.

b Loaned to Minneapolis when the Muskogee club dropped out of the W. A.

c Returned by Minneapolis to Little Rock.

d Optioned by Little Rock to Jackson and then sold to New York.

e Optioned by New York to Little Rock for 1928.

ABNER DOUBLEDAY: FATHER OF BASEBALL

A. Doubleday

BRIG.-GEN. ABNER DOUBLEDAY

BRIGADIER-GENERAL ABNER DOUBLEDAY

CHAPTER V

ABNER DOUBLEDAY: FATHER OF BASEBALL

By Harry Irving Shumway

How many momentous things have happened on that placid old institution, the Village Green. One vividly remembered is that still quiet and beautiful, verdant stretch in Lexington, Massachusetts. Certainly an important event took place there on a quiet morning in April. Every village green has its historical associations and memories; perhaps that is why we venerate them so much and why we refuse to allow anybody to change them in any way.

Important things have taken place on village greens. And possibly one of the most important in history (at least in sports history) had its birth on such a field in the quiet little village of Cooperstown, New York, on a sunny day in the year 1839. The scene was not, strictly speaking, the village green itself. It was an open field in a part of the town called Apple Hill.

On the morning in question, no battle flags fluttered in the breeze, no drums rolled, calling men to arms. Indeed, it would have taken a clairvoyant of most remarkable powers to have visualized anything at all important suggested by the actors and their actions. Yet what happened there caused a great business to be born. And more than that, this single occurrence gave to American boys and men something that probably contributes more happiness to their lives than any other single thing —at least, in the world of sports.

A crowd of schoolboys straggled onto the green field. One of them carried a long, thick club, somewhat wider than it was thick at one end, and fashioned to a double-handed grip at the other. It might be called a paddle. Another carried with some pride, a small leather covered ball. Those two items were all the paraphernalia they had.

One of the boys seemed preoccupied and more than a little determined. He was tall and remarkably straight of figure, something contributed by attendance at military school. But it was not soldiering that claimed his attention on this morning. It was an *idea*.

It was just about the best idea a human being ever had. And yet this young man, twenty years old at the time, was never to get a cent from his idea or discovery, nor merit fame until long after his death. However, on this morning he was just an athletic young fellow, full of his idea and determined to try it out on a gang of his own, though undoubtedly, some of them were openly critical.

"What are you going to do, Abner? Why all this secrecy and mystery?"

"You'll see," nodded the leader. "And there isn't any secrecy about it. Only I'd rather map it out on the field than tell it to you. It will save time —and a brain struggle with some of you fellows."

"But what is it?"

"It's a game."

"A new one?"

"Um—in a way," admitted the young man called Abner. "You see, this ball game we've been playing for years gets a little crazy now and then. Players dash around and crash into each other, which is all very foolish to me. Now I've got a scheme to straighten it out."

"Sounds good. How's it go?"

"Well, for instance, that big square we use, with a man on each corner: if the striker stands in the

middle of one side of this square, he can see
scarcely anything of the two men on his side of
it, so at least two men are out of his view. See
what I mean? It's awkward. In a game like this
each player should be in sight of the others.''

"Well, maybe it'll get clear as we go along."

"I think I've solved it by turning the figure
around. A sort of diamond-shaped square, see?
And have the striker stand at one corner. Now,
here's something else. Why have everybody roaming around like cows in a pasture? I've designated spots where players can stand. And no more
of this twenty or thirty on one side. That's just a
mob. It spoils the beauty of the game.''

"Beauty?" laughed one of the young men.
"Beauty?"

The dark eyes of Abner snapped. "I said
beauty and I meant it. You certainly were no
beauty when Soapy rammed his head into your
stomach the other day when you were both running
after the same ball. I tell you this plan will
straighten out the game, make it more understandable. And I think it will be more interesting
to play.''

They went to work. Minus precision instru-
ments, they used the old measuring device, the hu-

man foot. Soon several of the young men were pacing off designated numbers of feet under the direction of Abner. He sighted down the field on a center and used that as a basis on which to proceed. The sides of the diamond were made about ninety feet, somewhat longer than the old-time square.

"The thrower does not stand on the base line," informed Abner. "He stands within the diamond, around forty-five feet in front of the striker, on a line with second base."

"Base?"

"Yes. We'll have bases or flat stones instead of those old posts sticking up three or four feet. Then we can run right over them; no more running into posts or using them as spring-boards."

Accordingly, the boys got flat stones and sunk them into the earth at the points indicated by Abner. Four in all. Another husky lad made a sort of drag from a few stout saplings lashed together. Into the ends he put some pegs and summoned a small boy to sit thereon. With this improvised machine he dragged the base-line into a sort of path.

By now there was quite a crowd and everybody was intensely interested. They didn't have much idea of what it was all about but they knew Abner, who was one of those fellows who must have everything shipshape and definite.

He now explained his new game as best he could. "We'll have sides, with the same number of men on each side. Eleven will be about right, I think."

"Shucks. We had thirty-two the other day."

"Yes. And how many chances did you get to catch a struck ball? At one time I saw ten or twelve hands all reaching at once for one little ball. No, this idea is better. It will make every man sort of responsible for his territory."

"You do have the strangest names for games, Abner. Beauty. And responsibility. Well, let's get at it. That's a new ball and I'm aching to knock it into the orchard."

"That will give your side one point in the game," commented Abner. "Whoever rounds the bases without being touched by the ball scores a point for his side. Oh, don't look so stupid. It's all very simple."

"Yes. Clear as mud. Well, let's try it. I'll stand on one of these stones. I suppose I'm a stoner," laughed the fellow.

"No. I think base is a better word. It's military, you know. Consider yourself a baseman. We'll choose sides now and try it out. It won't be perfect at first but I'm sure it will be an improvement over the game we've been playing."

Thus was born the great game of baseball. The young man who evolved the scheme was named Abner Doubleday. All that day the young men of Cooperstown played this new game. They liked some of it—and some of it they didn't.

In the old days, the tireless exhibitionist; the all-over-the-field-rover, worked to his heart's content. He could zip around north, west, south and east, and the spotlight could be achieved by agility and good guessing. But now he had to stand in one spot in the field throughout the whole game, and this irked his ego. Standing out there among the clover of deep center was torture when pop-flies were falling all around the "thrower's" head. It didn't seem fair.

But soon it began to boil down into something pretty interesting. It did not work out perfectly all in one day. Abner worked over it, ironed out some of the kinks, and within a few days there was no more doubting. A new game had come to stay and it had splendid competitive features. It was neat; it was conclusive, and when a tussle was over, you knew which was the better team.

Abner Doubleday gave it its name—the one we know today. Baseball. It might have been called several other names, but these corners were suggestive. Men stopped there, they ran from there. The other side guarded them. They were the only tangible things in the big field. Hence it seemed logical to name the game after them.

The new game neither died out nor did it set the world afire. It was played at first in Cooperstown and the surrounding territory. At that time, the famous author, J. Fenimore Cooper, lived in the town that now bears his name, and died there some time later.

Challenges were offered and accepted. One of the first games on record was played in 1839, on a farm near Ostego Lake, near Cooperstown. Abner's team met the team of a Professor Green from one of the other schools near by. The Professor himself played in the contest. This was undoubtedly the first prep-school ball game, which makes prep-school baseball older than collegiate baseball.

Little could have been thought of it at the time, for why should anybody pay any special attention to a village green pastime, a boys' game of pelting a small, leather-covered ball around? Evidently, even Abner Doubleday, its inventor, paid little attention to his new game once he had put it on paper and seen it work. He had other things on his mind a lot more vital than ball-game promoting. He had already started up the ladder of a long military career.

It was almost immediately after the invention of this new game that he entered the military academy at West Point. The game was left behind him, and before long, this new life completely absorbed him. West Point cadets, then as now, had little opportunity for recreation. There is no record showing that young Doubleday played ball at the Academy, or showed the other cadets how to play it. But it is safe to guess that he did mention it. It seems likely, too, that a game or two might have been played there while he was a student. In that case, West Point would have the honor of having played the first college game of baseball— an honor, incidentally, that subsequently went to Amherst and Williams. The Big Three—the

Harvards, the Yales and the Princetons as they were then called in the sporting world—trailed the two smaller colleges by several years.

Abner Doubleday was graduated from West Point in 1842 and was assigned to the Third Artillery. Now he was to engage in throwing much larger and harder balls than that funny little one which was to give him so much belated fame. Active service came within a few years after he became an officer in the United States Army, and in the brief but sanguinary Mexican War he was in the thick of it as an officer in the First Cavalry. He saw service in two bloody engagements, Monterrey and Buena Vista. In 1847 he was appointed First Lieutenant and in 1855, he became a Captain. From 1855 to 1858 he saw more service against the Apache, and later, the Seminole Indians. At one time young Doubleday was in the same regiment as Stonewall Jackson and A. P. Hill, both of whom he met later on the battlefield. Before he was thirty he had served in one war; before he was forty, he had seen another long campaign, and was soon to be embroiled in a still longer and bloodier conflict.

For two or three years before the opening of the War between the States, Captain Doubleday was stationed at Fort Moultrie in Charleston Harbor, and was second in command. As hostilities became imminent he was ordered to withdraw his company to near-by Fort Sumter, and when that fort was attacked on April 12th, 1861, Captain Doubleday fired the first gun in defense of the stronghold.

Some weeks after the evacuation of Fort Sumter, he was made a Major in the Seventeenth Infantry. During the summer of 1861 he served with General Patterson in the Shenandoah Valley, taking part in many engagements, and after a few months of this service, he was transferred to a regiment which had been assigned the defense of Washington.

Early in the year 1862 he was made a Brigadier-General of Volunteers, commanding a brigade during that year. In this year he was in the Second Battle of Bull Run. Later, he commanded a division. In the hard fighting at Antietam he commanded a division with distinction, and later in the same year, was promoted to Major-General of Volunteers. Then followed the hard campaigns around Fredericksburg and Chancellorsville.

Late in June, 1863, it became apparent that a great battle would be fought in Pennsylvania. In vast numbers, the troops of both armies were converging in the vicinity of a small town called Gettysburg. Strangely enough, as the movements settled into place, it was seen that the Federal troops would be fighting towards the north and the Confederates under General Robert E. Lee, would be facing the south. The blue army was commanded by General Meade.

On July 1, General Doubleday was ordered to Gettysburg by General Reynolds, commanding the First Corps, to reinforce Buford's Cavalry which held a ridge west of the town of Gettysburg, and on that hot summer's day the great conflict began. The one-time fellow officer of Doubleday, A. P. Hill, now a General, led the attack against the First Corps. The battle was terrific from the very start, and General Reynolds fell early in the day. The command was taken over by General Doubleday, and for five hours the fight raged until the Federal troops were finally forced back to Cemetery Ridge, after capturing Archer's brigade, the greater part of Davis' brigade and almost annihilating Iverson's brigade. General Doubleday was relieved by his senior, General O. O. Howard.

On the third and last day of this greatest of American battles, came the famous charge by the

Confederate General Pickett. General Doubleday's troops took part in this awful engagement
and inflicted heavy losses.

The latter half of the War found General Doubleday engaged in less strenuous service. For
two years he had been in one engagement after
another, beginning at the very start of hostilities.
After this he served on courts martial and com-
missions, and later commanded the south-eastern
defense of Washington when the capital was being
threatened with invasion. In 1865 he was bre-
vetted Colonel in the Regular Army, and Briga-
dier and Major-General a short time later. In
December 1866, he was in command at Galveston,
Texas, and served as Assistant Commissioner of
the Freedman's Bureau until the summer of 1867.
After being mustered out of the volunteer service,
he was made Colonel of the 35th Infantry. Later
he was a member of the Retiring Board in New
York City and from 1869 to 1871 superintended
the general recruiting service in San Francisco.
After commanding in Texas he was retired from
active service December, 1873. He died at Mend-
ham, New Jersey, January 26, 1893.

There is a period of twenty years after his retirement from the Army. Yet in all this time his

name is never connected with the great sport he started. Biographies state his war record but not a word about baseball. Whether he ever saw it played is not known. Certainly he must have been interested in seeing the growth of the game, but he gave no word or laid any claim to being its discoverer. In his two books on the campaigns of the War Between the States he says nothing about himself. Like so many military writers he confines himself to technicalities.

But baseball was a lusty young fellow at the time of General Doubleday's death. Boys all over the United States were playing it. The baseball hero had come to stay. There was a National League, the same one we have today, and the clubs played to great, enthusiastic crowds. It was possible for General Doubleday to have seen both the New York Giants and the Philadelphia Phillies by merely taking a car ride. Perhaps he did, but nobody knows for sure. If he ever attended a game it must have given him a thrill to see that the game he had started at Cooperstown had become a national major sport.

At this time it might be well to go back to a period somewhat before that epoch-making event on the village green at Cooperstown. The story of baseball is quite hazy in its beginnings. We have claimants from England, and on our own side of the Atlantic, Massachusetts, where so many things were begun, had a very loud voice in the matter, and so did Philadelphia. They claimed to have originated something—but it was not baseball. Not *our* baseball. The English consider that rounders gave birth to the game of baseball. Rounders involves the use of a ball and a paddle, if that makes baseball!

Nobody knows very much about that most important article of the sport—the ball. Did a caveman pick up a round rock and playfully heave it at another husky? And did that other husky take a poke at it with the shin-bone of a dinosaur? Did a monkey throw a small, round coconut from a tree even before that?

Nobody knows. But the ancient Greeks played with a ball. Somewhere, sometime, a man or a boy stuck out his two hands and caught a throw. And somewhere, sometime, a man threw a round thing into the air and hit it with a club. There we have the two ingredients of the game. A club and a ball.

There were other early games that might have influenced the start of baseball. One of these was the ancient game of prisoners' base. This gave the important idea of a place of safety for a player. It also gave the idea of the possibility of a player getting tagged out—as when stealing second, for example. All these things were familiar to young Doubleday and other lads. A ball, a bat, a base, hitting a ball with a club, running, getting tagged, scoring and so on.

Balls were known in the 1830's. Not the kind we buy now, of course, but fairly round things made of any durable material. Generally they were string or yarn wound into a ball and covered with a leather cover. If you ever go to Cooperstown and visit the Baseball Museum there, you can see the original ball that Abner Doubleday used on that day in 1839. It is about half the size of the present baseball, and its cover is in four quarters.

In those days there were no sporting articles to be bought. You made your own or used an apple for a ball. Sometimes the village shoemaker or harnessmaker could fix up a pretty good article. At any rate, they had the right idea in the thirties. Something round, something hard which would sting the hands, and something tough enough to stand the repeated assaults of a bat. The early balls had this feature of being made with a cover composed of four quarters, stitched together. It can be seen that the two poles of such a ball would be a little knotty with so much stitching. The name of the genius who thought up that particular queer-shaped piece that makes the present day ball is not known. But he had a very nice idea. Perfect, in fact.

Early in the nineteenth century, perhaps before Abner Doubleday was born, there was a game called one-old-cat. Who devised this game (still good enough to play to this day) is not known. Undoubtedly it just happened—and perhaps like this: two boys were tossing a ball back and forth. Along came a third boy. "I wanta play. Let me play," he may have said. Perhaps they wanted to tease him; he may have been a younger brother or somebody they didn't like. He became belligerent at his unwanted status. Then he may have howled the early nineteenth century equivalent of "Oh, Yeah! Well, here goes your old ball game!" Whereupon he may have grabbed a tip-cart spoke, got in between them and whaled the ball out of the field.

This, as can be seen, would start something. And it did start something. A jolly game grew out of this. A base was fixed up, not too many feet away. If the batter could knock the ball, run to this base and return to his batting position before he was tagged with the ball, it could be counted one point for him. Everybody kept his own score. There were no credits for catches, or penalties for strikes or anything else. A caught fly retired the batter. When the batter was thrown out, the one who caught the fly took his place at bat.

This was in some ways, a most annoying game. It could bring tears of rage to smaller boys. Why? The stronger and better batter could stay in all the morning. He could become weary—but not weary enough to allow himself to be caught out. The other boys would have to keep pitching to him, which was no fun. The pitcher of today is the star performer; everybody wants his job. But in the days of one-old-cat, the star of the piece was the batter, while the pitcher was just the "maid of all work."

One-old-cat grew into two-old-cat, then three-old-cat, and finally four-old-cat. This last entanglement allowed for eight players, four on the bases and four hitters. It was lots of fun and provided a single game whereby several could compete.

But it still lacked the kick of competition as to

sides. Individual scores were kept but no team scores were possible. There was no mass rivalry, so dear to the heart of every male from five to eighty-five. However, it was something to while away the time with, something to pick up in the spring of the year, after marbles and top spinning had begun to pall.

But, as can be seen, it was nothing for the male with long pants and whiskers. He might, if nobody was looking, take a whack at it, just a mere taste, to show how it could and should be done. Then walk away with dignity—wishing with all his heart that he might stay and fill out a whole afternoon. The grown-up male needed a game with a ball and a bat in it. He yearned for it. All the cat-games were for kids.

Something had to be done in the matter of a game for the older male. There wasn't much of anything they could do outdoors, competitively, except fight duels and these were frowned upon. These always had such a disheartening, one-sided score. The time was ripe for the start of a game to whet the appetite of the most game-loving people on the face of the earth.

This was found and it grew out of the boys' game of old-cat. Four-old-cat contributed the form of the field—four bases in a square. Three of the batters were "killed"; only one batter was retained and he took his position in the middle of one side of the square. The pitcher, or thrower as he was called, took his position in the center of the big square. In the old-cat game the distance between bases was forty feet, and this was increased to sixty, making a bigger field.

The biggest improvement in the game came in the feature of sides or teams. One side could bat, in rotation as in baseball. And the other side could spread themselves out and do a spot of fielding. Any number could be on a side. Also they could, after the basemen were located, play any place in the field which suited their fancy. A Texas leaguer couldn't be missed, while a bunt would have hit somebody sitting down in the infield. However, there were no bunts. Those were invented many years later by a man named Tim Murname. There was, as can be imagined, just one batting technique—to knock the ball out of the field, about the only chance to make a score.

This *was* a game. It could be played at the present day and be worth the doing. Nomenclature was not forgotten. It was called town-ball, the name growing out of the custom of playing it on town-meeting days. It was a success. It provided an excuse for grown men to perform in a park. A boys' game had grown into a man's game. History does not say who was responsible for this, but, whatever his name, we owe him a lot. If this had not happened—well, imagine Babe Ruth, Ty Cobb and Tris Speaker playing one-old-cat! It makes one shudder.

Town-ball was a success. It became epidemic. Travelers got hold of it and introduced it to other sections of the country, especially the Eastern part. This was the game played in Philadelphia, which gave Philadelphians the idea that they were responsible for discovering baseball. This was the game played in New England, known as the "Massachusetts Game." Massachusetts, always stubborn and opinionated, threatened to secede or something when the real game of baseball knocked at their doors. They had the best beans, the best codfish, the best ball game and everything else, and they would play town-ball and make everybody else play it and like it.

Town-ball had its merits and also its excitement. One of the features was a unique method of tagging a base runner. The ball was thrown at him and if the connection was made, he was out

—sometimes both ways. This method of "plug-ging" base runners lasted for some years and many players were injured.

A fly-ball caught in the air or on the first bounce retired the batter. Of course there were no pro-tective articles of any kind. The paraphernalia consisted solely of one ball and a bat. The bat was shaped more like a paddle than like our modern bats. There were no restrictions as to the size of dimensions of anything.

It must be that Abner Doubleday knew of this game. From the shape of the playing field he may have evolved his own, better one, the diamond. This diamond-shaped square, with the batter at one corner, he worked out and put on paper. In this original plan he had eleven players on a side instead of nine as used later. These extra players stood between first and second, and second and third.

First, games were played in Cooperstown. There was a bit of visiting, too, for it is known that a team made up from a near-by school came to Cooperstown and played Doubleday's team. Un-doubtedly this was the first "World Series," as well as first in a lot of other things.

During the next few years little happened. The

younger boys had their old-cat game, the townies their town-ball and the disciples of the newer game had that. There is no data to be had on the subject, for there was no such thing as a sports writer in those days. Writers indulged in fancy or very heavy stuff. No historian could have seen the need of wasting any ink on a weird pastime played by hoarse-voiced yokels on the village green. Possibly J. Fenimore Cooper may have seen the game, but if so, he never mentioned it.

However, the germ had been planted. The serious-minded cadet of Cooperstown was in West Point, soaking up the hard courses of study there. All around him, sitting stiff backed in the halls, were future generals who would soon be trying their best to put each other out in a deadlier game. Grant was there at the same time; Sherman was an upper classman, as was Reynolds, whose place Doubleday was to take at Gettysburg; D. H. Hill; Ewell, against whom Doubleday was to fight; Longstreet, Hancock and many others.

In the years 1840 to 1845 the game of baseball was not much more than "getting ready to be liked." It was strictly a village pastime, something to do just for fun. But the American mind is very serious when it comes to sports. For some reason we cannot play, really *play* after we are ten years old. It is natural for us to take a nice game and immediately pass bylaws, organize clubs, and then challenge one another to immortal combat with it after we get organized. That is the American sports way.

Therefore it was inevitable that young Doubleday's village-green pastime should come in for a bit of serious consideration, once it got into the right hands. The point of incubation seems to have been in and around Manhattan. Town-ball was played there and over on the Jersey side, but the new game got a trial and took the fancy of many players.

The first organized baseball club in history was the Knickerbockers of New York City. They had been playing the new game for some time and in the early autumn of 1845, rules were drawn up and bylaws agreed to. This movement was started by Alexander J. Cartwright, who knew the game well. It has been said that Cartwright played with young Doubleday at Cooperstown, one story claiming that he was in the original game there. At any rate, he knew the new game of baseball and it was owing to his efforts that this first organized ball club, the Knickerbockers, came into being.

The players were enthusiastic. As they had jobs to attend to, practice had to be done at odd hours, but they played once a week. Other clubs were started in and around New York. Brooklyn had several in the next year or so. At first, the games were played in New York City but later a field was laid out at Hoboken, New Jersey, on a reservation happily called the Elysian Fields.

Once organized clubs got under way the enthusiasm grew and naturally, improvements came. For one thing there had to be a uniform, and in the early photographs we see the groups of players as they appeared on the field. Photography itself is the same age as baseball. People in New York were going wild about the new daguerreotypes and later, the sun prints, and probably Brady or Broadway took some of these early pictures.

The uniforms show it was a gentleman's game. A snappy slide into a base would have removed the trousers at once and probably the shirt. The trousers were full length, rather tight at the ankle, and some players wore a strap like a bicycle clip to keep the bottoms from flapping. The shirt was something like our modern polo shirt. There was a web belt. Oddly enough, the shoes were frequently identical with our present saddle-strap sport shoes. About one-third of the players wore beards—and what beards!

These photographs also show that something had been done about a bat. It was no longer a paddle, but a round, tapered bat, a good deal like the one of today. Some of them were very long, long enough to connect with a very wide ball.

The early ball was much the same as the one used today except for its size. It was a little larger and heavier. The ball has seen a good many minor changes and even now, the experimentation goes on. The latest one is in color.

The game of the 1850's differed from the modern one in many points. For example, take the pitcher and his work. He was compelled to throw underhand and with a toss. The point was to please the batter, mind you, not to fool him. Imagine this sort of thing today: "I say, old chap, where shall I put it?" "Well, pal, about knee high and say, two feet to the right, if you will be so good." And the thrower as he was called in the early days, would do that, or try to. Speaking of titles, the batter was called the "striker" in the very old days.

The thrower or pitcher had perquisites, though. He could roam around like a black panther on the loose. There was a twelve-foot line instead of a slab, marked forty-five feet from the home plate. He could take as many running steps as he liked to get up momentum. With this immense territory to work in, he could do a lot of things. But in those very early days it was not considered sporting to bemuse the batting gentleman or to perpetrate outrages of any kind. They actually wanted the batter to make a hit!

Another quaint feature was the method of counting strikes. There were no called strikes. The batter could stand there indefinitely until he got a sweet one and no penalty resulting therefrom.

It was a more open game, and for the players, perhaps more fun. Such pitching gave the outfielders plenty to do. Nobody stood out there, pulling grass and looking at the sky. They were usually out of breath running for hits. Scores at first ran to twenty-one; that is, the first club to score twenty-one runs won. But that was changed after a short time. The early scores often ran into the fifties and sixties and even higher. Games were long, four to five hours, and there was a delightful custom of a banquet following the early games.

There was no inter-city rivalry in the 1850's; indeed, there were no city names as we now have.

Instead the teams selected names like the old fire-tub associations. Some of these were the Gothams, Eagles, Baltics, Empires, Atlantics, Excelsiors, Continentals, Stars, Metropolitans, Hamiltons, Mutuals, and others.

Town-ball was out. New England, protesting to the last that it had been stabbed in a vital spot, finally had to come over to the new game. The Massachusetts Game was shelved forever, and soon the Yankees were busy at this upstart game from wicked Manhattan. Games were played on the very spot on Boston Common where boys play it to this day. There has been a ball game on the old Common every decent, mild day for the last ninety years.

It became apparent that some governing body must be established to make rules and regulations. In New York, the game was played differently from what it was in Boston. There was nobody or no body to tell what was right. So the National Baseball Association was formed in 1858, for the regulation of all regular baseball clubs. Playing rules were drawn up, and while these were crude, there did result some uniformity. The game was now definitely on its way. It became possible to charge admission to see important contests. It was ten cents in some places and even fifty cents in others. But even at this time it was a queer game, as we would understand it. There were many vital changes to come before it would be the fast, interesting thing which thrills our sport-loving nation today.

It was in the early 1860's that pitching began to get a little attention. That underhand toss which actually begged to be batted out of the park, had to be changed. A pitcher by the name of Creighton of the Brooklyn Excelsiors developed a fast under-hand delivery which sent the ball up to the batter with great effectiveness. It was just a straight, fast ball, but new to the batters.

But just as baseball was due to go places in the early 1860's something happened which put it on the shelf for a long time. Down in the Harbor of Charleston, South Carolina, were a couple of forts, and in 1861, forts were important. By April, the small garrison in Moultrie and Sumter knew that the conflict, which was anxiously awaited, had arrived. The second in command at Fort Moultrie under Major Anderson, was Captain Abner Doubleday, the founder of baseball. He was ordered to take his men from Moultrie to Sumter, which has already been told, and on the day the War opened, Captain Doubleday fired the first shot. It was a wild pitch and hit only the water!

The War occupied the attention of everybody, North and South, and baseball had a temporary setback. It was played here and there, but the big movement was arrested. However, it was only hibernating. Even in the armies it did not die. Battles were not fought every day and there were many opportunities for a game. Baseballs were not army equipment, but they were in many knapsacks. Federal troops played baseball whenever they had the opportunity. It is reported that during a game at Fort Fisher the bugles blew most inconsiderately in the middle of an inning, and the players had to rush from the field to the firing line. They played the game in the Confederate prison camps, where they taught it to their captors. On Roanoke Island, Hawkins' Zouaves formed two teams and played many hotly contested games.

The same thing was going on in the Confederate ranks. The New Orleans boys also carried baseballs in their knapsacks. Once a group of them, imprisoned in a Federal prison stockade on the Mississippi, formed a club and played daily. Some prisoners from Georgia and South Carolina watched them, became greatly interested, and got up a club of their own. These two outfits fought it out for the "World Series of the South" and the boys from New Orleans won.

There is no information as to whether General Doubleday ever played the game during the War. Probably he did not. If we can believe what we see in Brady's photographs of the War, no general could have lowered his dignity to do a plebeian thing like playing baseball.

After the War, clubs sprang up all over the land. Changes in the game came with great rapidity. One of the innovations arrived, and not as an invention, but as an accident. Without this important thing, baseball would not be what it is today. One day in 1866 a pitcher of the Excelsior Juniors discovered that the fast ball he was throwing had a break. So did the batters when they found they couldn't hit it. Unintentionally, this pitcher, Arthur Cummings, had evolved a curve. From that time on, pitchers began to concentrate on the antics of the sphere they threw. In the course of time many weird jumps were discovered in the pitch, all contributed by the fingers in conjunction with the friction of the air.

In the early 1870's came the regular rifle-like

throw which we know today. Pitchers developed speed and control. The idea now was to fool the batter, not to help him.

Naturally, with this speed and a much better ball, something had to be done about protection. Catchers got broken fingers, not to mention cracked heads and faces. It took a Spartan to stand behind the bat and pick off hot foul tips. The mask was invented by a member of the Harvard University ball team, Fred W. Thayer. Anybody who has ever taken a hot foul tip in the face or neck will offer up paeans of thanks to this inspired genius.

The big padded mitts were invented by a sporting-goods house. And the chest protector (you guessed it!) by an umpire who forgot to duck one day. As a matter of fact, baseball needs very few protective devices. Nearly all of it is needed at the plate. A good fielder can take care of nearly everything wth his bare hands, except the hot, line drive, and even this is sometimes taken with the ungloved hand. The most dangerous thing in baseball seems to be the bean ball. Fortunately it seldom happens. If it ever gets too prevalent, batsmen will have to wear helmets like their brothers of the football gridiron.

As the sport went through the sixties it began gathering its by-products. A baseball magazine was started in Boston in 1868 called, of all things, "The New England Base Ballist." It is a quaint sheet to look at now. Box scores appear in it, something like we have today. In one of these box scores for October 2, 1868, these items are set down among other vital statistics of the game: "Barked shins, 17—Lame hands, 19—Players winded, 14— Too much beer, 9!" Also these terms are generally used: "Put out on bases—Catches on strikes— Foul ball catches—Flycatches—Dropped flyballs."

Up to 1869, baseball was played as a sport. It offered no living or career to anybody. To be sure, money was sometimes offered to expert players for a game or a series. But in 1869 came the first salaried club, the Cincinnati Red Stockings. It had been a fine amateur club and now it became a marvelous professional outfit. It traveled all around the country, taking on all comers. This team never lost a game between April 1869 to June 1970, a record never beaten or equalled. Out of fifty-seven games played, they won fifty-six and tied one. George Wright, the famous shortstop, had a batting average of .518 and hit fifty-nine home runs. He was the Babe Ruth of his day.

It was this club that changed the uniform from that of something like the visiting firemen, to our modern one. Knickerbockers replaced the long trousers, and long red stockings adorned the legs. The cap was about the same as the one seen today.

Even when baseball was over thirty years old it was still an awkward child, not knowing exactly where it was going or when to stop when it got there. Professional teams with salaried players had sprung up but these teams were not welded together in any satisfactory whole. One year there would be eight clubs in the association, the next ten or twelve or thirteen. A city would have a team one year and abandon it the next. Some body was needed to give the thing unity, a body with authority and wisdom. So in 1871 the National Association of Professional Baseball Players was formed.

One of the big jobs the new Association had on its hands was to rid the sport of vicious gambling. This evil had grown to alarming proportions, and in the 1870's was ruining the game. Pool selling and betting were common, and the big gamblers were not content to play fair; they never are. They tried to bribe players to throw games and otherwise act discreditably. The Association went to work on this and after some years, cleaned it up. Gambling has persisted, of course, in some measure since then, but never in the manner of those early days. It would have killed the sport beyond redemption had it not been stopped. The history of the later days shows that unfair tactics do not succeed in baseball, and any player caught throwing a game or a series would be banned for life, and there have been instances of this where weak-willed and weak-minded players have succumbed. There is no appeal from a sentence passed on a dishonest ball player, no pardon or reinstatement. This is as it should be. Sport must be scrupulously honest and fair or the public will turn it down.

Baseball has had its troubles from the 1870's onward, but all in all, it has been a steady march. Every year or two saw some correction made, an evil cut out or an improvement installed. Paraphernalia became standardized. The ball was changed from time to time. First it was too lively, having an oversupply of rubber; with this ball scores up to two hundred or over were made and many games ran into darkness. The rubber was taken out and the ball became dead; so did the game. But eventually they got a proper ball, such as the one in use today.

One of the pleasant things in baseball was the formation of the American League in the first year of the twentieth century. At first, this was frowned upon. The National League was the old standby and people loved it. A new league, they thought, would upset the sport; it would be confusing. But, as we know, once it got under way the exact opposite was true. Cities like Boston, New York, Philadelphia and Chicago showed they could support two major league clubs and be loyal to both. And the World Series—well, where is there a sports classic that has the thrill of that? Life would be drab indeed without the clash between the National and American League pennant winners.

The formation of the two big leagues made the sport just perfect. People loved it. It was America's game; it had everything needed for our particular temperament. There was, however, something bothersome about it. It had a mystery.

The mystery? Nobody knew who invented it!

In the early part of the present century nobody seemed to have any idea where the game came from, who had given it to the world. Did it come from the English game of rounders? Or was one-old-cat with trimmings the source? A study of these two old games showed that somewhere along the line *somebody* had done a major operation.

Who was that person? How did he happen to 'think up' baseball? And after he had done the admirable deed, how come his name was not known?

The mystery could not be endured. Here was an American invention without the name of the inventor. So in 1907 a special Baseball Commission was appointed to investigate the matter. After months of research and sifting of evidence, the Commission reported that the game of baseball was invented by Abner Doubleday at Cooperstown, New York, in 1839. The members of this Commission were: A. G. Mills, the third president of the National League; Hon. Arthur P. Gorman, a senator from Maryland; Hon. Morgan G. Bulkeley, first president of the National League; N. E. Young, fourth president of the National League; A. J. Reach, famous ball player; George Wright, one of the greatest of the early professional players; and James E. Sullivan, president of the Amateur Athletic Union.

So now it was known. But who was Abner Doubleday, people wondered? A soldier, not a professional athlete. They dusted off the history books and read the meagre biographies of the General. Not a word in any of them about his connection with the national game.

He was, they discovered, a competent general. But competent generals were conspicuous by their generous numbers in the Civil War. He had aimed the first gun in the War, had fought in several sanguinary battles, had retired full of honors. And his funeral in 1893 had been a great ceremony, attended by hundreds of military and civic dignitaries.

General Doubleday was given credit for his discovery of baseball. The new encyclopedias hastened to mention his work. Had the General been living, suitable honors would have been bestowed upon him, but he was gone and nothing could be done about that.

However, as the years went on a few did not forget. And as the centenary of the great sport drew near, 1939, a movement was started to pay him fitting tribute. The question—where and what and how?

What better place than the birthplace of the

some contemporary account—say by J. Fenimore Cooper, for example.

But the very nature of the thing precluded such a possibility. All it was at the time was a boy's game. Any boy at this day could sketch out a proposed game on the ground with a pointed stick or show it on paper, and get no more recognition for it than did young Doubleday. It was not important *at the time*. But time has made it very important.

In the years to come many trophies of the great sport will go to Cooperstown, there to be added to the Museum of Baseball. It will become a Mecca for boys and men, and for all those who like to see the various articles worn or used by the immortals of sport. Everything there will be strictly baseball. Everything except one, that is. The exception is an oil painting of a man in the blue and gold uniform of a major-general in the United States Army of another day. And uninformed visitors will say "What did *he* have to do with baseball?" And the answer will be: "Just about everything." Because if he had not given out his conception of a good game, those who followed would have had no foundation upon which to build.

ROBERT WILLIAM ANDREW FELLER:
THE MAJOR LEAGUE MINOR

Courtesy American League

ROBERT WILLIAM ANDREW "BOB" FELLER

CHAPTER VI

ROBERT WILLIAM ANDREW FELLER: THE MAJOR LEAGUE MINOR

By Jerry Nason, Sports Writer, *Boston Globe*

On the fifth day of July, 1936, Bob Feller, to all intents and purposes, was just another youthful worker at a concession stand in the Cleveland ball park, selling soda pop and peanuts to the perspiring clients, and between sales, dreaming of the day when perhaps he, too, would stalk nonchalantly from the Cleveland dugout into the brilliant sunlight of the diamond.

Twenty-four hours later his dream was realized and his was a name that rolled glibly off the chattering tongues of those same baseball-fevered Ohioans at League Park.

For on the sixth day of July, Manager Steve O'Neil of the Cleveland Indians, of the American League, informed the cherubic, husky, young peanut vendor that he would definitely be one of the three pitchers to labor three innings apiece in an exhibition contest that afternoon with the famed and vociferous "Gas House Gang", officially the St. Louis Cardinals of the National League.

And that day is one the Cleveland Indians' ever-loving fans are never going to forget, for on that day, Robert William Andrew Feller, a farm boy from the unpretentious hamlet of Van Meter, Iowa, unveiled for the edification of major league hitters one of the fastest pitches in the history of the game.

It was a red-letter day, in every sense of the phrase, and before the summer was out, the name of Feller was to become almost synonymous with speed-ball pitching.

On July 6, 1936, Manager O'Neil elected to do the catching. The big farm boy was assigned to pitch the fourth, fifth and sixth innings.

History is very often made under such inauspicious circumstances. Who was to know that in this comparatively unimportant exhibition game one of the most widely-discussed pitchers of this era, or any other, was to bloom for the first time?

The fact of the matter is that the Iowa youngster, still a member of the junior class at Van Meter High School at the time, struck out eight

batters in three innings with a fast ball that
bolted over the plate in a style reminiscent of the
immortal Walter Johnson, with whom he was later
to be compared.

Eleven batters faced him. Eight fanned, Ogrodowski and Moore hit safely, Cleveland fans went
wild, and the pessimists entered a report that the
feat was far out of proportion to its worth since
the "Gas House Gang" was not bearing down at
the plate in so unimportant an exhibition game.

But none other than the great Jerome Herman
"Dizzy" Dean, then at the peak of his pitching
effectiveness for St. Louis, holder of the major
leagues' strike-out record, spoke encouraging
words of Feller's pitching.

So, too, did Manager Frankie Frisch of the
visitors, and Clarence (Brick) Owens, the American League umpire, made the rounds of the league
gushing praises for the unknown, seventeen-year-
old schoolboy.

Soon Feller was to rock the baseball world with
his "forked-lightning" fast ball, proving them all
prophets.

Before the month of August ran its course
Feller was to become an official representative of
the Cleveland Indians, and in his first major-

league start come within a single strike-out of
matching Rube Waddell's twenty-eight-year-old
American League record.

Before September vanished into October the
phenomenal Iowa schoolboy was to sling that
sizzling fast ball past seventeen bewildered members of the Philadelphia Athletics in breaking
Waddell's hallowed strike-out record.

That, briefly, was the dramatic bow made by
Bob Feller, 21-year-old, 185-pound, right-handed
pitcher of the Cleveland Indians, into the national
sportlight; a hasty sketch of the circumstances
surrounding the rise to fame, and probably fortune, of a typical American boy in a typical American game in a typical American way.

Before he had enjoyed the indescribable delights
of a first shave, Bob Feller had etched his name
beside those of baseball immortals; was insured
by his employers for the sum of $100,000, and was
earning a salary most mature men never hope to
earn.

Feller will be twenty-two years old on the third
day of November, 1940, a hoary veteran of four
years on the mound for the Cleveland Indians,
holder of his league's strike-out record of eighteen

batters made in 1938, and holder of the major leagues' mark for the same performance.

As this piece is written, probably the following seven dates stand out in bold relief in the ever-increasing pattern of his major league career:

July 6, 1936—First appearance in a major league uniform, three innings of exhibition against St. Louis Cardinals, registering eight strike-outs in pitching to eleven batters.

August 23, 1936—Made his first appearance as a starting pitcher for the Indians. Manager O'Neil, yielding to the terrific clamor of the Cleveland fans, started his fuzzy-faced recruit, but he had the veteran Denny Galehouse warming up in the bullpen before Feller made his first pitch. Net result: The schoolboy struck out fifteen members of the St. Louis Browns, allowed six hits, passed four men and won the game, 4-1. He was seventeen years old and missed the league strike-out record by one batter.

September 13, 1936—He faced Philadelphia Athletics in the first game of a double-header at Cleveland, and struck out seventeen batters in a masterful two-hit performance, which he won, 5-2. The feat erased Waddell's record and left the stocky youth co-holder of the major league mark with the incomparable J. H. "Dizzy" Dean of the St. Louis Cardinals.

April 24, 1937—In a game with St. Louis Browns, the team against which Feller had made his sensational debut a year before, the Iowa boy slipped while making a pitch and wrenched his arm. He lost the game, 3-4, and went onto the inactive list with a sore arm which kept him off the mound for two months. All Cleveland mourned. Critics claimed his career was clipped short, that his arm couldn't stand the strain of throwing such a fast ball on almost every pitch.

April 20, 1938—Feller had recovered and finished the 1937 season with a record of nine games won, seven lost. Today was his first start of the '38 campaign. The baseball world was tremendously interested, but Bob wasn't long in quieting the fears of the Cleveland fans. The Browns, coincidentally enough, were his opponents, even as they were when his arm went sore. This time he came within a whisker of that magic no-hit circle—the only hit being made off his delivery being a bunt in the sixth inning by Billy Sullivan, who won a close decision at first base.

August 25, 1938—Striking out sixteen Red Sox batters, Feller came within a hair of matching the major league record. He won the game, allowing four hits. Two such mighty sluggers as Jimmy Foxx, the league's leading hitter, and Pinky Higgins, struck out thrice each. Manager Joe Cronin, another competent batsman, fanned twice, once with the bases loaded in the seventh. Feller was seldom faster than on this date.

October 2, 1938—This day Feller mowed down eighteen Detroit batsmen to establish a new American and major leagues' record for strike-outs, passing by one the mark he held with Dean of the National League, who had fanned seventeen Chicago Cub batters in 1933. Feller retired the Detroit side on strike-outs in two innings, the first and sixth. Feller's eighteenth victim, marking the passage of the old record, was Chet Laabs, the Detroit center fielder, who fanned for the fifth time in the ninth inning. Strangely enough, Feller was beaten on this historic occasion. Detroit raked his delivery for seven hits in this season's finale, and took advantage of his seven passes for a 4-1 victory.

The feat did, however, allow Feller to lead the

major leagues in strike-outs for the 1938 season
by a margin of more than a dozen over Buck
Newsom, the big St. Louis Browns pitcher.

May 25, 1939—Well on his way to being the first
major league pitcher to win ten games, Feller
missed a no-hit game for the second time when
Bobby Doerr, the flashing second baseman of the
Boston Red Sox, spanked a single into center field
in the second inning at Fenway Park. It was the
only hit made off Feller, who struck out ten men
and won, 11-0. The day was otherwise conspicuous
for the fact that it was his first victory gained in
six starts at the Boston park.

These are dates of great significance in the
career of Bob Feller. On innumerable other days
of equal interest leading up to his affiliation with
the Cleveland Indians we will subsequently dwell
at some length, but first let us scan another mark
the youthful pitching sensation has achieved:

In the season of 1938, in which he won seventeen
games against eleven losses, Feller struck out
twenty-eight men in his last two starts, a record
for strike-outs in consecutive games. Again it was
his own standard he erased, for in his ''freshman''
season of 1936 he had bowled down twenty-seven
batters in two consecutive games.

And in 1938 big Bob led the major league pitchers in strike-outs, showing 240 for the year, but he
also had the questionable distinction of breaking
his league's record for lack of control, passing 208
batters, or thirty-seven more than had Irving
(Bump) Hadley seven years before.

And there was the kernel of controversy over
Feller's ability from the very start: Control.

Some of his greatest pitching achievements, as
witness his strike-out record against Detroit when
he passed seven batters, have been scarred by his
evident inability to control his blazing, fast ball.
But some insisted, and still insist, that this has
been of great assistance to Feller, for opposing
batters, knowing him not to be infallible when it
comes to locating the plate, have spent many un-
easy moments in the batting box. No batter takes
a confident toe-hold in the box against a fast-ball
pitcher whose control is likely to desert him without warning.

Yet the fact remains that Feller has studiously
prepared himself for a long and effective career as
a major league pitcher. The season of 1939 gave
evidence from the first of the wonderful progress
he has made.

When he made his debut as a schoolboy in 1936

his shortcomings were many. He knew next to nothing of the artistry of pitching with runners on bases, hence American League speedboys made many easy thefts of the bases around him.

He was as green as the Iowa grass in spring, but he could throw a baseball faster than any pitcher in his league. Bob knew that alone wouldn't be enough. He sought advice from the keenest baseball minds on his club, and, what's more, accepted it. On days he wasn't scheduled to pitch he carefully studied the form and tactics of the pitchers who toiled.

As a result, in 1939 Feller unfolded in full flower. He was the first hurler in the majors to win ten games. By the middle of June he had struck out one hundred batters, intimating that he was well on his way to pass his 240 mark of the previous season.

Incidentally, only twice did Walter Johnson, the immortal "Big Train" of the Washington Senators and presumably the fastest pitcher of all time, ever exceed Feller's seasonal mark of 243 strike-outs. In the season of 1910 Johnson fanned 313 American League batters. In 1912 he sent down 303. A year later he stopped 243 of them in their tracks, a record equalled by Feller in 1939.

The argument over the respective "fireball" merits of Feller and big "Barney" of the past have raged continuously ever since the former broke into the major leagues.

Steve O'Neil, who managed Feller during the first year or two of the schoolboy's career with Cleveland, does not consider him as fast as Johnson in his heyday. "Feller throws a livelier ball than Johnson did," says O'Neil. "Johnson threw more of a side-arm ball, so that the ball came in on the hitter. Feller's fast pitch hops upward, so that the batter is constantly swinging under it."

The only man in baseball today who saw both Feller and Johnson make their major league debuts is Charlie O'Leary of the St. Louis Browns. And Charlie agrees with O'Neil.

"Feller is fast, perhaps the fastest pitcher in baseball today," says O'Leary, "but he isn't as fast as Johnson was at his best.

"Johnson had the edge on Feller when he first broke into the league. He was taller and broader and heavier. He was also three years older and he had more experience.

"Neither of them had much more than a blinding fast ball at the start. Bob has developed a pretty fair curve and Johnson developed more stuff as he went along. Both were pretty cool customers, but Johnson had much better control.

"Feller will probably take on more speed as he grows older, but there never was a pitcher as fast as Walter Johnson. Old Barney was tops."

One thing above everything else that has impressed O'Neil about Bob Feller's pitching is the intensity with which the Iowa boy pursues knowledge of pitching.

"He listens and learns and has the memory of an elephant," the former Cleveland manager has been quoted as saying. "For example, he used to have the habit of holding the ball behind him before he pitched, where the coaches on the bases could see the position of his fingers. We only had to tell him once to hold it at his side and hide it."

And O'Neil never did agree with the critics who said Feller would not last long because his form put too much strain on his arm in throwing a speed ball.

"Bob's delivery is as smooth as silk. He follows through perfectly. It was nothing more than his youth and eagerness to make good that caused him to press and hurt his arm in 1937!"

With the whole baseball world discussing his speed and strike-outs you'd naturally expect that

Feller's big thrill of his four seasons of pitching would be the day he broke the major league mark by fanning eighteen Detroit Tigers.

On the contrary, Bob is like most pitchers in that a hit is an infinitely greater pleasure than a fistful of strike-outs, and one of the high lights in his opinion came in 1936 when he made two hits in one inning against the Chicago White Sox.

One hit was made off Vernon Kennedy, who had entered the Hall of Fame with a no-hit game previously. The second was off Johnny Whitehead. Cleveland won, 17-2.

"That was a real thrill," says Feller. "I always did love to hit. I recall when I was eleven how Dad built a batting cage on the farm with some boards from the barn and a mess of chicken wire. We had five or six baseballs, and I'd hit away until the supply was exhausted, then we'd go hunt up the balls."

And thus is introduced "Dad", or Bill Feller, the man to whom untold credit is due.

Bill Feller himself had never been a famous ball player. He probably saw little if any major league baseball played. He was an Iowa farmer with 640 acres of farm land to cultivate and that is a task that doesn't allow one to cultivate such extravagant hobbies as journeying away to see the big leaguers in action.

But Bill Feller had more than the average American's love for the game, for which the Cleveland Indians are extremely thankful.

Bob was born at Adel, Iowa, where the Feller farm is located, just outside Van Meter, on November 3, 1918, and when he was seven years old his father abruptly dropped the homely but tricky game of pitching horseshoes to play "catch".

This must have been a sacrifice on the part of the elder Feller for his skill at slinging the celebrated "mule slippers" was common knowledge throughout that section of the State of Iowa.

Two years later Bob was working behind a tractor on the farm, tending the countless chores to which a farm boy is assigned, and was already displaying a special aptitude for throwing a baseball.

One evening before twilight, Bill Feller gazed contemplatively at a haystack some distance away and then at the brown fist of young Bob as it encircled a baseball.

"All right," said Bill Feller. "Let's see how far you can throw it."

So Bob wound up and flung the ball hard and high in the direction of the haystack. The sphere passed serenely over that objective and landed in a furrow some distance beyond.

They measured off the distance as best they could and found the ball had journeyed a matter of approximately 275 feet, give or take a few.

When he was eleven, young Bob was with the American Legion junior team of Adel, and again he had the opportunity to marvel at the power with which he could throw a baseball.

At that time, however, he had given no thought to pitching, but was playing center field for the Adel juniors. One afternoon the opposition worked a man around to third base at a critical moment in the juvenile contest. The hitter at the plate drove a long, hard fly into center field. Young Feller took it on the run, whirled and drove the ball toward the plate with all his strength.

At the impact of the catch the runner left third on a mad dash for home, but the ball sped on a dead line into the catcher's glove from center field; the runner was out, and the boy from the Feller farm had again demonstrated his uncanny faculty for throwing a baseball.

Working long hours on the farm had allowed Bob to develop extremely powerful hands, wrists, arms and shoulders. Before he was twelve he could hoist the rear end of a car off the ground, although he hastens to explain that this feat was about two-thirds trick and one-third strength.

"The idea is to back up to the car and push hard against it as you lift," he remarks.

One of the brightest hours on the farm was the day Bill Feller told Bob he was going to plow up a piece of land near a grove of oaks on the farm where the youngster could have his own baseball diamond.

"That was in 1931," recalls Bob. "What a thrill that was! But that's about all we did do that year toward completing the diamond where I really commenced to develop as a baseball player.

"Meanwhile, Dad gave me almost as big a thrill when he said he was going to organize a ball team of his own to play on the field.

"The next spring we got down to the business of making the field. We plowed and rolled it, and Dad bought a lot of lumber and chicken wire for a backstop. As I think of it now, it was quite a backstop—extending more than a hundred feet along each base line from the plate."

What was more natural, considering the location, that the new, homemade field be called Oak View Park and the team the Oakviews?

"When it came almost time for the opening of the season and the new park Dad bought a dozen uniforms. The first time I tried mine on I guess I felt just as wonderful as that day later when the Cleveland Indians handed me a big league uniform!"

Well, Bob Feller wasn't confirmed a pitcher even then, although the diamond and stands on the Feller farm were ready in 1932. In the sixth grade he organized a team of boys not old enough to play for the high school at Van Meter, mostly sixth graders like Bob.

The high school coach suggested practice games, pointing out the advantages for both sides. Bob and his boys agreed, and in the course of eight such skirmishes the lower graders won seven times.

"I had a mighty good catcher handling me in those games," reminisces Bob. "After every game his hand would be red and swollen, because I was just a thrower. I put everything into every pitch. But he hung onto that ball swell all the time. I guess I was pretty wild at times, but the high school batters were aiming at a lot of bad pitches."

Bob still liked to play in the infield, either third or shortstop, and he loved to hit. He was playing shortstop with the Oakviews under his father's management, and not pitching, until a very critical situation arose one evening in a game at Winterset, Iowa, in 1934.

The Oakviews' hurler slumped badly in the early stages, filling the bases and failing to retire a batter. Manager "Bill" Feller looked out at his shortstop and offspring, wagged his hand and yelled: "See what you can do as a pitcher, Bob." The younger Feller stalked to the mound, took his warm-up pitches and fanned the next two batters on six pitches and put out the runner on third base attempting to steal home.

From then on Bob Feller was a pitcher. He started on the mound for the Oakviews the next game, allowing one hit and striking out twenty-one batters. In his next start he struck out twenty-three men and allowed two hits.

"I guess all those hundreds and hundreds of times Dad had played catch with me on the farm were beginning to pay off," he says. "I can recall how I used to pester him every night to play catch, hardly giving him a chance to finish his chores. I couldn't wait. I used to be out bouncing the ball off the side of the barn until he was ready.

"And another thing: Dad never let me throw

anything but a regulation baseball at any time. He insisted on it. My target was the catcher's mitt he put up for me to aim at. He used to let me throw until I made a mistake, then he'd walk up and correct some faulty part of my delivery.''

It wasn't all honey and cakes for Bill Feller. His husky son threw a ball so hard that you had to be on the alert every second. Once one of Bob's dazzling fast pitches skinned off the end of his father's glove and smashed two of the latter's ribs.

A brief history of Feller's play with the Oak-views shows that he played the infield in 1932 and 1933, hitting .321 the second season and getting an extra base hit here and there. Then in 1934 the situation as described a short time ago diverted Bob into other playing channels . . . pitching.

He was fifteen years old now, weighed 145 pounds, and this was in 1934.

In 1935, after the school sessions at Van Meter High had closed, the boy joined the Farmers' Union team of neighboring Des Moines. The schoolboy's prowess was household conversation throughout that section of the state. The Des Moines team hoped to compete at Dayton, Ohio, for the national amateur title, and needless to say felt it necessary to enlist the services of the boy from Van Meter.

"To even get to Dayton," Bob says, "it was necessary for us to win the amateur championship of our own section. For that purpose they conducted a tourney at the Iowa State fair grounds.

"We were challenged to a game by a good team from Bennett, even before the tourney started. We accepted. Since there was to be a big Farmers' Union picnic at Tipton, Iowa, we decided to play the game there. It was a good game, despite the score of 8-0. We had the eight."

Feller pitched it, too, striking out twenty-two batters and allowing three hits. He pitched the first game of the ensuing tournament, was wild, but held the opposition to three hits and seven runs. He pitched and won the final game the next day, getting three hits, driving in the winning run, and allowing the foe only four hits.

So the Fellers and Farmers' Union nine journeyed to Dayton, Ohio, which was quite an event for most of them.

The park, like many others, was haunted by scouts from the major league clubs seeking promising amateur timber for major league payrolls of the future, and it was here they saw Feller for the first time, and in a losing game. The Iowans drew Battle Creek, Michigan, one of the best teams in the tournament, in the opening game.

Young Bob Feller mowed the Michiganders down with his blazing fast ball, inning after inning, but the Iowans couldn't get a run for the phenomenal youngster. Finally the Farmers' Union center fielder dropped a fly ball to let in a run and Feller, although he struck out eighteen batters and allowed only two hits, lost, 1-0.

"The scouts from all the big league clubs seemed to think my pitching was more important than our losing the game, although I didn't feel that way about it," Feller recollects. "We all felt pretty bad about it, our center fielder worst of all. We didn't ride him, because he sure was heartbroken over his miscue.

"At any rate, the scouts went after Dad. They kept him so busy listening to arguments and propositions that I guess he didn't have time to sleep!"

The upshot of it was the Fellers returned to the farm and talked plenty of baseball through the long, cold winter nights in the cozy kitchen. Mrs. Feller was in the middle of it, for Bob's mother knows baseball. So was his younger sister, Marguerite.

Bob played basketball throughout the season at the high school, as a means of keeping in good condition, because a big league opportunity had virtually been promised him as a result of the tourney at Dayton.

On the occasion of the first warm day of spring, 1936, Bill Feller and his boy were out by the barn with their baseball gloves for the first game of catch of the year. It might be their last under such circumstances for some time to come, if the rosy picture painted by the scouts was fulfilled. Bob's dog, Tagalong, sat by and watched, as was his habit. Incidentally, one of those scouts had been Cyril C. Slapnicka of Cleveland, now the general manager of that American League team.

Bob pitched five games for Van Meter High School that spring, and he won five. They were all no-hit games. In three games not a man reached first base. Between times he sat in the cool classroom in the high school, puzzling over English composition and listening to the morning train wailing its way eastward, wondering if a day would really come when he would journey on it to a big leagues' destination.

That day was not long in coming. He had an agreement to play with the Fargo-Moo⌐ team of the Northern League. Larry Gilbert o⌐ ⌐ne New Orleans club, Southern League, had purchased his contract from Fargo-Moorland, but Bob, in his junior year at high school, preferred to get his diploma, and Gilbert endorsed that ambition.

So, when the Cleveland Indians management, one day in 1936, extended an invitation for the boy to travel to Ohio at their expense and take a summer job in a concession stand in the ball park there were no objections from New Orleans or elsewhere.

Later there was to be much ado about it, so that Judge Kenesaw Mountain Landis, supreme ruler of the baseball kingdom, was to be called into the case to lay down a monumental decision.

"Well, I guess we were pretty excited getting ready for the trip to Cleveland. I know I was. It was to be my first trip alone. I'd be on my own this time," comments Bob. "While Mother was packing my things Dad and I took a little stroll over the diamond we'd made four years before. Then we walked slowly around the base paths. I figure both of us were doing plenty of thinking.

"Then we went to the depot. I kissed Mother

and Marguerite goodbye and shook hands with Dad. None of us were breaking down or anything, but it sure was a real moment in my life. Oh yes, I gave Tagalong, my dog, a hug. This would be one time he wouldn't tag along.

"I could tell Dad was feeling pretty proud of me. I knew I would throw my arm off at the socket to make good for him if I ever got a chance in Cleveland."

During that train ride to Cleveland young Feller's thoughts skipped around like grasshoppers in a field of clover, between the picture he'd conjured up of the ball park at Cleveland and the homemade diamond back at the farm.

When he finally got inside the Cleveland ball park the immensity of it almost took his breath away. He worked out with the Cleveland players and found them kindly and considerate, and ready with valuable advice.

"I can't begin to say what a great help those Cleveland players were. The size of the city itself was enough to scare the dickens out of a lonesome boy from Iowa, but they made me feel right at home. Just putting on a Cleveland uniform alone gave me a big thrill."

But Feller's job was to sell soda pop and peanuts, and he did. But it wasn't natural for him to throw the ball only in occasional workouts with the Indians. He needed and wanted plenty of pitching. So he joined a team in the Cleveland amateur league.

Bob lost the first game he pitched for the Rosenblooms, the team with which he had become attached. The score was 3-2. But he won the next start, struck out sixteen batters, allowed four hits. He batted .486 in those two games.

It was shortly after this that Manager Steve O'Neil of the Indians spoke the words Bob Feller had dreamed of hearing for a decade: That probably he would pitch against the St. Louis Cardinals in an exhibition game on July 6.

Of that inspirational debut we have already written. But let Bob recall it for us:

"When I say I wasn't nervous, I don't mean I was cocky. I warmed up just as I used to back on the farm. I wasn't frightened of the crowd, as I had become accustomed to big throngs. I made up my mind I wasn't going to attempt to be a 'Fancy Dan': I'd just slam that fast one in there and not throw many curves.

"I got a couple of strikes on the first batter to face me, and it was pretty encouraging. I struck him out and picked up a little more confidence. I just kept wheeling that ball in there as fast as I could. Munns and Garibaldi struck out twice. Collins and Martin and Durocher also struck out. So did Gelbert. Moore and Ogrodowski got hits, so I had a chance to make it nine strike-outs in three innings. But the last batter attempted a bunt and was thrown out.''

It wasn't until ten days had passed that Manager Steve O'Neil signed the boy to a Cleveland contract, however.

The team had gone on a road journey without the schoolboy and he was feeling pretty low when a wire from O'Neil instructed him to join the team at Philadelphia. Cleveland had purchased his contract from New Orleans, a team for which he had never donned a uniform.

Charged with the enthusiasm of youth, Bob crammed his clothes into a suitcase, along with his glove, penned a lengthy and exuberant letter to the folks at home, then caught the first train for Philadelphia.

In his mind he probably started and pitched his first game of major league baseball before he ever reached the suburbs of the eastern city.

But those are the dreams of youth. Actually,

the Iowa schoolboy sat many an afternoon on the Cleveland bench, aching to take a turn on the rubber for the team. Idleness fostered impatience, but he did not waste the hours on the bench. Instead, he asked questions, watched the great pitchers of the league and observed everything.

Two or three chores of relief pitching, the first at Washington on July 19, served to acquaint him with the art of pitching in American League competition.

Finally, upon returning home, the clamor of the Cleveland fans for a look at the Iowa farmboy in a starting role became so loud that on August 23, Manager O'Neil decided to start him against the St. Louis Browns.

And history, as we have already written, was made that afternoon.

Years before, Waite Hoyt had pitched a no-hit game at the age of fourteen and was signed by the New York Yankees a year later. Feller was determined to finish his senior year at Van Meter High School, an attitude which the Cleveland officials, it must be said, encouraged.

That meant that in 1937 Bob would join the team late in February at the New Orleans training camp only after completing his courses necessary to get him a diploma, then return in May for graduation exercises.

But meanwhile a storm cloud had gathered on the hitherto unblemished horizon of his future.

The Des Moines team of the Western League had protested Cleveland's right to sign Feller to a major league contract, claiming a violation of a ruling which forbids major league clubs snatching players off the nation's sandlots at the expense of the minor leagues.

Cleveland was covered there, because it had purchased Feller's contract from New Orleans, which in turn had purchased it from Fargo-Moorhead, two teams for which Feller had never pitched.

Des Moines also protested that its efforts to contact Bob for the purpose of having him play for that neighboring nine had been frustrated by Cleveland's signing him.

For many unsettled weeks it looked as though Feller would be declared a free agent. Many wealthy clubs in the major leagues were prepared to bid as high as $100,000 for his services.

Then, on December 10, 1936, Commissioner Kenesaw M. Landis prepared and delivered a decision of three closely typewritten pages that left Feller in the hands of the Cleveland team, which paid Des Moines $7,500 balm, so to speak.

When he learned he was to stay with Cleveland, Bob cried: "Good! It was a fair decision. I'm glad to be with Cleveland!" although he probably would have benefited greatly as a free agent sought by every club in baseball.

He says that one of his biggest moments since joining the Cleveland team to equal, then better, the strike-out record, was his return to Van Meter High School in May 1937, to graduate with his senior classmates.

Almost everybody in the vicinity dropped his or her chores when the train bearing Bill Feller's boy chugged into the station.

The members of the senior class journeyed eighteen miles to Des Moines, the state capital, for the class dinner, which was held in a cafeteria. Bob consumed seventy-two cents worth of "groceries," as the ball players put it, but was most dismayed to learn that he had been outdistanced by a matter of six cents by a classmate.

"That dinner certainly put quite a hole in the class treasury," said Bob, "but we had enough left to hold a wiener roast the next night."

Bob's big moment was to be when his diploma

was passed to him, with appropriate words on the part of the principal.

An even bigger moment he had not expected was when the principal reached out to a long cord, pulled it, and an American flag was raised revealing a color portrait of Robert William Andrew Feller, class of 1937.

It was a gift of the class to Van Meter High School, from which Feller was and is its most famous graduate.

Bob in turn had a gift for the school. He had made a careful selection of a handsome trophy case for the gymnasium.

And so, with his prized diploma in his possession, Bob said goodbye to school days forever. The train made a special stop at Van Meter to pick him up, while the entire countryside waved its partings from the depot.

He was off to far away Boston to rejoin his team and pick up the threads of a career so promising that Robert William Andrew Feller, the likable farmer boy from Iowa, may yet surpass the pitching feats of baseball's immortals.

Feller fulfilled the promise of his youth in 1939 when he rose to the top rank in the American League with twenty-four victories as against nine defeats, held his strike-out form and showed better control. The Iowa lad won his twenty-fourth game on the final day of the season, whipping Detroit, the team which on June 27 he had held to one hit.

The baseball world was in the hollow of his capable hand.

ROBERT WILLIAM ANDREW FELLER

Born Adel, Iowa, November 3, 1918.
Bats Right. Throws Right. Height, 6 feet, 1 inch.
Weight, 185 Pounds.

YEAR	CLUB	LEAGUE	G.	IP.	W.	L.	PCT.	SO.	BB.	H.	AVG.
1936	Cleveland	A. L.	14	62	5	3	.625	76	47	52	.334
1937	Cleveland	A. L.	26	149	9	7	.563	150	106	116	.338
1938	Cleveland	A. L.	39	278	17	11	.607	240	208	225	.408
1939	Cleveland	A. L.	39	297	24	9	.727	246	142	227	.285

HANK GREENBERG: MODERN HOME-RUN KING

HENRY "HANK" GREENBERG

CHAPTER VII

HANK GREENBERG: MODERN HOME-RUN KING

By Harold Kaese, Sports Writer,
Boston Evening Transcript

THE late John McGraw, one of baseball's shrewdest executives, harbored throughout his career as a leader of the New York Giants, an ambition to discover a great Jewish player. Years passed quickly; the Giants won pennants and World Series; money rolled into the club's treasury; turnstiles spun; McGraw discovered Jewish ball players, but never a *great* Jewish player.

Why did McGraw want a great Jewish player?

"Think what it would mean," he once told a friend, "to have a Jewish player—say one as good as Babe Ruth or Ty Cobb—playing before New York's Jewish millions. Wouldn't such a player be a tremendous attraction here in New York? Think what an idol he would become."

McGraw had competition in his quest. The

211

Yankees and the Brooklyn Dodgers, who also performed before the New York multitudes, joined the search for a great Jewish player. Every corner of the land was examined. The scouts of these three clubs did not miss the smallest town in the smallest league. They gave tryouts to the few Jewish players they uncovered. None of them became a star. Perhaps Andy Cohen, who played second base for the Giants, had the most promise, but his big league career was short, if not sweet. In vain the search went on and on. When finally a great Jewish ball player was found, he did not join the Giants, the Yankees, or the Dodgers; he joined the Detroit Tigers.

Ah, the irony of it! While the scouts of the New York teams were combing the hinterlands, a fifteen-minute ride away from Yankee Stadium and the Polo Grounds, at Crotona Park in the Bronx, a lanky Jewish lad—a lad with fine features, dark brown eyes, black hair, thin straight nose, high cheek bones, and dark skin—was learning the fundamentals of America's national game, fundamentals which he was later to use with telling effect against one of these metropolitan teams: the Yankees.

The great Jewish ball player John McGraw

paid his scouts to find, the one they missed because he was under their noses, was Hank Greenberg. But the New York clubs did not miss him altogether. The irony is still furthered by the fact that Hank Greenberg's father visited John McGraw in the Giants' offices, asked for a tryout for his son, then nineteen years old, and was refused as McGraw said, "My scouts have seen your boy play, but they don't think he'll ever be a prospect. They say he is too awkward."

Thus did John McGraw slam the door in the face of fortune. The Brooklyn Dodgers never were interested in Hank Greenberg when he was trying to break into professional baseball, although the first semi-professional team he ever played for, the Bay Parkway Club, was a Brooklyn outfit.

With the Yankees, it was a different story. They not only saw in Greenberg the makings of a powerful slugger, but they bid high for him. It was Paul Krichell, chief Yankee scout, the man who had signed Lou Gehrig to a contract, who negotiated with Greenberg. "If we hadn't signed Lou Gehrig and had him playing first base for us," says Krichell; "we would have landed Greenberg."

In the spring of 1929, a woman visited the Yankees' offices and explained that she was a wel-

fare worker attached to James Monroe High
School in the Bronx section of New York City.
She not only was interested in baseball, but she
could tell a good player from a poor one, she said.
In short, James Monroe High School had a pitcher
who deserved a trial with the Yankees. She did
not mention the James Monroe High School's first
baseman.

Krichell was inclined to laugh at the woman,
but he was too experienced to pass over any sort
of a tip. He decided to see Monroe High play
Morris High and watch the talented young pitcher.
When the game was over, Krichell asked the
woman, "Who's the boy playing first base?"

"Oh, that's just a big awkward kid who plays
basketball. How did you like the pitcher?" said
the woman.

"Not so good," replied Krichell, and to himself
he added, "This kid may be another Gehrig. I'd
better get busy."

Krichell saw Greenberg in the locker room
immediately, but could not sign him at once. The
boy wanted to go to college, and he needed time to
think over the Yankee proposition. When Krichell
returned three weeks later, he learned that Greenberg had graduated from high school, with a

scholarship for his scholastic and athletic preeminence, that was designated for Princeton, and that Greenberg was now playing for the Bay Parkways, owing to the insistence of a friend, Isadore Goldstein, who was a pitcher for that team.

The Yankees were not in favor of Greenberg going to college, but Krichell nevertheless offered to help him through the School of Commerce at New York University. One night Krichell visited the Greenberg home in the Bronx and ate with the family, but he could not win over the young slugger. In the end, Jean Dubuc, connected with the Tigers, gave him $900 to play with East Douglas, Massachusetts, promising to protect his amateur standing. East Douglas was an independent team playing in the Blackstone Valley League.

The Yankees, Washington Senators, Pittsburgh Pirates, and Tigers competed for Greenberg in that summer of 1929. Greenberg explained why he accepted the Detroit offer in these words:

"Krichell started with an offer of $1,000 and worked up to $5,000. He stopped there, and I was not interested, because I knew Lou Gehrig would play first base for the Yanks for a long time. Washington wanted to give me $10,000 to sign and $800 a month, but Clark Griffith also wanted me to quit school. Bill Hinchman, the Pittsburgh scout, also made me a fine offer.

"I liked Frank Navin's terms best, however. I got $6,000 down and I was to get $3,000 more when I finished college. I was not to start in a lower league than AA, and I was not to be farmed out for more than three years."

In the fall of 1929, Greenberg entered the School of Commerce of New York University, the Princeton scholarship never having materialized. When he promised to play for Detroit, he also agreed that he would not take part in football or basketball while he was in college. As a high school boy, Greenberg was a five-letter athlete, competing in soccer and track, as well as in baseball, football, and basketball.

Hank's college career was short lived. His contract with Detroit failed to inspire him in the classroom. He was like a boy with an ice cream cone in his hand; he had to go to work on that cone. One winter of studying was enough for him, and when the chance came to attend spring training with the Tigers at Tampa, Florida, in March of 1930, he took it.

"Going to college four years was not going to do me any good as a baseball player," Greenberg explains now. "When I was in high school, I never figured that I'd earn a dime playing baseball. My folks had always emphasized education, not the playing of games, so it was not until I had the scouts chasing me that I realized what I might do if I didn't waste my chances. So after going to college for a few months, I realized that the sooner I started playing professional baseball, the better off I'd be."

Greenberg, then 20 years old and a tall, awkward youth nearly at the six-foot, four-inch mark he was to reach at maturity, did not rush into the big leagues in sensational fashion. Indeed, Manager Bucky Harris of the Tigers, after watching the youngster in practice sessions, decided he was several years away from the majors. Although Detroit had agreed to send him to no league lower than AA, Greenberg understood that he would do well to start at the bottom, like many another potential star.

And thus Greenberg was optioned to Hartford, Conn., in the Eastern League, a Class A organization. Strangely, Lou Gehrig, after graduating from Columbia and joining the Yankees, also had made his professional start at Hartford. If Greenberg thought he was doing Hartford a good turn when he agreed to play there, he was mistaken. After the first seventeen games had been played, he had an average of .214, and as his fielding was ghastly even when compared to such a poor batting figure, Detroit wisely shipped him far away to Raleigh, N. C., in the Piedmont League, where the fast balls were not quite so fast and the curves not quite so sharp.

In slower company, Greenberg was able to hold his own his first year in professional baseball, and when the season closed he sported a .314 average for 122 games played with Raleigh. The Tigers recalled him in the fall, and he got into a big league uniform just in time, he says, to lift a nice high fly to Tony Lazzeri of the Yankees, on his first trip to the plate in the American League. He was not asked to pinch hit again for the Tigers before the sands ran out on the 1930 campaign.

The Tigers originally intended to play Greenberg at their Beaumont, Texas, farm in 1931, but afraid of rushing him too fast, they moved him to Evansville in the Three-I League. At Evansville it was Greenberg's good fortune to play under an exceptionally able developer of young players, Bob Coleman. He improved so much as a fielder, base runner, and heads-up player, that he won the first base job with Beaumont the next year, on the strength of his .318 average with Evansville in 1931.

Beaumont was in the fast Texas League, one of the best minor leagues in the country, and a circuit that sent such star performers as Beau Bell, Rudy York, Zeke Bonura, Harland Clift, Pete Fox, Don Gutteridge, Pinkey Higgins, Pepper Martin, Wally Moses, Al Simmons, Bill Terry, Elden Auker, Dizzy and Paul Dean, Lee Grisson, Carl Hubbell, and Willis Hudlin to the big leagues. Greenberg had one of his most embarrassing moments in the Texas League.

In 1932 there was a huge Italian youth by the name of Zeke Bonura playing for Dallas. He had just graduated from Loyola College in New Orleans and he was an even poorer fielder than Hank Greenberg. Bonura was a jolly chap and one day made the faux pas of laughing too loud and too long at an error committed by Greenberg. Big Hank, a strapping fellow and a spirited competitor, resented the idea of the likes of Bonura laughing at him, and started after the rival first baseman. Still laughing and thinking it a great joke, Bonura back-pedalled.

But forwards or backwards, Bonura never was

very fast on his feet, and Greenberg quickly caught up with him. "And that is where Greenberg made his mistake," said an observer of the bout which followed. "When Hank caught Zeke and hit him, Zeke stopped laughing and really went to work. By the time we'd got them separated, Zeke had done a lot of scoring with his fists, and Hank was wishing he'd let Zeke go on laughing at him."

Greenberg was a better player than boxer when he was with Beaumont in 1932, but he was not a sensation. His average was a mediocre .290 and he still was below the big league fielding standard. His best point was power, and the thirty-nine home runs he hit kept alive Detroit's interest in their $9,000 investment. At the close of the season he was voted the most valuable player in the Texas League.

In the spring of 1933 he reported for spring training with the Tigers at San Antonio. He thought his chances of making the grade were small. The Tigers had an experienced first baseman, Harry Davis, who was an artist in the field and a reliable producer at the plate.

"I've been out three times, and you can't release me again," Greenberg reminded Frank Navin, then head of the Tigers.

Navin laughed, and answered, "That's what our contract said, and we'll live up to it."

"Will you trade me, or sell me?" asked Greenberg. "I don't want to hang around here and sit on the bench."

"No, we're not going to trade you or sell you, not right away, anyhow," answered Navin. "You wait awhile. They'll be throwing some left-handed pitchers against us and we'll need a right-handed, hitting, first baseman."

Navin was right; Greenberg's pessimism was unwarranted. At the end of the first month of the American League season, Greenberg crowded Davis off first base. He played 117 games for the Tigers in 1933, batting in 87 runs and finishing with a .301 average. When the Tigers had their spring training in 1934, Davis was gone. Greenberg was the only first baseman in camp. The job was his—if he could hold it. "I made up my mind to hold it, and I did," recalls Greenberg.

The confidence the Tigers placed in Greenberg seemed to inspire him. He improved as a fielder, he stopped chasing bad balls, he learned how to wait out a pitcher, and he gained poise. Thereafter his place was definitely with the great first basemen in the league. As this is written, Greenberg has played seven years with Detroit and has never batted under .300. It was not high batting averages that earned him yearly contracts calling for $25,-000 and more, however, but the power of his hits. In 1935 he batted in 170 runs to lead the league hitters, and repeated in 1937 when he drove 183 runs over the plate, just one run short of the American League record set by Lou Gehrig in 1931.

"I'd rather lead the league in runs batted in than in homers or average," admits Greenberg. "When you drive in runs, you are coming through in the pinch. A man can have a high average by making his hits when they don't count. Or he can hit a lot of home runs when they are not important. But knocking runs over the plate really counts in the success of a team, and when it comes to making out contracts, most of the owners know it."

But if Greenberg places more stress on runs batted in than he does on hits and homers, it is unlikely that the baseball public agrees with him. To the man in the bleacher, the greatest of all records is the home-run record set by Babe Ruth in 1927 when he drove out sixty four-masters. The home run symbolizes power. Power, a huge bicep, a tremendous blow, great strength—these give sports fans their maximum thrill. The heavyweight in the ring, the line crasher in football, the weight lifter, the tennis player with the crashing service, the golfer who hits them a mile off the tee, and the home-run hitter all have something in common.

There have been three strong challenges to Ruth's home run record. In 1930 Hack Wilson of the Chicago Cubs came close, with fifty-six homers. In 1932 Jimmy Foxx, then of the Philadelphia Athletics, approached still nearer, with fifty-eight homers. And in 1938 Hank Greenberg had the record in his grasp, only to stop at fifty-eight when he slumped the last week of the season. Undoubtedly Foxx and Greenberg are the hardest hitting, right-handed batsmen modern baseball has had. If American League parks did not favor left-handed hitters, they might have broken Ruth's mark, a mark thought unapproachable when it was established.

Babe Ruth was one of Hank Greenberg's boyhood idols, just as he was the idol of millions of American sports fans, old and young. While Greenberg was still in high school, he used to sit in the bleachers at Yankee Stadium and watch with awe this king of sluggers, never guessing that some day he would wear the crown, that some day he would challenge the record set by the Bambino.

"When I saw the Babe struck out," Greenberg recalls, "I always felt sorry. It didn't seem right. But when he hit a home run out to us in the bleachers, I used to stand up with every one else and yell. After the game I used to wait around the players' entrance, just to see Ruth come out. We all worshiped him."

In 1938, when it seemed that Greenberg might break Ruth's record, a sports writer referred to Big Hank as another Babe. It was a comparison that aroused Greenberg. "I'm not another Ruth and I'll never be another Ruth," he told the writer. "Ruth was in a class by himself; no one will ever come close to him, even if they do break his record. Don't ever refer to me as another Babe Ruth."

Greenberg thinks that some one will break Ruth's record some day, but he does not think any batter will be as consistent over the years as was the man who transformed baseball. Ruth hit 714 homers during his lifetime. Four times he hit more than fifty homers in one season; eleven times he hit more than forty homers. "The rest of us sluggers can't carry Ruth's bat," said the modest Greenberg one day during a dugout conversation.

The baseball world looked on tensely in the last

month of the 1938 season, when Greenberg aimed at sixty-one homers. There was a growing excitement as the weeks passed, and when Greenberg reached fifty-eight homers with five games to play, the fans were holding their breath. Would he make it? Some thought he would, some hoped he would. But there were many worshipers of the picturesque King of Swat who hoped this young challenger would fail.

On the street corners, gangs of men debated the possibility of a new home run record. Tempers became short; knuckles were skinned.

When Mr. Jones met Mr. Brown in the subway, instead of talking about the weather, they talked about Hank Greenberg. Would he hit three homers in the next five games?

The question, as stranger talked to stranger in the railroad stations, was: "Did Hank Greenberg hit a home run today?"

The pressure was on Greenberg as it had been on Foxx in 1932, as it had been on Wilson in 1930, but as it had not been on Ruth in 1927. Furthermore, Greenberg was contending against other disadvantages: he had played nearly 150 games and was tired; it was late September and shadows which covered the diamond made it difficult to follow pitches; the ball was less lively in the cooler weather than it had been in midsummer.

In the last five games of the season, Greenberg had to bat against Howard Mills and Buck Newsom of the Browns, Dennis Galehouse, Bob Feller, and John Humphries of the Indians. All were good pitchers. Mills walked him three times. Newsom was after his twentieth victory and put the pressure on the whole way. Feller was so fast he set a new strike-out record of eighteen men. Galehouse and Humphries were no easier. When the season ended, Greenberg still had fifty-eight home runs, no more and no less.

The baseball world relaxed again. Babe Ruth's record was still there for the kid sluggers to shoot at. It was just as well. "Nice try, Hank," said the fans, and turned to the World Series.

Although Ruth was his idol, Greenberg did not copy the Babe's style. Greenberg and Foxx use different styles, also. To this leading Jewish ball player, it is significant that few good hitters bat alike. One reason, of course, is that they are not built alike. Some like to stand over the plate, like Jimmy Foxx; others like to stand back from the plate, like Rogers Hornsby. Some uppercut

the ball and hit huge flies, as did Ruth; some strike
into the ball and hit line drives, as does Greenberg.

Greenberg says he uses the same batting style
now that he employed when he was sixteen years
old. He was fortunate to have a lot of practice
when he was a boy, and he quickly found the stance
and swing that suited him best. For this he credits
Tom Ellife, his baseball coach at Monroe High.
Ellife saw to it that the boys had plenty of opportunity to practice.

Because he stands six feet, four inches, Greenberg has unusual leverage. When he meets the
ball on the nose, he hits it as far as anyone, even
Ruth. One of his longest drives was into the left
center field bleachers at Yankee Stadium, a feat
that was unprecedented, and through 1938, un-
equaled. Greenberg overstrides, and as a result
often strikes out, but he more than makes up for
these lapses. He has the ability to relax, which is
necessary to good hitting.

In big league inner circles, Greenberg is called
a "guess" hitter—one who tries to figure out what
the pitcher is going to throw, a fast ball, a curve,
or a change of pace. Greenberg likes to know what
is coming. The year he hit fifty-eight home runs,

there was a great deal of talk about Del Baker, third-base coach for the Tigers, stealing signs or detecting what the pitcher was going to throw. Greenberg and Baker both denied that the homers pouring off the former's bat were the result of the coach's sagacity, yet they admitted that occasionally they worked together. This is the system:

Sometimes Baker standing in the coaching box can see the catcher giving his signals to the pitcher. More often, the shrewd Baker, by constant study and observation, discovered little give-aways in a pitcher's style. Supposing, for instance, that a pitcher keeps his wrist flat when he is about to throw a fast ball, but sidewise when he is about to throw a curve.

In a pinch, when a base hit probably will mean victory, Baker will watch the pitcher wind up. Seeing the wrist flat, he will shout, "kill it," and Greenberg will know that a fast ball is coming. Or, if the pitcher's wrist is turned sidewise, Baker will shout, "come on," and Greenberg will know that a curve is coming. It is a great system, so long as Baker does not make any mistakes. If Greenberg steps in to hit a curve and the pitcher throws a fast ball, he probably will have to fall flat to avoid being hit by the pitch, if it is inside.

There was a tremendous celebration when Henry Greenberg was born in Greenwich Village, but it was not for Henry Greenberg. The tooting, and horn blowing, and whistling, and bell ringing was to welcome in New Year's Day in 1911. Yes, Henry Greenberg was born on the first day of the year, amidst a tumultuous noise, and thus the roars of approval which greet his home runs each summer come naturally to him.

Greenberg's mother and father were both born in Rumania, but did not become acquainted until they met in New York City. David and Sarah Greenberg lived at first near Fourth and Barrow streets. They had four children: Benjamin, the oldest, who is a lawyer; Lillian, who is now married; Henry, of whom we are writing; and Joseph, the youngest, who is also a professional baseball player, although not a big leaguer. When Henry was seven years old, the Greenberg family moved to the northern end of Manhattan, to the Bronx. Each summer they spent a few weeks at Red Bank, New Jersey.

Henry's father made progress in business while

his family was growing up, and when Henry reached high school, after graduating from Public School No. 44, he spent his summers driving a delivery car for his father's establishment, the Acme Textile Shrinking Works. He did not have a great deal of time in which to play baseball, only a few minutes at sundown in the P.S.A.L. Stadium, which was near his home. Hank now says, "I stumbled into baseball. It was just luck that I joined the Bay Parkway team in 1929 and the scouts started following me."

Oh, yes, Hank Greenberg thinks himself fortunate to have entered professional baseball. "Where else is there a better paying game or business in which a man can get so much enjoyment?" he asks. Through a succession of yearly salaries ranging between $20,000 and $30,000 for six months of work, Greenberg has saved enough to be financially independent, has contributed generously to the welfare of his family, and is still unmarried in 1939. Greenberg has helped baseball, but baseball has been good to Greenberg, too. The Tigers paid him $25,000 when he played only twelve games in 1936.

A broken wrist was responsible for the giant

first baseman's inactivity in 1936. In the very
midst of his career, at the very moment when he
seemed about to shoulder his way among the immortals, Greenberg suffered an injury that threatened to end his playing of baseball. In the 1934
World Series, which the Tigers lost to the St.
Louis Cardinals in seven fierce games, Greenberg
had not been a sensation, although he batted .321.
When the 1935 series opened, between the Tigers
and Chicago Cubs, the experts said, "Watch
Greenberg go this time. Maybe Dizzy Dean and
Paul Dean made him look bad, but he's just got
through leading the American League in home
runs and runs batted in, and he'll get his revenge
now."

Greenberg hit a home run in the first World
Series game against the Cubs, but in the second
game, as he made a desperate slide for the plate,
he jammed his wrist against Catcher Gabby Hartnett. It was discovered that the wrist was broken;
Greenberg was out of the World Series. It speaks
volumes for the courage and ability of the Tigers
to say that they went on to beat the Cubs and win
the championship in six games without their first
baseman and hardest hitter.

Greenberg kept his left arm in a cast for months. There was much conjecture as to whether or not the injury would hamper the slugger the next season. In spring training there were indications that Greenberg's hitting was not normal; he was not snapping his wrists as he swung. Yet he made a good start when the 1936 season opened and was batting for .348 when he broke his left wrist again. It was in the twelfth game of the season, in Washington, that Greenberg caught a throw from an infielder just as Jake Powell, the batsman, crashed into him. Unintentional though the collision was, Greenberg was seriously hurt; X-ray photographs showed that his wrist had been broken again.

He played no more that season. It was a sad sight for visiting players to enter Navin Field and see the lanky slugger running about the field chasing flies and doing his best to keep in condition with his left arm in a cast. Greenberg caught the ball in his right hand, took off the glove, and tossed the ball in. He thought he would play late in the season, but the break was slow in mending and doctors advised him not to risk breaking it again, so Greenberg's record for 1936 reveals that he played in only the first twelve games of the season. Detroit won the World Series without him the previous fall; it could not win the American League pennant without him in 1936.

Many days stand out in Greenberg's memory: the day he hit a home run to left center at Yankee Stadium; the day he hit a line drive over the center field wall at Fenway Park in Boston; the day Bob Feller struck him out four times; the day he hit a line drive at Fred Ostermueller, Boston pitcher, and shattered the pitcher's cheek bone; the day in 1938 when he hit two home runs in a game for the eleventh time in the season, thereby setting a big league record. But no day does he remember more vividly than Rosh Hashana of 1934.

This sacred day of Jewish atonement and sacrifice came near the close of the season. The Tigers were leading in the pennant race, but they had not clinched the championship when the holiday arrived. The Tigers were playing the Boston Red Sox in Detroit that day, and great was the furor aroused when Hank Greenberg announced that he might play baseball that day, contrary to Jewish religious dictates.

Advised by sacred and secular counselors from

all parts of the country, Greenberg was in a fog of bewilderment as he debated with himself to whom his greatest debt lay, his teammates or his church. In 1933 he had not played on either Rosh Hashana or Yom Kippur. Mickey Cochrane, manager of the Tigers, told Greenberg to settle the problem himself. Whatever he decided would be all right with Cochrane. Greenberg finally decided to play; some rabbis gave him encouragement.

"I don't mind telling you I was upset in mind and in heart when I went into that game," relates Greenberg. "I felt sick and I was confused. The very first throw to me I muffed, and umpire Harry Geisel asked me what was wrong. After that I pulled myself together. Some divine influence must have caught hold of me, because I hit two homers and just about won the game with my hitting. I never regret having played that day; I would never have forgiven myself if we had lost the game and then failed to win the pennant. I had my teammates to consider as well as myself."

In 1939 the mental alertness of Greenberg brought a ruling from Judge Kenesaw Mountain Landis, high commissioner of baseball, on the size of gloves. Never a very artistic first baseman,

Greenberg devised a glove that other players called a "rat trap," because the size of the webbing between the thumb and main body of the glove was so large and tangled that a ball striking near it became ensnarled and could not be dropped. The restriction, after this event, in the size and shape of the webbing was a handicap to Greenberg and many other first basemen.

From the time he started playing baseball, Greenberg was a first baseman. Unlike most boys, he never wanted to be a pitcher. He was unique in another respect: unlike most ball players, he has never wanted to be a manager. Perhaps when his playing days are finished he will be ambitious to lead a big league team, but while he is still a slugger, he is satisfied to concentrate on hitting home runs and knocking runs over the plate.

Asked one day if he would like to manage Detroit, Greenberg exclaimed, with an injured air, "What? And be blamed for everything that happens?"

With his size and leanness, his free swing, and his fine competitive spirit, Hank Greenberg should not have to worry about managing for several years yet. He should be playing a good game until he is thirty-eight or forty years old, which would bring him up to 1950. After that he probably will not have to worry about his financial future; he should be able to take his managing or leave it, for he is not a money waster.

Greenberg typifies the modern baseball player in that he keeps an eye on the future; he is clean living and intelligent. He hustles at his work; worries more than ordinary players when he is in a slump, and is kind and generous to those he loves.

He probably would be an executive in the Acme Textile Shrinking Works today, if professional baseball had not come between him and the college education he was so eager to have. Now he is at the height of his career, an inevitable threat to Babe Ruth's home-run record for several seasons, and a probable big league slugger until 1950. It must seem a long time to those three New York clubs who so badly wanted a great Jewish player and then missed one who lived within their precincts. Especially it must seem a long time to the New York Yankees, who have to put up with this big fellow's bleacher-moving line drives; this Hank Greenberg, who grew up in their backyard, who idolized their Babe Ruth, who refused their $5000 terms way back in 1929, and who says he is perfectly happy playing for the Detroit Tigers.

HENRY GREENBERG

Born, New York City, N. Y., January 1, 1911.
Bats Right. Throws Right. Height, 6 feet, 4 inches.
Weight, 215 Pounds.

YEAR	CLUB	LEA.	POS.	G.	R.	H.	R.B.I.	S.B.	AVG.
1930	Detroit	A. L.		1	0	0	0	0	.000
1930	Hartford a	E. L.	1B	17	10	12	6	0	.214
1930	Raleigh	P. L.	1B	122	88	142	93	6	.314
1931	Evansville	I. I. I.	1B	126	88	155	85	18	.318
1932	Beaumont	T. L.	1B	154	123	174	131	11	.290
1933	Detroit	A. L.	1B	117	59	135	87	6	.301
1934	Detroit	A. L.	1B	153	118	201	139	9	.339
1935	Detroit	A. L.	1B	152	121	203	*170	4	.328
1936	Detroit	A. L.	1B	12	10	16	16	1	.348
1937	Detroit	A. L.	1B	154	137	200	*183	8	.337
1938	Detroit	A. L.	1B	155	*144	175	146	7	.315
1939	Detroit	A. L.	1B	138	112	156	111	8	.312

	YRS.	G.	R.	H.	R.B.I.	S.B.	AVG.
Major League Totals .	8	882	701	1086	852	43	.323

World's Series Record

YEAR	CLUB	LEA.	POS.	G.	R.	H.	R.B.I.	S.B.	AVG.
1934	Detroit	A. L.	1B	7	4	9	7	1	.321
1935	Detroit	A. L.	1B	2	1	1	2	0	.167
World's Series Totals .				9	5	10	9	1	.294

a On option from Detroit.
* League leader.

RALPH GULDAHL: A GOLFER'S GOLFER

Courtesy "Groove Your Golf", International Sports, Inc.

RALPH GULDAHL

CHAPTER VIII

RALPH GULDAHL: A GOLFER'S GOLFER

By Tom Fitzgerald, Sports Writer, *Boston Globe*

LATE in the afternoon of June 12, 1938, a slope-shouldered giant of a young man smilingly shoved his way through a cheering mass of spectators that ringed the eighteenth green of the picturesque Cherry Hills course in Denver to take his place with the immortals of American golf.

The huge young man was Ralph Guldahl, a twenty-six-year-old professional, with a slow Texas drawl and a big-boned frame that told of his Norwegian ancestry, and that afternoon he had rounded out one of the greatest feats in golfing history by clinching his second successive National Open championship.

The full significance of Guldahl's achievement is readily understandable to even the most casual follower of the ancient game that had its origin so many years ago on a gorse-grown Scottish heath. For the Open is the blue ribbon event on America's golfing calendar; it compares, in sporting analogy with the World Series of baseball; the heavyweight championship of boxing, and the Derby of horse racing.

The Open is a seventy-two-hole medal play test, spread through three days, with eighteen holes on each of the first two days and a grueling grind of thirty-six holes on the third. In it, the master shot makers of the country, professionals and amateurs, battle not only against one another, but against the inexorable standards of par as well.

It takes a real master of the links to win the Open, a man sure of every shot, a man calm and poised and with plenty of courage. For it takes plenty of courage to wage this lonely battle in which you're fighting by yourself—and against yourself to a great degree.

And Ralph Guldahl had just established himself as the master in this meeting of the masters, for two years in a row!

In the long history of the Open, which dates back to 1895, only one man has ever bettered this record, and that was in the early years of this century when the fabled Willie Anderson ran off three successive victories from 1903 to 1905. Only two other men ever won two in a row, Jack McDermott in 1911-12, and the greatest amateur of them all, "Emperor" Bobby Jones, who won in 1929-30.

In some respects, Guldahl's feat surpasses all of these. Certainly he has scored in more sensational fashion, for in his first victory at the Oakland Hills course outside Detroit in 1937, he set a new championship record of 281 for 72 holes, and at Denver he used just 284 strokes. Thus, for 144 holes in two years of championship play he used up 565 strokes, or an average of 70.6 per 18 holes.

Added to this is the fact that in both cases big Ralph has been forced to come from behind to attain victory, and in both cases he has responded in true championship fashion, carding sub-par rounds of sixty-nine for the last eighteen-hole stretch each time to pull away from his hotly pressing challengers.

In view of these events and of the fact that the slow-speaking boy from the Southwest also had to his credit two successive victories in the Western Open—which comes as close to the National Open in importance as any other professional golf event —it is little wonder that the sports writers galloped off to their typewriters to hail Guldahl as the new "super man" of the golf world.

Yet, amid all this glory shouting and the clatter of shattering records, Guldahl himself was probably deriving his greatest and sweetest enjoyment from the fruits of another subtler but much more satisfying victory he had gained in a fight against the adversity of fate and a gloomy golfing precedent.

For once before, Ralph Guldahl had rapped upon the door of golfing opportunity and had come away empty handed. It was back in 1933 when, as an unheralded youngster of twenty-one, he had burst into view at the scene of the Open, threatening a sensational upset, and then faltering just when the pot of gold loomed biggest before his eager young eyes.

The Open was held that year at the North Shore Country Club, near Chicago, and all the greats of the game had gathered, headed by Gene Sarazen who was riding high as the defending champion. But Gene, and the other established stars were destined to take a back seat in that dramatic Open. The spotlight was to fall on two youngsters.

One of these was Guldahl. The other was a swashbuckling young amateur from Omaha named Johnny Goodman who was known as the "box-car kid" because he had blithely made his way to the scene of the championship as a "guest" of the railroad in a freight compartment.

Goodman pushed up into the battle at the start, and when he finished his final round with a 72-hole total of 287, he seemed to be safely set for the crown, for Sarazen and the others had already checked in and had failed to shade that mark. Then suddenly the new threat loomed in the late afternoon as the youthful Guldahl who had been known only to a few of his brother pros up to that time, started storming home.

Running off an imposing array of pars and birdies that set a rapidly gathering gallery gasping, the shambling young Texan closed in on the Nebraskan amateur. They said he couldn't keep it up, but he did, and when he came to the eighteenth tee he needed a par four to force a tie.

It wasn't a hard par four. Any fairly capable amateur could have made it with ease. But this was the Open, where things are a lot different— especially for a twenty-one-year-old kid—and Ralph didn't make it. As it was, he had only a five-foot putt for that four, but still he didn't make it. Careful and methodical, as he continued to be in the later stages of his career, the big fellow sized up the putt from all angles, while the gallery waited apprehensively. Then he stepped up, took one last glance, and stroked the ball towards the cup. But the pellet never found its destination. While the onlookers let out a stifled groan, it curled far to the right side of the hole.

So Goodman won the 1938 Open, but since he was an amateur he couldn't accept the top-prize money. That went to Guldahl, but it's easy to believe Ralph would rather have had it the other way around, for, among the professionals, there's a dread significance attached to finishing second in the Open. The old timers will tell you the tales of other youngsters who came up fresh and promising as Guldahl did to barge their way into the fight for the big prize. They'll tell you, too, how they failed in much the same manner, and how they never did manage to get back again. So of Guldahl, the sages said early in the summer of 1933, "It's too bad. He's a nice boy, but he's all through."

From what happened thereafter, it seemed as if their prediction was all too true. Ralph tried an exhibition tour after that Open, but it failed. People don't pay to see the runner-up. Things went from bad to worse. He lost his job, and jobs were scarce. He cast about for anything that offered itself in an effort to make a living, and became in turn, an automobile salesman and a carpenter. He even sold his golf clubs.

It looked like a gloomy end to a career that had hardly begun, but Guldahl somehow never lost faith, even when things were worst. In addition, he had a real asset in a charming wife who retained her full trust in him and in his golfing destiny. She it was who deserved much of the credit for the hope that buoyed them both in those dark days. Laverne Guldahl has some claim to those two Open championships which Ralph Guldahl has won. And Ralph is the first to admit it. Thus, it was something of a corporate triumph when big, quiet Ralph did crash through to the top in the championship, to the amazement of the gloomy experts and in defiance of the awful jinx of having finished second in 1933.

Much of the secret of Guldahl's success probably lies in the fact that he has been forced to fight life for practically everything he's ever got out of it. He was born in Dallas, Texas, in 1912, to immigrant parents who had come from Oslo, Norway in the traditional quest for better living in the New World. Although he is a pretty taciturn fellow and not given much to talking about his personal history, it's easy enough to read between the lines that while Ralph's folks gave him the best they had, they had to work hard to keep the family going.

At any rate, Ralph, at the age of ten, started off in the path of so many other great golfers when he enlisted in the caddy ranks at Tenison Park, a golf club near his home. It wasn't long before the serious, brown-haired youngster with the big soft eyes was deeply interested in the game, learning all he could about it, while he carried bags for the few dollars he could earn. Gradually, as he grew into a vigorous large-framed youth, young Ralph attracted attention as a promising young golfer in a section where a particularly fine crop of bright young stars was rising—youngsters like Guldahl and Dave Goldman and Gus Moreland, who were to rush into prominence in the national scene later on.

As a matter of fact, in his first (and as far as anybody knows, his last) tournament appearance as an amateur, young Guldahl appeared in a municipal championship against Moreland and Goldman. Unfortunately the results of that tournament aren't immediately available. That same year, 1928, despite his youth, Ralph became a pro, accepting a berth at the Oak Grove club in Dallas, and a year later, he moved away from his home town for the first time, and became an assistant at the Franklyn Hills club in Detroit. In 1930, he made his initial tournament appearance as a pro when he finished tenth in the Texas Open.

In 1931, he was entered in three big events, the Western Open, the Canadian Open and the National Open, finishing in a tie for 32d in this last event with a score of 308. He took over another job at the St. Louis Country Club the following year, and while he was far down in the list of finishers for the national championship at Fresh Meadow, he did manage to win his first purse that year when he annexed top money in the Phoenix, Arizona Open.

It is little wonder, then, in view of his unimpressive record up to this point, that Guldahl created such a sensation when he suddenly appeared, to make a serious challenge for the Open crown. And after he had failed, it is quite easy to understand why the experts put him down as "flash in the pan" who had been extended the glad hand by Lady Luck and failed to grasp it.

It shouldn't be supposed, of course, that immediately after his heart-breaking failure to overtake

Goodman at North Shore Guldahl plummeted downward in one fell swoop to the depths of privation and despair. As disappointing as the experience was, there was at least the fairly substantial consolation of the top purse of $1000 that went to Ralph, since Goodman, as an amateur, was ineligible to share in the monetary awards. To a young couple like the Guldahls that $1000 was an important consideration, although they'd have gladly given it all to gain Ralph another chance at that five-foot putt which cost him his chances for even greater pots of gold and a greater share of glory.

Furthermore, Ralph and Laverne, full of the confidence and optimism of youth, planned an exhibition tour around the country. After all, Ralph was the top-ranking pro in the Open, and he had a fine golf game. The public would want to see him play, and later, they thought, perhaps there'd be a chance for a good berth at some club and chances, too, in other Opens to come.

Unfortunately, the public didn't respond quite in the manner they expected. Ralph's appearances met with indifference, for the average golfing fan, more than any other member of his species, demands nothing less than the very best at all times.

He'll pay to watch the head man, and he'll patiently trudge in his wake up and down the fairways, but generally, Mr. Fan hasn't much time for the fellow who failed to come out on top.

Eventually, Ralph gave up the tour in disillusionment, and he went back to a pro's job in St. Louis. It wasn't long before he lost that, too, and with his $1000 long since melted away, things looked very bleak indeed. He still loved golf and firmly believed that his future lay in the game. But golf, just then, was giving him a cold shoulder.

With no cash on hand, Ralph had to seek a living in other fields. He tried his hand as an automobile salesman, but he quickly found he wasn't suited to that profession. Sports writers later claimed that the only car he sold was one he bought himself. After a while, at the insistence of his wife, who never let her spirits sag in the face of all these reverses, they moved to California. To Hollywood, to be exact.

There are those who say that Ralph migrated to Hollywood with some idea of getting into the movies, a story which probably was prompted by the fact that Guldahl was really a nice-looking chap with his massive build and his shock of wavy hair. As it was, Ralph did break into the movies —but as a studio carpenter. And that job wasn't always steady.

Meanwhile, during this desolate period, Ralph managed each year to get to the Open to try once again for the prize that had so nearly been his. In 1934, the year after his Chicago downfall, he finished in a tie for eighth place with a score of 299 and the following year, badly in need of practice he dropped far down into a tie for fortieth place.

Guldahl has some sturdy Norse blood in his veins, and he's no part of a quitter, but after that miserable showing in 1935, he decided that he and golf would go their separate ways. He sold his clubs then and settled down to the serious, and wholly disheartening, business of scraping out a living.

He couldn't shake the golf fever, though, and one day he borrowed a set of clubs and entered a small country club tournament near Hollywood. He won first prize, and while the prize wasn't a whole lot, the victory went a long way towards replenishing his sadly depleted store of confidence.

As a start back on the tournament trail, he finished sixth in the True Temper Open in Detroit, winning a purse of $240, which doesn't amount to much the way pros figure purses. But it meant a lot to the Guldahl of that day. In the 1936 Open at Baltusrol he finished eighth, still well out of sight of that elusive crown and almost forgotten by experts and public alike.

Just about this time, however, something important was happening to the big, quiet lad with the sad eyes. He felt himself ''getting good'' again. His game was coming back. He couldn't tell you just how—golf is a matter of so many intangibles —but he knew it was so.

This was significant, for Guldahl has always been his own best critic. Although he's not given to bragging and swaggering—generally he is a laconic, retiring fellow—he has confidence in himself. When he's good and he feels as if he's going to win, he'll say so in a straightforward, uncolored statement as if he were rendering a verdict on some other golfer. When he feels his game is off, he says so in much the same manner, not to alibi, but merely to explain.

After the Open he went on to the Shawnee event where he finished second with a fine score of 289, which left him just one stroke behind Ed Dudley, the winner, and he followed this up by finishing fourth in the General Brock Open.

Then came the Western Open at Davenport, Iowa, which was to prove the turning point in Guldahl's career; the start of a period in which he was to sweep back from rock bottom in his profession to its heights, and in which, incidentally, he was to fulfill a strange augury.

That augury business, no doubt, will stand some explanation. Some time previously, Mrs. Guldahl, in womanly fashion, had wandered into a fortune teller's tent, more as a lark than anything else. In uncanny fashion, the elderly palm reader told the young wife that her husband was a professional athlete, and that while he had been having some hard luck, things were going to change for the better very soon.

As a matter of fact, the seeress told Mrs. Guldahl her husband's luck ran in "two's and three's" and that he was going to win the big championship in his sport two or three times in a row. Furthermore, she said he was going to score a great victory very soon, and that eventually the young couple would have plenty of money.

The Guldahls aren't any more superstitious than the rest of us, and they probably didn't take the prediction too seriously, except to hope that in time it would prove partly right. As far as they were concerned, they laughingly told each other, they'd settle for one victory in the Open.

Whatever the worth of the fortune teller's prophecy, the fact remains that the Guldahl fortunes immediately took a turn for the better. For, with every club in his bag behaving as if it were possessed of some magic of its own, Ralph slammed through that 1936 Western championship to an impressive victory with a score of 274, one of the lowest ever made. It was his first major triumph, and it put him right back with the leaders of the profession, for a victory in the Western carries with it no little prestige.

Through the rest of the fall of 1936, he was a regular member of the professional tournament caravan, and while a tie for first in the Seattle Open was the nearest he came to a victory for a while, he was managing to win his share of the smaller purses, and he was scoring consistently well.

Just before the year's end, when the scene had shifted to the Southland, Guldahl established himself as something pretty close to the number-one pro of the moment when he won both the important Augusta and Miami-Biltmore Opens with identical scores of 283, to become the scoring champion of 1936. A singular achievement, indeed, for a young man who, a year before, scarcely knew how he was going to get the next meal for his little family.

As the spring of 1937 rolled around, this amazing young giant continued at a great pace, and in five important tournaments, he was lower than second place only once, although his best effort was a tie for first in the St. Petersburg Open.

The concluding event on that stretch was the so-called Masters tournament at the Augusta National course where a selected group of the country's leading shot-makers compete in a fixture that had its inception as a kind of testimonial to Georgia's favorite golfing son, Bobby Jones. Ralph set the golf world talking once again when he finished second, a stroke behind Byron Nelson.

The National Open, which was held that year at Oakland Hills, near Detroit, was the next date on the golfing calendar, and Guldahl arrived on the scene with calm confidence. He felt that this was his year at last, and Mrs. Guldahl likewise was convinced. Her "woman's intuition" told her that her Ralph was going to take the big prize this time.

They couldn't find many to agree with them.

The experts all realized that Guldahl had set the tournament trail afire during the past year. They knew he had the game. But, man alive, this was the Open and Guldahl had had his chance before and muffed it. They never come back in the Open, they pointed out.

The attention of the golf writers was occupied chiefly with a sensational young "freshman" of the professional fraternity, a lad named Samuel Jackson Snead just one year out of the mountain country, and whose tremendous power and low scoring were the talk of the golfing set.

There was, in addition, dapper little Tony Manero who had won the year before with a record-breaking score of 282, along with such others as Harry Cooper, Gene Sarazen, Henry Picard, and Ed Dudley, all of whom were rated as strong favorites.

Even when the boy who had failed in '33 was still up there at the halfway mark in a tie for the leadership with a 36-hole score of 140, the sages around the scoreboard said, "Watch him fade when the pressure's on."

Still the quiet Norseman from the Cottonwood trail hung on grimly, holding to a searing pace that found Ed Dudley the leader at the end of 54 holes with a total of 211. And Guldahl was just a stroke behind, while Snead, Sarazen, Cooper, Picard, and Goodman, Ralph's old nemesis, were still in the thick of the fight not so far back.

When that tense finishing stretch of eighteen holes started on Saturday afternoon, the pressure started to exert its influence—but not on Guldahl. Dudley felt it first when he started with a faltering 6-5-5 that presaged a complete collapse. One by one, the others fell away until all were gone except big Ralph and Snead, the precocious newcomer.

Snead had finished his round when Guldahl had only gotten as far as the sixth green. They told Ralph that Slammin' Sam had finished with 283 and he'd need a sub-par round to tie.

If they waited to watch him crack they were sadly disappointed. Upon receiving that information he roared through the next three holes with a par, an eagle and a birdie, and he was two strokes up on Snead's mark for that point.

He never lost the lead thereafter. He did have some shaky moments on the tenth and eleventh holes, but he rallied again and when he came to the last tee, he needed only a six to win and a five to break Manero's record.

By this time everybody knew Guldahl wouldn't fail again. His drive off the eighteenth tee was just in the edge of the rough, but he made a nice recovery that left him just off the putting surface. His chip went twenty feet past the cup, but then he rolled up a putt that just missed dropping for a birdie four.

He stopped for a moment before he addressed the ball again for the almost unmissable putt that would give him the championship—and the record as well, and he must have thought back a little to that open four years before. As he paused musing and unmindful of the crowd that banked the green, he absently took a comb from his pocket and stroked it through his thick, ruffled hair. Then he stepped up and almost casually tapped the ball into the cup.

Then while the crowd roared its approval and the reporters went scurrying off to the press tent to pour out their burden of praise, Guldahl, smiling quietly, walked off to share his glory with his greatest allies, pretty Mrs. Guldahl and "Buddy," their young son.

Right at that moment, Guldahl could have rested content, assured of a place in golfdom's annals as the man who made one of the greatest comebacks in history.

But he didn't stop there. By virtue of his Open conquest he was named to the Ryder Cup squad which staged a successful invasion of England, and Ralph contributed his full share to the American victory. He paired with Tony Manero in the foursomes to beat A. J. Lacey and W. J. Cox and then as the number-one player in the United States line-up in the singles he scored a resounding eight and seven verdict over the celebrated Alf Padgham, one of Britain's finest professionals.

When he returned home, he picked up where he had left off, by tying Horton Smith in the Western with a score of 288 and then winning the play-off for his second consecutive conquest in that event.

In the early part of 1938 he continued his fine surge, although he finished second in the Master's tournament again—this time tied with Harry Cooper at 287, two strokes behind the victorious Henry Picard.

When the time came for the 1938 Open, held on that eye-filling Cherry Hills course in the shadow of Pike's Peak in Colorado, Ralph was an overwhelming favorite to stage a successful defense. And though he was four strokes behind handsome

Dick Metz when three rounds had been completed, nobody was willing to sell Guldahl short again.

It was just as well that there were few hardy souls to bet against the heavy-shouldered Texan's chances, for, living up to his title, the champion put on another of his characteristic spurts, like a thoroughbred in the stretch. For the second year in a row, he posted a dazzling 69 for his score in the last round of the Open to win with a total of 284. True, he hadn't made another record, but he probably would have if he had been pressed hard enough. As it was, his 284 was the third best score in the Open's history, yielding only to his own standard of 281 and Manero's 282 at Baltusrol.

With that second straight victory under his belt, Guldahl was almost inevitably tagged as the "super golfer" by the critics. Still, he was hardly the perfect golfer. It was difficult, in a manner of speaking, to see what really made him tick.

Certainly he was no great stylist in a game where style and form count for so much. With his heavy, stooped shoulders and his slouching stance, he seemed awkward on the tee, and while he did hit a powerful tee shot it wasn't as long as Sammy Snead's or Jimmy Thompson's. His iron shots were accurate but not as deadly as silent Denny

Shute's. He chipped well and he was careful and consistent when he was on the green wiggling a putter. But there were at least a trio of his brother pros who excelled him in both departments.

So, the analysts came to the conclusion that Ralph was the great golfer he was because he did everything well, though he was master of no one particular trick of his trade. He lacked that indefinable quality called "color" by the sporting authors, but he had a rare power of concentration that the glamour boys sometimes lack.

Concentration was the key note of Ralph's great success, no question about it—that and a courageous willingness to gamble when a gamble meant the difference between certain defeat and chance for victory.

The baseball people have a nice term which fits Guldahl's case very adequately. When a ball player performs all the functions expected of him in a competent manner without creating a sensation, the boys put him down with awesome respect as a "ball player's ball player."

By the same token, Ralph Guldahl would have to be regarded as a golfer's golfer.

When you break it right down, Ralph's old

friend, the fortune teller, would probably ascribe
his success to the fact that his luck ran in "twos
and threes." In any event, after his second victory in the Open, he calmly proceeded on to his
third straight Western championship, winning
with a score of 279.

Early in 1939, he won the Masters' tournament
at long last, with a stirring finish that was the
masterpiece of all his performances. With this
crown to his credit, Ralph had won all the high
honors that a professional aspires to in American
golf. All, that is, except the P.G.A. championship,
and that is held as match-play competition while
the Guldahl forte is stroke competition.

With all these honors behind him it is small
wonder that Guldahl was an almost prohibitive
favorite to score the second "triple" in the history of the National Open when the 1939 championship rolled around.

But the man was human, after all, and as he
frankly admitted, he lost his putting touch entirely to fade out of the contention, finishing in a
seventh-place tie with a score of 288.

Meanwhile, he saw a duplication of his own failure of 1933 when the brilliant Snead blew his seem-
ingly certain chance for the title by taking a dis-

astrous eight on the home hole of the Spring Mill
course in Philadelphia, thus paving the way for a
triple tie among Craig Wood, Byron Nelson and
Denny Shute, the first three-way deadlock since
the youthful Francis Ouimet shook the golf world
to its foundations in 1913 by defeating Vardon
and Ray, the English professionals in a play-off
at Brookline, Massachusetts.

It took two play-off rounds in the 1939 championship before Nelson finally won out over Wood.
It was a signal triumph for Nelson, but in the eyes
of most golf devotees, it paled in comparison with
the feat of the man who preceded him as the Open
king, Ralph Guldahl, the man who came back.

RALPH GULDAHL
Born Dallas, Texas, 1912.

EVENT	FINISHED	SCORE
1930		
Texas Open..................	10th	——
1931		
U. S. Open.................	tie for 32d	308
Western Open...............	——	——
Canadian Open.............	——	——
1932		
U. S. Open.................	45th	314
Phoenix (Arizona) Open......	1st	——

EVENT	FINISHED	SCORE
1933		
U. S. Open...............	2d	288
1934		
U. S. Open...............	tie for 8th	299
1935		
U. S. Open...............	tie for 40th	318
1936		
Los Angeles Open..........	tie for 16th	293
Catalina (California) Open....	tie for 9th	261
True Temper (Detroit) Open..	6th	291
Shawnee (Pennsylvania) Open	tie for 2d	289
General Brock (Canadian) Open....................	4th	290
U. S. Open...............	tie for 8th	290
Western Open..............	1st	274
St. Paul Open..............	10th	283
Vancouver (B. C.) Open......	tie for 8th	283
Victoria (B. C.) Open........	tie for 9th	280
Seattle Open..............	tie for 1st	285##
Portland (Oregon) Open......	tie for 4th	280
Glen Falls (New York) Open..	tie for 4th	286
Hershey (Pennsylvania) Open.	tie for 6th	291
Canadian Open.............	tie for 10th	287
Augusta (Georgia) Open......	1st	283
Miami-Biltmore (Florida) Open....................	1st	283
1937		
Los Angeles Open..........	tie for 2d	279
Oakland (California) Open....	2d	272

EVENT	FINISHED	SCORE
St. Petersburg (Florida) Open.	tie for 1st	284##
North and South Open......	tie for 6th	295
Masters' Tournament........	2d	285
Inverness Fourball...........	3d (with Sam Snead)	—
U. S. Open.................	1st	281*
British Open...............	tie for 11th	300
Chicago Open...............	tie for 8th	299
St. Paul Open...............	tie for 7th	288
Hershey (Pennsylvania) Open.	2d	283
Canadian Open.............	2d	287
Western Open...............	tie for 1st	288#
Oklahoma City Fourball.....	6th (with Billy Burke)	—
Miami Open.................	tie for 2d	272
Hollywood (Florida) Open....	tie for 5th	282

1938

St. Petersburg (Florida) Open.	tie for 4th	284
Hollywood (Florida) Open....	tie for 8th	281
Greensboro (North Carolina) Open.....................	tie for 3d	281
Masters' Tournament........	tie for 2d	287
Metropolitan Open..........	3d	292
U. S. Open.................	1st	284
Western Open...............	1st	279

1939

Greensboro (North Carolina) Open.....................	1st	280
Miami Fourball.............	1st (with Sam Snead)	—
Masters' Tournament........	1st	279*
U. S. Open.................	tie for 7th	288

RECORD IN RYDER CUP MATCHES (1937)

Singles—defeated Alfred Padgham, Great Britain 8
  and 7
Foursome—with Tony Manero defeated A. J. Lacey
  and W. J. Cox, Great Britain 2 and 1.

  *—Established record
  #—Won in play-off
  ##—Lost in play-off

DONALD RAY LASH: THE HOOSIER HURRICANE

DONALD RAY "DON" LASH

CHAPTER IX

DONALD RAY LASH: THE HOOSIER HURRICANE

By Jerry Nason, Sports Writer, *Boston Globe*

COACHES and critics alike are agreed that if any American distance runner of this era is destined to smash the Finnish monopoly of the coveted Olympic races at 5,000 and 10,000 meters, that runner is Donald Ray Lash of Bloomington, Indiana.

From one to six miles this sandy-haired state policeman from the banks of the fabled Wabash is no doubt the most competent foot racer in American track and field history.

Holder of five native records for distances of two miles or longer; a 4 minute, 7 seconds miler in his own right; having the distinction of running man's fastest indoor two miles; and at one time holder of the world outdoor record as well, Lash is, nevertheless, a racing enigma.

He is the human bombshell of track, destroying

271

records without warning, and then suffering defeat when his legion of admirers are singing most lustily of his invincibility. He is, in short, unpredictable, a foot runner of unlimited possibilities who has yet to fully exploit his talents.

In street apparel, or in his sweat clothes preparatory to a race, Lash does not conform to the picture one conjures up of a mighty foot racer.

He gives the impression of shyness, for by nature he is quiet, extremely modest and somewhat reticent. Street clothes belittle his physique. He looks little. But when the Hoosier Hurricane breaks away from the starting line his chest appears to have suddenly taken on inches, and his legs the power of pistons as he churns up the cinders.

Like Glenn Cunningham, the marvelous miler whom he has the distinction of having defeated, Lash is a product of the farm. He was exhibiting prize onions and tomatoes at Purdue University's agricultural shows before his name was a household word wherever there abides a lover of track and field athletics.

He was born in Bluffton, Indiana, on August 15, 1914, when the world was prepared to pitch headlong into the disaster known as the World War. That makes him twenty-five years old in 1939.

He was a student at the University of Indiana at the time he made his most notable efforts in track, and thus is the special pride and joy of the Hoosier State, outside of which he has never resided.

When he attained the dignity of a five-year-old, Don Lash moved with his parents to Auburn, a small community in the lakes district of Indiana, fifty miles north of his birthplace.

Lash's father was a moulder in an iron foundry, but the family lived on a farm in the outskirts of Auburn. There, unconsciously, began the training that seventeen years later was to send him tearing madly around a mud-puddled track at Princeton, New Jersey, to win world recognition and a record of 8m, 58.3s for two miles.

From five years on, or until he was of college age, Don Lash did the chores around the farm in Auburn, much as Glenn Cunningham, whose career served as an inspiration for many years, had labored in the Kansas wheat bowl as a youngster.

Cunningham, the incomparable miler, was not Lash's original inspiration, however. Like most boys, his admiration for an older brother knew no bounds, and in this case, the brother's name is Charles, four years Don's senior.

"Charles certainly was an inspiration to me," recalls Don. "He was a football, basketball and track man, was a 4m, 40s miler at Auburn High School, and afterward attended Purdue.

"With my brother so versatile it was only natural for me to attempt to play the same sports. I liked football, but found I was too light to play it well. I tried basketball, which as you know, is a thriving sport in the Indiana high schools, but the game was hard on my legs. So I turned to track and there found myself."

Don was a member of perhaps the most famous track triumvirate in the history of Auburn High School. There were three boys who often whipped the big Fort Wayne squad in the interscholastic district meets, and had the versatility, if lacking the numbers, to finish second and third in the State meet team scoring.

"How well I remember those years," remarked Lash, pointing to the past with evident relish. "There was a boy named Williams, who participated in the weight events. Then there was Trovinger, who was a fine dash man. I ran the half and mile events, and among us, we managed to score a lot of points."

At Auburn High School the coming American distance-running champion naturally became intensely interested in the career of Glenn Cunningham, then a famous runner at the University of Kansas.

"It was Cunningham's running which made me interested in the mile," said Lash. "In my senior year at Auburn High I managed to run the mile in 4m, 23.7s, to beat Glenn's world school record made at Chicago in 1930. It was only natural that I should be tremendously interested in running this distance as a result of that victory."

And ever since that time, Lash has been secretly fond of the mile event, as evidenced by his constant willingness to double up against major opposition in the big meets, frequently defeating his two-mile foemen, then coming back to race the great American milers.

A checkup of his record proves that the majority of Don's defeats have been in the mile, an event for which he has rarely made concentrated preparations. Close observation of his efforts in the past also accentuates the one instance in which he did make careful plans for the mile, and on that day, he beat Cunningham.

It was in Princeton's famous invitation mile race of 1937, on the site of his world, two-mile record the year previous.

Don raced Cunningham and Archie San Romani, the dark-eyed, little Kansas cornetist, in what developed into the fastest three-man mile in the annals of track.

San Romani won it, but his margin of victory over Lash was so minute that the officials conferred many minutes before announcing their selection. But they gave Lash the same time as the winner—4m 7.2s, at that time the second fastest mile ever raced. Cunningham, third, was timed in 4m 7.4s.

Critics have since insisted that Lash's unusual style of finishing, with his head back and torso straight from the waist, cost him a memorable victory. Had he lunged forward at the tape, as did San Romani, he doubtless would have been proclaimed the winner. At it was, his leading foot was across the line before his adversary's, but San Romani's body crossed the line first.

"I think that 4m, 7.2s race proved that I can run a good mile when prepared for it," says Lash now.

"It is nearly impossible for a runner—at least I find it so—to come down the distance scale from two miles and run a fast mile if he has not put in speed work.

"For that mile race at Princeton I dropped my regular training routine for two miles and trained especially with the idea of breaking the mile record at Princeton.

"I was pretty confident I was capable of doing it, and had I run my race a little differently I might have broken Cunningham's record. As it was, I let Glenn and Archie pass me near the end, seeing too late that both of them were weakening, and that I probably had more speed and strength left than either of them!"

And so he did. Lash uncorked a mighty spurt on the home stretch, swinging wide on the outside and around the two battling Kansans he had allowed to pass him.

The stretch was not long enough. Lash had made his move a second too late. He burst past Cunningham charging toward the tape like a mad buffalo. A yard from the worsted he came bounding up even with San Romani and they slammed across side by side, virtually a tangle of thrashing arms and legs.

Had Donald Ray Lash won that race we have no doubt that he might suddenly have denied his pledge of allegiance to the longer events and trained exclusively for the mile. And there is even less doubt that Princeton's mile race of 1937 would have stood forth among his many competitive memories as THE race of his life to date.

But to return to Auburn, Indiana, and the high school miler of 1933: Brother Charles was a senior at Purdue University and, all things being equal, it seemed logical that Don, too, would seek his college degree at Lafayette, Indiana. But, the University of Indiana under E. C. (Billy) Hayes, the incomparable coach of distance runners, was turning out a long line of nationally famous runners, so it is not surprising that Don elected to seek his degree at this renowned incubator.

In his visits to see Charles at Purdue, though, the younger Lash had been bitten by the cross-country bug, so badly that even to this date he insists the greatest enjoyment he has known as a runner has been as a hill-and-daler.

"Of all the events in track, I enjoy cross-country running the most," Don relates. "In the first place, cross-country provides a marvelous foundation for the winter and spring races. Secondly, it is a real sport, in my estimation.

"Track is, or should be, essentially for the athletes, not the spectators, and this one thing is emphasized in cross-country running. Unfortunately, this is not so of track itself."

This is typical of Lash's viewpoint of athletics where the stars are lauded at the expense of the lesser gifted. This is especially true of indoor track, where complimentary invitations are rarely issued to other than established athletes.

As we have said, Don caught the cross-country "germ" early and at Purdue. While watching the Purdue runners defeat a conference rival at cross-country he puzzled over the picture of two rival varsity runners nearing the finish, neither apparently expending every ounce of energy to win the race.

"Running, to me, meant striving with every ounce of energy to win," confesses Lash today. "I knew that if I was in the position of either of those men I would tear my heart out to win, as the saying goes. From then on my thoughts gradually turned to the longer distances."

Lash has been eminently successful as a cross-country runner, too. Disregarding his innumerable collegiate championships, he has won the national A.A.U. cross-country title six times consecutively, a record never matched in this country.

As a freshman he finished third to Ray Sears, a Hoosier also, from Butler University, who was destined to surrender the American native two-mile mark (indoor) to Don. That was in 1933. Ever since Lash has won the title, in rain, fog and snow. Conditions overhead or underfoot rarely trouble this dynamic young state trooper of the Bloomington barracks.

Don was likewise bitten early by the desire to represent law and order, and while relating the incident somewhat upsets the sequence of events in this story, we take the liberty to tell it, since it more or less explains his appearance in an Indiana patrol car today.

In his sophomore year at Indiana he had the unfortunate experience of being victimized by a pair of holdup experts in the Stygian darkness of Bloomington's outskirts.

Returning from his Christmas vacation to his college classes, Don swung off the train at the depot and decided to walk more than a mile to the

Delta Chi fraternity house. That was one of two decisions he made that night.

Obviously having waited until the appropriate moment and the proper setting, a car whisked up the road, shrieked to a halt beside Lash and discharged two citizens of questionable motives. At gun point they relieved Don of not only his purse, but his hat and overcoat as well, then disappeared rapidly down the highway.

It was a crisp December night, with the thermometer flirting too close to zero to be comfortable, and Don was still a mile from Delta Chi's warmth and hospitality, but before doing the perfectly natural thing and running, Don reached his second decision in an hour: some day he'd not only chase records, but criminals as well.

So today he wears the snappy regalia of the state police, glistening Sam Browne belt and all, drives his own patrol car, and makes an average of twenty arrests a week.

(Ed. Note—Almost four years later, the gentlemen who robbed an Indiana sophomore named Lash were caught in the web of the law, identified by Don, and eventually paid the law's penalty.)

Incidentally, that was the year the Hoosier Hurricane first generated enough velocity to make a national impression as a runner. He blazed the trail to the first of six A.A.U. cross-country championships that fall, then journeyed east in January with Charles (Chuck) Hornbostel and Ivan Fuqua, two famous Indiana upper classmen, to make his indoor track début. The three Indianans hit Boston for the Knights of Columbus indoor track games with Hornbostel and Fuqua, national figures, the center of attraction.

Lash, of a retiring nature in the first place, and probably a trifle overwhelmed on the occasion of his initial journey to a major meet, wasn't a particularly conspicuous figure. But buxom Bill Kenney, manager of the Boston games, and noted for the number of future stars he has introduced to the public in his meet, had a friendly word of warning for this writer.

"Lash is his name," we clearly recall Kenney's advice, "and take good note of it. He may be unknown now, but someday he will be one of our great runners. I saw him win the cross-country race last fall. He is a wonderful possibility."

It would have been fitting, of course, had the youngster from Indiana won his event, the two-mile race for the glittering Billings trophy, but Hornbostel won the trophy for the 1,000 yards, Fuqua the 600 yards cup, and Lash, in his début, finished second to the redoubtable Joe McCluskey, veteran campaigner and Olympian.

Board-track running is vastly different from cinder-track competition, to which the Hoosier sophomore was accustomed. Yet Don made a creditable showing, it being only the second time he had dug his spikes into the pine planks.

Boston was to see more of this sandy-haired Hoosier. He was to return at a later day and ruin all recorded marks for two miles on the green-banked track at Boston Garden.

It was not until the outdoor season of his sophomore year that Don blossomed forth in real glory on the track. Once the spring rains had been sponged off the Indiana track and the warm sun heralded the approach of outdoor competition, Lash commenced to take strides toward something akin to track immortality.

Truly an "iron man," with the speed and endurance one would hardly suspect lurked in that compact 145-pound frame, Lash startled the veteran observers in the Western Conference with "twin killings" in the annual outdoor championships, one of the few sophomores ever to achieve that distinction.

The physical education student from Auburn knocked the mile record down to 4m 14.4s in his first important race as a collegian at that distance, then returned to win the two miles handily.

He had annexed the Conference indoor championship for two miles five months before, so he showed a prolific haul of three titles in Big Ten competition for his first season of competition therein.

That was the start. Like the average sophomore, Don was not at all consistency's twin. He was badly beaten in the national collegiate championship that season, and ran fourth at Princeton's invitation race. But he was to gain ample revenge in the proper course of events.

Probably Lash's best running for any period of time was done in his junior year at Indiana, the year he lowered the American records for the 10,-000 meters and the two miles, the latter on two occasions.

That would be 1936, which he inaugurated on the first day of January by winning the Sugar Bowl two miles. At the Drake Relay Carnival in

April the durable Hoosier ran in 9m, 10.6s, the fastest an American had ever raced the distance.

Eureka! But it was still some distance to the world record of 8m 59.6s made eleven years before by Paavo Nurmi, the immortal Finn, and, incidentally, a mark no American had dared hope of touching until Lash came along.

Don slashed his way through his intercollegiate competition from the day of his Drake effort in April until the close of the season. He again doubled successfully in the Western Conference championships, setting new records of 4m 10.8s for the mile and 9m 19s for the longer race. He was undefeated on the eve of Princeton's invitation meet on June 13, 1936.

June 13, 1936. It was a day of days in Lash's meteoric career, but it was no day for record running. Or so thought the critics. The rain drove across the cement crater that is Palmer Stadium in New Jersey. The wind from the east whistled a raw, cheerless tune, and even the quick-draining Princeton saucer of which the grounds keepers are so justly proud, was dotted with puddles.

The race of the program, the centerpiece, was to have been the mile event. Of course, everybody was anxious to see Lash run, on account of his fine efforts in preliminary races. But the press had not publicized the two mile race as other than a guest appearance of a star newly risen in the track firmament.

Norman Bright, a graduate of Leland Stanford University, who had been running splendidly on the Coast, was Don's leading opponent. Bright, now an Alaskan school teacher, was undoubtedly the finest distance runner ever produced on the Pacific Coast to that time.

The upshot of it all was that Lash went berserk in the rain. Where the pundits of the press had anticipated an interesting race, and perhaps time comparable to, or a trifle faster than, his mark at Drake, the Hoosier Hurricane raised havoc with their predictions.

It was more a rout than a race, for Don left Bright some two hundred muddy yards behind, and cracked Nurmi's supposedly impregnable record by more than a second.

Smashing through his final lap in the breathless time of 62.7s, Lash sailed serenely through the rain drops to a mark of 8m, 58.3s . . . a new world record.

Lash, the unpredictable, the human bombshell of track! Here was the perfect illustration. Without warning, the Indiana junior had catapulted from the rank of a promising Olympic prospect to a red hot American hope for the 5,000 and 10,000 meter races at Berlin that summer.

Naturally, he was compared with Nurmi, the peerless. Actually, these two great runners—the American of the present and the Finn of the past—had nothing in common save speed and endurance, unless it would be the erect head carriage for which both are conspicuous.

Lash, like Nurmi before him, runs with his arms high, but brings his forearms far back with each stride. And almost in direct contrast to the "old master," the American runs high on his toes, in the manner of a half-miler.

In tactics, too, they differed, the old record holder and the new. Nurmi's plan was almost always to run his race in evenly proportioned quarters. Lash invariably bursts away from his field, sets a torrid pace for the first mile, lays low for a spell, then plans to bolt home with a fast-finishing spurt.

This run to a new record, then, was instigated directly on the eve of the Olympic games of 1936 at Berlin, Germany.

America's hopes in the distance runs, dominated for twenty-four years by the Finns, suddenly soared. Here at last was an American with the stamina and speed to break a Nurmi record.

Until Lash had negotiated the distance under nine minutes at Princeton, the fastest two miles ever raced by a native was the 9m 7.4s made by Ray Sears of Butler University, Indiana, two years before, and that feat was performed indoors on boards.

Only once had an American harassed the accomplished Finns in the Olympic distance runs on the flat. In 1932, Ralph Hill, a collegiate miler from Oregon, had turned to the 5,000 meters for the Olympics, and almost succeeded in running down Lauri Lehtinen on the home stretch, finally losing by two feet.

Lash was just as eager as any to bring one of those titles back to America for the first time. Destiny ordered otherwise, but certainly his subsequent races after the Princeton event justified the confidence of the critics.

In the national championships he lowered the American record for 10,000 meters to 31m, 6.9s and won the national collegiate 5,000 in 14m, 58.5s after having raced and placed third in the 1,500.

But America's new hope, determined as he was, produced no upset when he finally squared off against the mighty Finns at Berlin. He ran eighth in the 5,000 meters, his time being more than thirty seconds slower than his American record, and later finished almost twice as far back in the longer event.

Lash, to give him credit, has never tried to alibi his disappointing performances in Germany. Those who know claim they were the result of one of two things, perhaps both: the fact that he had injured a nerve in his leg while training, and his lack of opportunity on the boat to train as rigorously as was his wont.

Few runners could stand up under the heavy training program to which Lash subscribes. In the first place, Coach Billy Hayes is an ardent advocate of "over distance" training, that is, running distances longer than that at which a forthcoming race is to be run.

Lash quite frequently puts in a brisk workout the morning of a race, and few runners "warm up" so long and thoroughly as this Hoosier.

Speaking now of the Olympics of 1940 the Indiana state policeman has some very definite ideas about racing the Finns, whom he still aspires to defeat.

"I think I can say without boasting that I am

as good at 10,000 meters as any American," he says, "and yet I feel we haven't a chance to beat those Finnish runners on their own track, or anywhere else, unless we have ample time to train under conditions existing at the site of the Olympic games.

"I'd feel pretty confident of winning one of those Olympic races were the American Olympic committee to send me to Finland from four to six months before the games to train, and run in competition with the Finns.

"America has never had a 10,000-meters man anywhere near the top in the Olympic games and this appears to be the logical solution. Japan placed a runner third at Berlin. He was a little fellow, but he had been in Germany training for six months under Olympic conditions. That would seem to prove my point."

At the time this was written the Olympic games committee had either chosen to ignore Lash's proposal or had failed to act upon it. At least his idea is endorsed by any number of track coaches, who agree that America's top prospect should benefit from such a privilege.

In 1937, Lash catapulted back from his Olympic failures, presumably a better runner than ever.

He concentrated on indoor competition in the East from January until March, and ran up a string of two-mile marks that were of breathless quality, including the fastest time—indoor or out —made by man to that moment.

At the hoary Boston A. A. games in February, he unreeled an 8m, 58s race, winning by a tremendous margin from Norman Bright. That record still stands for board-track running, but Gunnar Hockert, the Finn, ran the distance in 8m 57.4s and Miklas Zsabo, the Hungarian, in 8m 56s that season, for world marks outdoors.

Lash had made careful speed preparations before he uncorked his stunning record in Boston. On the same track two weeks previous he had elected to race Glenn Cunningham, the mile monarch, at the latter's distance, and promptly provided one of the strangest spectacles we have ever witnessed in track.

Lash broke on top from the gun and set a terrific pace. Cunningham ignored his rival's rashness until far into the race, but Don sped past the quarter post in 58.2 seconds, the half in 2m 1s, and rushed by the three-quarter mark in 3m 6.4s— world-record pace on a small track that measured 12 laps per mile.

Cunningham became frantic. The master miler found himself fully eighty yards behind his red-shirted opponent who was apparently going strong. Then commenced one of the most stirring pursuits in which Cunningham, or probably any runner, ever figured.

The Kansan summoned all his resources for a grim sprint to make up this almost insurmountable margin. Yard by yard he brought the flying Lash back to him while 13,000 staid Bostonians howled in delight at this epic of foot racing.

Don, having made insufficient preparations for the mile, and paying the penalty for his savage opening pace, commenced to falter in the last lap. Cunningham finally caught and passed him thirty yards from the finish, but was forced to smash the all-time Boston record down to 4m 11.9s.

But with that speed workout under his belt Don was ready to launch a devastating barrage at the two-mile trophy events. He returned to Boston two weeks later, found the track had been enlarged until it was eleven laps to the mile, and much faster as a result of reconstruction.

The 8m 58s record, he says, was not his idea. Sid Robinson, an old Billy Hayes runner at Mississippi, was the chap who urged Don to make a supreme effort that night.

Sid, now a professor at Indiana, was then taking graduate work at Harvard University near by. He knew the track was fast and Lash prepared for a record effort.

"Sid convinced me this was the time to try for a new two-mile record, provided I could get in a fast opening mile," reveals Don.

Don rushed to the front at once, piling on the pace furiously that night. He planned to hit the mile mark in 4m 27s, and so accurately did he judge his pace that his time was four-tenths of a second faster than he had planned.

Robinson was at the side of the track, posting Lash on his time by laps. "This was of invaluable assistance," recalls Don. "At the conclusion of every lap I knew exactly how fast I was running and could plan to distribute my strength properly over the entire distance."

Lash blazed such a path around the green saucer of pine that night that en route to his world record of 8m 58s he shattered Nurmi's indoor 1¾ mile record in the process. Don fled past that station in a blur of red and white, being timed in

7m 52.2s, or approximately two seconds under the Finn's record for that distance.

As we mentioned, Lash ran his opening mile in 4m 26.4s. His last was negotiated in 4m 31.6s, or about five seconds slower than the first. That is his usual tactics, so often criticised by some, lauded by others. It is similar to Cunningham's revolutionary idea of running the mile, and discussed in the sixth volume of this series.

"Some of my critics may be right, but a runner should know himself better than an outsider," says Don in defense of his tactics. "I have found by experience that I make my best time when I crowd my best running in the first half of the race.

"For me the toughest part of a two-mile race comes in the fifth quarter-mile, or the step into the last half of the race. It is my plan to run my opponents out early in the race, and then use my kick at the finish."

One of the few important two-mile races Lash has ever lost was due to his failure to stand by the plan he had found so satisfactory in the past.

That was in a special race with Glenn Cunningham, the miler, at the indoor intercollegiate championships in New York, March, 1939. It was Cunningham's first race in several seasons at the distance. Instead of carrying his opponent at a fast early clip to tire him out, as is his custom, Lash somehow allowed the early pace to be slow. As a result Cunningham had plenty of running left when the race had two laps to go. He sprinted past Lash in a surprise move and was in the lead like a flash.

Don responded with his own sprint, a dreaded burst of speed that had mowed down many an aspiring runner. But he had to run on the outside and Cunningham stood him off in a mighty stretch battle, winning by two feet in the average time of 9m 11.9s.

"Glenn ran beautifully," said Don in the dressing room after the race, "but the race was run to order for him. I was wrong not to have kept on the pressure during the middle stages of the races, making it work for him to stay up with me. I thought I could catch him napping with my finishing kick. Instead, I was caught napping."

Unpredictable Don! Prior to that special race, he had slashed many seconds off the native American record for 5,000 meters, indoors or out, in the national board-track championships with a record of 14m 30.9s. Then Cunningham had beaten him at his own patented distance, avenging his mile defeat by Lash at Princeton earlier.

Lash was married in June, 1938, immediately after racing at Palmer Stadium, Princeton. Margaret May Mendehall, a pretty, blue-eyed Indiana co-ed, accompanied him to that famous "The Little Church Around the Corner" in New York for the ceremony.

During his first two or three years at Indiana the social functions on the campus concerned the boy from Auburn very little, if at all. Dancing had no special attraction and dates were something to be eaten from a package.

But Don one day gave his fraternity pin away to a certain party, and after graduation they were married. Today Mrs. Lash, slim and smiling, makes the trips east for the big meets, talks interestingly and informatively of running—especially the running done by Donald Ray Lash.

"In many instances my duties as a state trooper in Indiana have kept me from putting in the proper amount of training for my races," informs Lash, discussing his manner of combining his work and running. "One reason for my being especially anxious to be connected with the Bloomington barracks was to be handy to the Indiana track and the coaching of Billy Hayes, who is undoubtedly the greatest of them all. Unfortunately, this hasn't worked out so well in a number of instances. I recall planning my training schedule for several important races in the east last winter, but of the three workouts I had planned I managed to get in only one. On two other days my orders took me far out of town and I did not return until long after dark.''

Lash makes a good policeman. Years ago in the C.M.T.C. camp which he attended he won marksmanship medals. Now he has a patrol car of his own, radio and all.

''He makes a fine-looking officer, too,'' said petite Mrs. Lash to a New York scribe some time ago in a moment of confidence. ''He has a handsome dark blue tunic, gray breeches with a blue stripe, a snappy cap, Sam Browne belt and revolver.''

Wearing the badge of the state police was one of Don's first ambitions. He has now realized it. His second is to be the first American to win an Olympic running event on the flat beyond 1,500 meters.

It is a worthy ambition, certainly, and a lofty

one. America has pinned its hopes on several athletes in years gone by, but perhaps none whose determination and whose ability are so outstanding as that of Donald Ray Lash, the Hoosier Hurricane.

DONALD RAY LASH

Born Bluffton, Indiana, August 15, 1914.

1934

National Senior Cross Country	1st	32m	17.2s
A.A.U. 5,000 Meters, indoor	3rd		

1935

National Senior Cross Country	1st	32m	42.6s
Boston K. of C. Two Miles, indoor	2nd		
Millrose A.A. Two Miles, indoor	3rd		
Ohio State, dual, Two Miles	1st	9m	35s
A.A.U. 5,000 Meters, indoor	7th		
Big Ten Two Miles, indoor	1st	9m	21.3s
St. Louis Relays, Two Miles	1st	9m	43s
Big Ten Mile, outdoor	1st	4m	14.4s
		(New Record)	
Big Ten Two Miles, outdoor	1st	9m	23.1s
Central I.C., Mile	4th		
Northwestern, dual, Two Miles	1st	9m	17.6s
Princeton Invitation Two Miles	4th		
National College Two Miles	Failed to place		

1936

Sugar Bowl Two Miles	1st	9m	19.5s
Boston K. of C. Two Miles, indoor	2nd	9m	27.2s
Millrose A.A. Two Miles, indoor	4th		
National Senior Cross Country	1st	32m	37s
Drake Relays Two Miles, outdoor	1st	9m	10.6s
		(New American Record)	

Big Ten Mile, outdoor.....................	1st	4m	10.8s
		(New Record)	
Big Ten Two Mile, outdoor................	1st	9m	19.9s
		(New Record)	
Indiana Intercollegiate Mile...............	1st	4m	17.5s
Indiana Intercollegiate Two Mile...........	1st	9m	19s
		(New Record)	
Central I.C. Mile..........................	1st	4m	19.3s
Central I.C. Two Mile.....................	1st	9m	20.2s
Princeton Invitation Two Mile.............	1st	8m	58.3s
		(World Record)	
National Collegiate 1,500 Meters...........	3rd		
National Collegiate 5,000 Meters...........	1st	14m	58.5s
National A.A.U. 10,000 Meters.............	1st	31m	6.9s
		(American Record)	
Final Olympic Tryout 5,000 Meters.........	Tie 1st	15m	4.2s
Olympic 10,000 Meters....................	8th	31m	39.4s
Olympic 5,000 Meters.....................	15th	No Time	
		Taken	
Princeton Invitation Mile..................	Dropped Out		

1937

National Senior Cross Country.............	1st	32m	57.4s
Sugar Bowl Two Miles....................	2nd	9m	14s
Brooklyn K. of C. 3,000 Meters, indoor......	1st	8m	32.4s
Boston K. of C. Mile, indoor..............	2nd	4m	13s
Notre Dame, dual, Two Miles..............	1st	9m	23s
Millrose A.A. Mile, indoor................	4th	4m	15.7s
Millrose A.A. Two Mile, indoor.............	2nd	9m	13.6s
Boston A.A. Two Mile, indoor..............	1st	8m	58s
		(World Record)	
New York A.C., Two Mile, indoor..........	1st	9m	1.6s
		(New Record)	
A.A.U. 1,500 Meters, indoor...............	5th	3m	54.2s
Seton Hall 1½ Miles, indoor..............	1st	6m	47.9s
Chicago News Two Mile, indoor...........	1st	9m	24.3s
Big Ten Mile, indoor.....................	2nd	4m	12.9s
Big Ten Two Mile, indoor.................	1st	9m	19.7s
New York K. of C. Two Mile, indoor.......	1st	9m	00.9s
		(New Record)	

Penn Relays Special Mile, outdoor..........	1st	4m	24.3s
Michigan, dual, Mile......................	2nd	4m	11.2s
Northwestern, dual, Mile..................	1st	4m	9.7s
Big Ten Mile.............................	1st	4m	14.4s
Big Ten Two Mile.........................	1st	9m	21.4s
Central I.C. Mile.........................	1st	4m	13.4s
		(New Record)	
Central I.C. Two Mile....................	1st	9m	13.3s
		(New Record)	
Princeton Invitation Mile.................	2nd	4m	7.2s
East Lansing, Michigan, Four Miles........	1st	19m	17.3s
		(American Record)	

1938

National Senior Cross Country.............		34m	33.2s
Sugar Bowl Mile..........................	3rd	4m	14.8s
Sugar Bowl Two Miles....................	1st	9m	21.7s
Brooklyn K. of C. 3,000 meters, indoor......	2nd	8m	27.4s
69th Regiment Two Miles, indoor...........	1st	9m	11s
Boston K. of C. Two Miles, indoor..........	1st	9m	4.6s
		(New Record)	
Boston K. of C. Mile, indoor..............	Failed to finish		
Millrose A.A. Two Mile, indoor.............	1st	9m	6s
Millrose A.A. Mile, indoor.................	Failed to finish		
Penn A.C. Mile, indoor...................	1st	4m	22.3s
Boston A.A. Two Mile, indoor.............	1st	9m	3.6s
Providence (Rhode Island) Mile, indoor.....	3rd	No time taken	
New York A.C. Two Mile, indoor..........	1st	9m	4.1s
Seton Hall (New Jersey) Two Mile, indoor ..	1st	9m	12.6s
		(New Record)	
A.A.U. 5,000 Meters, indoor...............	1st	14m	39s
		(American Record)	
New York K. of C. Two Mile, indoor.......	2nd	9m	2.1s
Indianapolis 3,000 Meters, indoor...........	1st	8m	32s
Chicago News Mile, indoor.................	1st	9m	10.7s
Penn Relays 3,000 Meters, outdoor.........	3rd	No Time	
Kansas Relays Mile, outdoor...............	3rd	4m	24.2s
Compton Relays 1,500 Meters..............	1st	3m	57.8s

Compton Relays 5,000 Meters..............	1st	15m	7s
Princeton Invitation Two Miles............	Failed to finish		
Toronto (Canada) Three Miles.............	1st	14m	37.6s

1939

National Senior Cross Country.............	1st	32m	26s
Sugar Bowl Mile..........................	3rd	4m	13.2s
Sugar Bowl Two Mile......................	1st	9m	23.3s
Brooklyn K. of C. 3,000 Meters, indoor......	1st	8m	28s
69th Regiment (New York) Two Miles, ind...	1st	9m	17.4s
Boston K. of C. Two Mile, indoor..........	1st	9m	8.8s
Millrose A.A. Two Mile, indoor.............	2nd	9m	9.3s
Penn A.C. Mile, indoor....................	3rd	4m	16.7s
Boston A.A. Two Mile, indoor..............	1st	9m	8.4s
Providence (Rhode Island) Mile, indoor.....	3rd	4m	17.7s
New York A.C. Two Mile, indoor..........	1st	9m	6s
Seton Hall (New Jersey) Two Mile, indoor...	2nd	9m	16s
Boston V.F.W. Two Mile, indoor...........	2nd	9m	13.6s
A.A.U. 5,000 Meters, indoor...............	1st	14m	30.9s
	(American Record)		
ICRA Two Mile Special, indoor............	2nd	9m	11.9s
New York A.C. Two Mile, indoor...........	1st	9m	2.4s
Dartmouth Invitation Two Mile, indoor.....	1st	9m	1s
Chicago News Two Mile, indoor............	1st	9m	5s
Portland (Oregon) Mile, indoor.............	2nd	4m	25.6s
Compton Relays 1,500 meters, outdoor......	Twisted Ankle		

THE TENNIS CAREER OF ALICE MARBLE

ALICE MARBLE AND MRS. SARAH PALFREY FABYAN

CHAPTER X

THE TENNIS CAREER OF ALICE MARBLE

Our Fourth Super-Star in Twenty-five Years of Women's Tennis

By J. Brooks Fenno, Jr.

Member National Ranking Committee, United States Lawn Tennis Association

THE remarkable fact about women's tennis in the United States during a period of a quarter of a century has been its dominance by a small group of American players: to be exact, just *four* in number. Consider that in the twenty-five-year period intervening between the two major European wars of 1914 and 1939, our national women's singles championship has been won by no more than a quartet of our own players, if you except the year 1919 when Mrs. Hazel Hotchkiss Wightman staged her great comeback, inasmuch as she really belonged to an earlier epoch. Amazing as it may seem, Mrs. Molla Bjurstedt Mallory, Mrs. Helen

Wills Moody, Helen Jacobs and Alice Marble have won among themselves no fewer than twenty-two United States singles titles, as well as countless national women's doubles and mixed doubles championships.

Mrs. Mallory was the first of these tennis queens to reign and still holds the all-time record of eight national singles titles to her credit, some of which, to be sure, were won during the World War years when international competition was effectively stifled. Mrs. Moody, whose sovereignty came next, is close behind, being the winner of seven singles titles. Her bid for an eighth championship, in 1933, was frustrated when because of a back injury she was forced to default to Helen Jacobs in the third and deciding set of what proved to be a sensational final round match at Forest Hills.

Miss Jacobs succeeded to the throne after Mrs. Moody abdicated and won four singles titles in a row, thereby equaling Mrs. Mallory's record of consecutive triumphs. Lastly, in 1936, there came upon the scene a tall, well-built, good-looking blonde, Alice Marble, to fulfill an early promise and wrest the title from Helen Jacobs, thus accounting for the first of her three United States singles championships. Indeed, after being crowned national champion for the third time last September, Alice Marble's dynasty is now in full swing, and as the tennis season of 1940 makes its appearance upon an internationally troubled horizon she stands supreme among the women players of the world.

These, then, are the Big Four among American women tennis players during the past quarter of a century. Add to them only the names of Mrs. Wightman and Mary K. Browne, and you have in that group the super-stars of this nation since those days way back at the turn of the century when Mrs. May Sutton Bundy ruled the courts.

The daughter of a cattle rancher, Alice Marble was born in Plumas County, California, on September 28, 1913, and thus was only a few days short of being twenty-three at the time of winning her first national singles championship. She attended the Polytechnic High School of San Francisco and began playing tennis at the age of fifteen on the Golden Gate Park courts of that city where Maurice McLoughlin, Donald Budge and many other outstanding players have started on the road to fame. Somewhat tomboyish in her early girlhood, she became a baseball enthusiast and got her exer-

cise chasing flies for the San Francisco Seals'
sandlot ball team rather than in playing lawn tennis or engaging in other feminine sports. In due
course she became the team's official mascot and
used to warm up with them before game time,
even learning to give the ball a resounding swat
with the bat and to throw a fast curve from the
pitcher's box.

Meanwhile, at home, when she had a chance she
practiced singing and revealed a real talent in this
respect. Her mother had a fine voice which had
been professionally trained, while her father had
musical tastes, so that they enthusiastically encouraged their daughter in the cultivation of her
voice, with the result that she sang in the choir
as a youngster and in public school. Little did she
then dream that some day she would capitalize on
this talent and for a season become one of Broadway's most talked of attractions.

Eventually her family put its collective foot
down upon her close association with the baseball
world, which rightly was no place for a girl and
which certainly offered her no future. Accordingly it was an auspicious day when one of her
brothers presented her with a tennis racket and

thus managed to induce her to forsake the diamond
for the public tennis courts.

Alice Marble had regarded tennis as somewhat
of a sissy's game, but when she came to learn the
thrill and strenuousness of it she was quickly converted into an ardent devotee of the sport. She
best enjoyed playing with the boys and men inasmuch as their style of play was more vigorous
than that of the girls; a natural athlete, she was a
good imitator and liked nothing better than to hit
the ball hard. This preliminary training and her
own inherent strength and muscle account for the
masculine type of game she plays. Her fast, hard-
kicking American-twist serve and the finality of
her smashes give her an advantage never before
enjoyed by any other woman player in the history
of the sport, for she stands supreme in overhead
play among the immortals of the game. Besides,
she can hit her flat, Eastern, forehand drive with
the severity of a Mrs. Moody—though perhaps
not of a Jadwiga Jedrzejowska, the strong-armed
Polish girl. Her backhand has frequently proven
itself to be the most reliable of her ground-strokes,
with her most glaring weakness over a period of
time, a certain lack of consistency, which is why

we cannot place her quite yet on the same topmost pinnacle with Mlle. Lenglen and Mrs. Moody to vie with them as the greatest woman player of all time.

Although Miss Marble "loves to volley," to use her own expression, she has sometimes run up more errors in this department than a great champion should, but judging by her 1939 performance, she is still improving and showing signs of steadying down. To any comparison between herself, Mrs. Moody and Mlle. Lenglen must be added the statement that when Miss Marble strikes a run of her very best tennis, her sheer power of stroke production gives her, in my opinion, a margin of superiority over anything ever before demonstrated on the tennis court by a female exponent of the game. Give this alluring and gracious Californian another few years at the top, and her record may well transcend that of either of her two most illustrious predecessors.

Mention should be made at this point of the great friendship which Miss Marble had already struck up with Eleanor Tennant, a student of the sport and a former national ranking player who subsequently taught tennis for a livelihood in California and is widely and popularly known as

"Teach." She has been a very successful teacher, too, and immediately took Alice Marble under her wing visualizing immense possibilities in her game. Eventually, the latter became Miss Tennant's secretary and their intimacy has continued to grow with the passing of the years until they are now virtually inseparable. Miss Tennant is, of course, no longer the superior on the tennis court, but she remains her pupil's coach, manager, constant adviser and very close friend. She has had much to do with shaping Miss Marble's mental attitude and getting her into the proper frame of mind to withstand the strain of tournament play.

It was in 1931, at the age of seventeen—only two years after she had taken up the game—that Alice Marble first came into the sports limelight when she and Bonnie Miller, another Pacific Coast player, won the national girls' doubles championship at Philadelphia, although the girls' singles title eluded her. In the singles she was decisively defeated in the final by Ruby Bishop, a fellow Californian, who, curiously enough, has scarcely been heard of since. "Brilliant but erratic" was a then current description of Alice Marble's play. Thus her early career differed from those of her immediate predecessor champions, Miss Jacobs and Mrs. Moody, both of whom shone more brightly as junior players, each having annexed two national girls' singles titles.

But beginning in 1932 Miss Marble's play improved rapidly, and she won for herself a number seven place in the national senior rankings of that year. Moreover, she learned and absorbed many lessons through the hard knocks of defeat. Her cockiness and the sometimes scornful confidence of her junior tennis years were disappearing and so was the indignation which formerly used to grip her when she made errors and missed set-ups on the court. In other words, she was rapidly maturing and profiting by example and experience, particularly in her match-playing temperament. She had always been a good sport but now she was becoming more restrained in her actions and less nervous and vexatious over mistakes and errors committed under the stress of competition.

In these early tennis years Miss Marble continued to enjoy greater success in doubles play than in singles, being a finalist with Mrs. Marjorie Morrill Painter in our national doubles championship of the 1932 season, and incidentally, losing then to Sarah Palfrey, partnered by Helen Jacobs, who as Mrs. Fabyan was destined at a later date to become part and parcel of the famous Marble-Fabyan duo, undoubtedly one of the greatest women's doubles teams ever to tread the courts.

I recollect seeing Miss Marble play early in the season of the ensuing year at the Longwood Cricket Club in her first New England appearance, and it seemed to me then that she had a potentially brilliant game, needing only more experience and greater steadiness to reach the top.

This was the year that Alice Marble had her first taste of international competition, being chosen for our Wightman Cup team in the annual tennis matches between the United States and England. She was selected to play only in the doubles with Mrs. Van Ryn, but did not fare very well, losing to the Britishers, Betty Nuthall and Freda James, in straight sets. Yet she had definitely "arrived" as a player of topnotch caliber and as a championship contender to be reckoned with. She ended the season with twenty wins and five losses in singles competition and a number three place on our national ranking list just behind Miss Jacobs and Mrs. Moody. She had won two important turf-court events and in the quarter-final of the national singles championship at Forest Hills had gone down to defeat in a grueling and thrilling three-set match before the British luminary, Betty Nuthall, herself a former United States singles champion. It was a battle not readily to be forgotten by those who witnessed it, in that Miss Marble led 5-1, 40-15, in the third and deciding set when Miss Nuthall staged one of the greatest uphill rallies ever seen in the tennis arena to take six straight games for the match. Miss Marble faltered badly at the very end and it became apparent that she had not completely recovered from the physical ordeal she had undergone at Easthampton the latter part of that July. For there, due to the pressure of an exacting and all-too-crowded tournament schedule, she had been forced to play two semi-final and two final matches on the same day, which had unfortunately turned out to be the hottest of the year with the thermometer at the 100°-mark in the shade. In this sweltering heat she played a total of 108 games, entirely too much for a tennis committee to ask of any player, male or female, under the circumstances. She suffered a sunstroke and as a result was unable to take her place in the Wightman Cup singles line-up a few days afterwards. Even later in the season, as at Forest Hills, she continued to show the effects of the taxing grind she had been through.

But all in all, the 1933 season offered Miss Marble's adherents a good deal to be enthusiastic over. The conviction had grown that if she could only acquire greater control of her shots and bolster her defense a little, she would become unbeatable.

In the spring of the following year, after sojourning in the Florida sunshine and playing some light tennis during the winter months, she appeared to have recovered from the ill effects of the previous summer and in May sailed for Europe with the American Wightman Cup team to compete in the French championships before going to England. But in France under a broiling sun she collapsed on the court in the middle of the first set of a team match against Mme. Henrotin, the French player. She was carried off the court and rushed to the American Hospital in Paris where she remained for three weeks and was pronounced to be suffering from pleurisy. At the end of her convalescence there Miss Marble took the first steamer home and was met in New York by her faithful friend, Eleanor Tennant. Physicians now ordered her to take a long rest in the warm climate of Southern California and to forego all tennis for many months. The realization of the serious aspects of her illness came like a bolt to her many well wishers who were fearful that she might never be able to play again. It seemed incredible that a young career so full of promise was to be cut short just as greater successes appeared on the immediate horizon. But, fortunately, this tragic sequence of events resulted only in postponing the date of her ultimate triumph in our national championship, and not in forever forestalling its arrival.

When the next season came around, Miss Marble was none too strong and had to refrain from serious play although she was able to take her racket in hand and participate in friendly knock-ups and in not too arduous practice sessions. An exhibition doubles match marked one of her few public appearances on the tennis court, but it was not until the early spring of 1936—just twenty-two months after she had been stricken in France— that she returned to singles competition. In her first tournament at Palm Springs, California, she gave an inkling of the glory that lay ahead of her by winning it without the loss of a set from a strong field of home talent, including the Misses

Babcock, Wheeler, Bundy, Workman, and Cruick-
shank. She went on from there to win the Southern
California championship preparatory to packing
her belongings and starting the long trek east for
the grass-court circuit. In fact, her first defeat did
not come until August when at Rye she lost to
Mme. Henrotin, the identical player against whom
she had been playing two years previously when
she collapsed on the court at Auteuil. A defeat by
Helen Jacobs ensued shortly afterwards, yet it
was a match in which Miss Marble actually won
more games and scored more earned points than
her adversary. She had the satisfaction of taking
one set at love by a magnificent display of tennis,
varying her speed with chops and drop shots, as
well as going to the net for winning volleys.

It was evident that Miss Marble had diversified
her game and was no longer dependent solely upon
speed of stroke and serve to pulverize her opposition. She had changed her stroke, too, from a
Western top-spin to a more effective, flatter, Eastern drive. Today hers is an all-court game. She is
equally at home at net as on the baseline and just
as capable in doubles as in singles.

Next came the 1936 national championships. At
Longwood she and Gene Mako won the national

mixed doubles title but Miss Marble lost out in the semi-finals of the women's doubles when Katharine Stammers and herself were defeated by Helen Jacobs and Mrs. Fabyan in a grueling match, one set going to the record-breaking score of 21-19, which was a veritable endurance test and left the four combatants in a state of exhaustion, as well as the spectators—and the umpire, too, for that matter!

Then on to Forest Hills—to the realization of her long-cherished ambition and to the delayed fulfillment of her girlhood dreams! In this national singles championship all the leading American players, with the exception of Mrs. Moody now in temporary retirement, were contenders, in addition to Katharine Stammers who was regarded as a serious foreign threat. Yet both Miss Marble and her arch-rival, Helen Jacobs, the defending champion, advanced with equal impressiveness to the final round, neither losing a set en route and the latter eliminating Miss Stammers in the semi-finals.

In this first of their several epochal championship matches Miss Jacobs won the first set 6-4 and led 2-0 in the second when Alice Marble started to play in brilliant fashion, varying her length nicely,

executing some perfect drop shots and rushing to
net for the kill. Many fine rallies ensued since both
girls were at their peak. In spite of Helen Jacobs'
miraculous "gets" Miss Marble took the second
set 6-3 and then the third more easily at 6-2, with
her opponent tiring toward the end and missing
the lines with her chops where earlier she had been
making the chalk fly.

It was a great victory for the elated Alice
Marble and proved her fighting qualities and
ability to come back after a disheartening start.
Yes, a new and worthy champion had been
crowned; she was acclaimed on all sides for her
grit and determination as well as for the sheer
power and beauty of her game.

The ensuing year, 1937, marked two events of
importance in Alice Marble's tennis career. The
first was her début in England as a tournament
player and the opening of her campaign in quest
of the British championship at Wimbledon. The
second was the winning of her first United States
women's doubles championship, with Sarah Palfrey Fabyan, this pair beginning a partnership
which may possibly go down in lawn tennis history
as the greatest team of all time, and one which at
this writing has gone through three seasons of

major national and international competition without defeat. When both these girls are playing in top form (and Mrs. Fabyan is prone to lapse occasionally from her best game) it is hard to visualize any team—past, present or even future—able to defeat them. Miss Marble, with her American-twist serve, powerful strokes and severe overhead, acts as the battering ram and creates the openings through which Mrs. Fabyan is invariably ready to slip the winning volley. The latter has no peer today in net play and, being a disciple of Mrs. Wightman, is well versed in the knowledge and tactics of the doubles game. Often, too, she works the opponent out of court with her deep or angled volleys so that Miss Marble will have a setup to pounce upon for the winner. Each effectively supplements the other and no matter which one makes the opening you can rest assured that her partner will take full advantage of it. Nor is there anything defensive about their style of play. One is always at the net even when her partner is receiving. *Attack, volley, smash* is their creed: the net position at all costs!

During 1937 Miss Marble continued to improve and played better tennis than in the previous season, and yet, due to stiffer competition from foreign players, lost a good many matches including her national singles title, which went to Anita Lizana of Chile. But she took her defeats graciously and was definitely becoming a more and more popular figure. This was the year marked by a series of terrific battles with the sturdy Polish player, Jadwiga Jedrzejowska. They met five times, three encounters being in England and two in the United States. The stocky Polish lady won four of them but all the matches were furious struggles with three of the meetings requiring extra sets and the remainder containing deuce sets.

Special mention should also be made of her hard-earned and sensational victory at Wimbledon over Fru Sperling, the German girl. It was a match the memory of which should last a lifetime. After the German star had taken a lead of 5 games to 4 in the first set Miss Marble came back to win it at 7-5 by dint of magnificent drives and well-timed advances to the net. The former then gained a lead of 3-2 in the second set, with Miss Marble falling into errors on her ground-strokes, and from there the German player went on to take six straight games to even the sets and establish a lead of 3-0 in the final set. At that point, just as her own cause appeared hopeless, Miss Marble suddenly found herself, and uncorking one of those inspired streaks of which she is capable, ran off six consecutive games, in her turn, to take the match. It was one of the most spectacular reversals of form and magnificent displays of tennis ever seen on a Wimbledon court.

Miss Marble subsequently fell a cropper to Jadwiga Jedrzejowska in the semi-finals, 8-6, 6-2. A description written at the time of this encounter ran in part as follows and is quite typical of all their matches:

"Mlle. Jedrzejowska started hitting on her own account with real beefy thumps that sprang from her Western forehand grip. Miss Marble, however, besides having the strokes of a man, had a manlike pace about the court. She retrieved these thumps and returned them with interest."

Miss Marble salvaged the Wimbledon mixed doubles title with Donald Budge, this pair sweeping through the tournament without losing more than four games in any set. In fact the scores of their last four rounds ran as follows: 6-1, 6-1; 6-2, 6-2; 6-3, 6-2; 6-4, 6-1; so one-sided was it.

In the Wightman Cup competition of that year Miss Marble was victorious in all three of her matches but her game was still spotty and she would alternate between mediocre and topnotch performances. She struck a tartar in the national singles championship when she lost to Dorothy Bundy 1-6, 7-5, 6-1 after apparently having the match well in hand. However, she secured revenge shortly afterwards by trimming Miss Bundy in California in the Pacific Southwest championships. And yet, despite the unevenness of her play as a whole, her season's record clearly entitled her to a number one ranking among the American players, just ahead of Helen Jacobs who was awarded second place over Dorothy Bundy.

A great season was predicted for Miss Marble when she arrived East the following spring en route to England to start the 1938 campaign. She stopped off at the West Side Tennis Club at Forest Hills in May and played some practice matches with Frank Hunter, former national doubles champion. "She is the strongest woman player I have ever seen," said he, after she had taken a set from him during one of their practice sessions.

This opinion was corroborated from London a month later when in a pre-Wimbledon tournament Miss Marble's form was summed up in the following sentence: "She produced as good tennis as has ever perhaps come from a woman's racket."

It was a tournament in which she was victorious against a strong international field including Mrs. Moody, Miss Hardwick, the English girl, and the South African star, Mrs. Miller.

And yet inconsistency was still to dog her trail along the path of international conquest, for immediately after playing such invincible tennis Miss Marble went down to defeat before Katharine Stammers in the Wightman Cup matches. Gaining a lead of 6-3, 5-4, and deuce—just two points from victory—Miss Marble, after chasing her opponent all over the court, foozled some easy shots and lost that set and eventually the match.

Again, in the Wimbledon semi-final shortly after, she missed a simple smash and some important volleys against Helen Jacobs, who was in one of her steadiest moods, and as a consequence lost in straight sets. This was the tournament in which Mrs. Moody staged her great comeback and defeated Miss Jacobs in the final, although, to be sure, only after the latter had suffered an ankle injury during the course of play. And yet Miss Marble showed her all-around class by winning the doubles with Mrs. Fabyan and the mixed once more with Donald Budge, the latter event again without losing a set. Among their victims were

Mrs. Moody and Jean Borotra as well as Mrs. Fabyan and her German partner, Henner Henkel. In looking over the roster of Wimbledon mixed doubles winners since the World War days of 1914 I would select Alice Marble and Donald Budge to play those French immortals, Suzanne Lenglen and Jean Borotra in the heyday of their career, as a dream match of matches.

But upon leaving the shores of England Miss Marble's defeats ceased entirely and once home she won the Seabright, Rye and Essex tournaments, and then topped off these victories by regaining her national singles title. In the United States she had the satisfaction of winning twice from Kay Stammers to gain ample revenge for her defeat by the English girl overseas. Like their earlier meeting, both of these encounters were free-hitting duels, although in the last set of their match at Forest Hills Miss Marble purposely slowed up the tempo of her game and by so doing succeeded in breaking up her adversary's attack. The wonder was that she had not tried it before as Miss Stammers has always thrived upon hard hitting.

In our national singles championship, with Mrs. Moody not competing and Miss Jacobs the victim of an early round upset, Alice Marble's sternest competition came in the semi-final from her good friend and partner, Mrs. Fabyan. The latter excels as a doubles player since her forte is volleying and her back-court game at best is an uncertain factor. But every once in a while she puts on a beautiful exhibition of singles play and this match was probably her supreme effort. It was easily the high light of the tournament and Miss Marble eked out victory by the slimmest of all possible margins : a single solitary point. Down one set and behind 2-5, 15-40 in the second, the Californian staved off two match points, one of them by a remarkable backhand volley. Yet her difficulties did not end until the last point had been played, for the Boston girl hung on tenaciously to the very end of this epic encounter. The score of 5-7, 7-5, 7-5 speaks for itself, and so close was it that the point tabulation showed that each player had won exactly the same number of points during the entire match!

The final round at Forest Hills was a terrific anti-climax and it took Miss Marble just twenty-two minutes to annihilate Nancye Wynne, the Australian player, who had defeated Dorothy Bundy in the semi-finals. High tribute was paid the Californian's devastating attack in this match when Wallis Merrihew, editor and publisher of *American Lawn Tennis,* wrote in part: "It is possible that never has a woman displayed such controlled average speed of shot as Miss Marble."

So once again the California blonde had the supreme satisfaction and high honor of being national champion. In successive matches she had demonstrated that she had the *heart* of a champion in extricating herself from the jaws of defeat against Mrs. Fabyan and the *strokes* of a champion in running roughshod over Miss Wynne in the final.

The National Ranking Committee of that year, of which I was a member, decided unanimously to rank Alice Marble in the number one position among American competitors and yet not to rank either Mrs. Moody or Miss Jacobs because of insufficient playing data. But in a world's ranking for that year, published by *American Lawn Tennis,* Mrs. Moody was placed at number one, Miss Marble at number two and Miss Jacobs in the number three position. This seems to me the logical order although there was at the time no unanimity of opinion as to whether Miss Marble, Miss Jacobs or possibly Fru Sperling should hold the place directly behind Mrs. Moody who, in spite of her limited tournament participation, unquestionably deserved to head the list by virtue of her Wimbledon victory.

With another tennis season over, Alice Marble engaged in a brand new venture when, capitalizing upon her pleasant contralto voice, she made her début as professional supper-club singer in the Sert Room of the Waldorf-Astoria Hotel in New York. This was on December 1, and her contract lasted for about two months, at the end of which time a trifle homesick she left for California for a rest and change as well as for three months of intensive practice on the courts—preparatory to making another effort to break the Wimbledon jinx and win the All-England singles title, the only major championship to elude her onslaught. But her New York stay was a wonderful experience for her and gained her much publicity as well as plaudits for her smooth performances. The newspaper writers took particular delight in describing her as a ''glamour girl.'' Although her tennis fame certainly paved the way for her début as a songstress, she unquestionably made a successful start at her new-found vocation. The poise she acquired in singing gave her, in turn, a new self-confidence which stood her in good stead on the courts the next summer. To put it in her own words:

"I felt that if I could do well in something which was really new to me, then I did not have to fear for anything in tennis, the game to which I was so accustomed."

Her singing success included some radio broadcasting and was the forerunner of her entering the field of designing sports clothes. There were rumors that it might be the movies next. And though Miss Marble may be inclined to emphasize that her interests are now turning from sport into other channels, and even to reveal an ambition to become some day an opera singer, yet at heart tennis is, in reality, still her prime concern. Just how long this interest will continue as she grows older depends to a certain extent on her final and lasting place among the immortals of the game when viewed in retrospect many years hence.

Upon her return home from New York Miss Marble resolved to put in a lot of practice on the tennis court improving her defense in particular, so that she would not again be the victim of the steady type of player personified by Helen Jacobs. She worked hard on her forehand drive and the next season revealed better footwork in executing this stroke. Above all things she has always been conscientious and thorough in her practice and in her training, even to the extent of doing setting-up exercises.

Miss Tennant said at Wimbledon the beginning of the following summer: "When Helen Jacobs beat Alice here last year I took her home and worked for several months on her defense. Now she's got it and as a result she's a more complete player. Another thing is that it has taken these extra two years since Alice's serious illness to get her nerves padded well enough to withstand any championship emergency, although she had fully recovered physically."

For it was at the 1939 Wimbledon championships that Miss Marble first showed convincing proof of her improvement when she dominated the tournament from start to finish. Her game here reached its crest. Suzanne Lenglen and Helen Wills Moody in their most glorious moments never gave a more superb demonstration of lawn tennis. Alice Marble's decisive victories speak for themselves. In the quarter-final she defeated her old rival and nemesis Jadwiga Jedrzejowska 6-1, 6-4, while in the semi-final she quickly blasted Fru Sperling's strong defensive game 6-0, 6-0 with the loss of only fourteen points in the match—the same player, mind you, who had carried her to three sets in the 1937 Wimbledon tournament; and then she literally swept Katharine Stammers (victor over Miss Jacobs and Mrs. Fabyan) off the court by dint of withering drives and a powerful net attack, to take the final 6-2, 6-0. Better all-around control, an improved forehand and a deadlier volley were the features of Miss Marble's new game compared with her Wimbledon performance of the previous year. Aptly enough, *Murder on the Centre Court* was the title of a serial running in the London newspapers at the time of the English championships and it certainly applied most appropriately to Miss Marble's sterling exhibition. She also defended successfully her women's doubles title with Mrs. Fabyan and proceeded to win the mixed doubles tournament for the third time in a row, on this occasion with Robert Riggs.

Later, back home, Alice Marble never really duplicated her Wimbledon form for any sustained period. Yet she won the Maidstone tournament in which she competed for the first time since that

eventful day six years before when she had suffered her first collapse as a result of the dangerous
combination of too much tennis and too much sun.
In the final she met and bested her old rival, Helen
Jacobs. For two sets this pair played on even
terms, each winning one of the sets. Then as Miss
Jacobs' shots lost some of their sting and depth
Miss Marble went to net on the shorter returns and
won the deciding set at love.

National Doubles week at Longwood followed
and with it a third victory for herself and Mrs.
Fabyan in the women's doubles as well as a mixed
doubles triumph in partnership with the Australian veteran, Harry Hopman. Next came the
Wightman Cup competition at Forest Hills, which
the United States won by five matches to Great
Britain's two and in which Miss Marble contributed toward three vital points, her aid being indis-
pensable to ultimate victory. A three-set win over
Miss Stammers, who had defeated Miss Jacobs the
previous day, was the feature of this series. Further triumphs that season added more silverware
to Miss Marble's rapidly expanding collection.
Incidentally, her generous nature is well revealed
by the many gifts of hard won trophies she has

donated to her friends, keeping for herself only those of national and international import.

Then it was back again to New York for defense of her national singles title. This time matters at Forest Hills progressed smoothly enough until the final round when she found herself opposed once more by the chops and wiles of her arch-rival, Helen Jacobs, whose game had always proved the hardest kind of nut for her to crack. Sweeping through the first set at love by superb tennis and leading 3-1 in the second it looked like clear sailing for the defending champion, when she fell suddenly into an avalanche of errors. Her control deserted her and she missed the easiest kind of shots both at net and in the back court. It is true that a high wind made it difficult to play good tennis; but she had not played as badly for a long time. Helen Jacobs, improving noticeably at this point, fought a brave, resourceful battle despite marked weariness and physical distress as the match advanced. Yet it was a losing battle for the latter—although in a sense a moral victory in which she had the gallery pulling for her as the underdog, and because of her never-say-die spirit. The final score of 6-0, 8-10, 6-4 for Miss Marble had the spectators on tenterhooks and was sterling competition, though not always championship tennis. It was her greater stamina this time, and not her superior strokes, that ultimately brought victory to the champion. It was proof, too, of her ability to keep a level head and pull herself together despite adversity and an obvious loss of confidence in her own game.

To top off her many honors, she was voted the outstanding woman athlete of the year in any field of sport. And so richly did she deserve this award that she was far out in the lead when the final tabulation of votes was recorded.

This triumph gave Alice Marble the unique distinction of being the first player of her sex to win in the same year the English and American women's singles, doubles and mixed doubles championships. A truly remarkable feat and something for posterity to aim at.

With Mrs. Moody now finally retired from active competition after a glorious career and Helen Jacobs already a veteran in her early thirties and her game definitely on the decline, despite her great comeback fight of 1939, the grand old guard of American lawn tennis has left a clear field for

Miss Marble. The younger generation may claim numerous budding stars but at the moment no apparent satellites.

It was bad luck that Miss Marble had to lose two of her best tennis years because of illness but, still, several seasons of active tournament competition lie ahead of her and, if she keeps up an unflagging interest in the game, she has a possible chance of equaling or surpassing Mrs. Moody's record of winning seven national singles titles, and even Mrs. Mallory's all-time high of eight championships. But this is dependent upon many totally unpredictable things, including the state of the world in the years immediately ahead. Yet be it peace or war, lawn tennis will not only survive but reach out ultimately to new heights, and already Miss Marble has won a niche for herself among the immortals of the game. Whether or not she betters the record of Mrs. Moody she will be remembered by posterity as the first female exponent of the American-twist serve. And personally I doubt that in the next ten, or even twenty, years we shall have the privilege of witnessing a girl whose style of game is more masculine, forceful and interesting than hers, nor, I might add, a

player of her own sex capable of playing finer
tennis than Alice Marble at her best.

ALICE MARBLE

Born Plumas County, California, September 28, 1913.

1931	U. S. National Girls' Championship (final) lost to Miss Bishop..........	6—1, 6—4
	U. S. National Championship (1st round) lost to Miss Greef.................	6—2, 6—2
1932	U. S. National Championship (2d round) beat Miss Palfrey (now Mrs. Fabyan)	6—8, 6—4, 6—2
	(3d round) lost to Miss Ridley......	3—6, 6—4, 6—3
1933	U. S. National Championship (quarter-final) lost to Miss Nuthall..........	6—8, 6—0, 7—5
1936	U. S. National Championship (semi-final) beat Miss Pederson...........	6—1, 6—1
	(final) beat Miss Jacobs............	4—6, 6—3, 6—2
1937	British Championship (quarter-final) beat Fru Sperling.................	7—5, 2—6, 6—3
	(semi-final) lost to Jadwiga Jedrzejowska..........................	8—6, 6—2
	Wightman Cup Team Match (U. S. vs. England) beat Miss Hardwick.......	4—6, 6—2, 6—4
	beat Miss Stammers..............	6—3, 6—1
	U. S. National Championship (3d round) beat Miss Lumb..................	6—1, 7—5
	(quarter-final) lost to Miss Bundy...	1—6, 7—5, 6—1
1938	British Championship (4th round) beat Miss Hardwick....................	7—5, 6—4
	(quarter-final) beat Mme. Mathieu..	6—2, 6—3
	(semi-final) lost to Miss Jacobs......	6—4, 6—4
	Wightman Cup Team Match (U. S. vs. England) lost to Miss Stammers.....	3—6, 7—5, 6—3
	beat Miss Scriven.................	6—3, 3—6, 6—0
	U. S. National Championship (quarter-final) beat Miss Stammers..........	6—8, 6—3, 6—0

     (semi-final) beat Mrs. Fabyan....... 5—7, 7—5, 7—5
     (final) beat Miss Wynne............ 6—0, 6—3
1939 British Championship (quarter-final)
     beat Jadwiga Jedrzejowska.......... 6—1, 6—4
     (semi-final) beat Fru Sperling....... 6—0, 6—0
     (final) beat Miss Stammers........ 6—2, 6—0
   Wightman Cup Team Match (U. S. vs.
     England) beat Miss Hardwick....... 6—3, 6—4
     beat Miss Stammers............... 3—6, 6—3, 6—4
   U. S. National Championship (quarter-
     final) beat Miss Hardwick.......... 6—3, 6—8, 6—2
     (semi-final) beat Miss Wolfenden.... 6—0, 6—1
     (final) beat Miss Jacobs............ 6—0, 8—10, 6—4

ALICE MARBLE
AND
MRS. SARAH PALFREY FABYAN

1937 Wightman Cup Team Match (U. S. vs.
   England) beat Miss Dearman & Miss
     Ingram........................... 6—3, 6—2
   U. S. National Championship (semi-
   final) beat Miss Stammers & Miss
     James............................ 6—3, 7—5
   (final) beat Miss Babcock & Mrs.
     Van Ryn......................... 7—5, 6—4
1938 British Championship (quarter-final)
   beat Miss Coyne & Miss Wynne..... 4—6, 6—2, 6—2
   (semi-final) beat Mrs. Miller & Miss
     Morphew......................... 7—5, 6—4
   (final) beat Mme. Mathieu & Miss
     Yorke............................ 6—2, 6—3
   Wightman Cup Team Match (U. S. vs.
   England) beat Miss Lumb & Miss
     James............................ 6—4, 6—2
   U. S. National Championship (semi-
   final) beat Miss Stammers & Miss
     Lumb............................ 6—2, 6—2

	(final) beat Mme. Mathieu & Jadwiga Jedrzejowska......................	6—8, 6—4, 6—3
1939	British Championship (semi-final) beat Mrs. Hammersley & Miss Stammers..	8—6, 6—3
	(final) beat Miss Jacobs & Miss Yorke	6—1, 6—0
	Wightman Cup Team Match (U. S. vs. England) beat Miss Stammers & Mrs. Hammersley......................	7—5, 6—2
	U. S. National Championship (semi-final) beat Mme. Henrotin & Mrs. Andrus...........................	6—3, 6—1
	(final) beat Miss Stammers & Mrs. Hammersley......................	7—5, 8—6

MELVIN T. OTT: THE MIGHTY MITE

MELVIN T. "MEL" OTT

CHAPTER XI

MELVIN T. OTT: THE MIGHTY MITE

By Harold Kaese, Sports Writer,
Boston Evening Transcript

THE screen door opened, then drifted lazily shut behind a husky boy. A scarred suitcase in his hand, he surveyed the hotel lobby calmly, until, seeing no familiar face, he crossed to the desk to register. A small group of men in a shadowy corner stopped talking, the better to observe him. They noted his broad shoulders, a lithe physique not hidden by street clothes, a strong chin and an uptilted nose, large and powerful hands.

"Well, Mac," said one of the men, speaking to a pudgy companion with a red face who occupied the most comfortable chair, "I didn't know you were bringing a bat boy to training camp."

"Bat boy!" exclaimed John McGraw, famous manager of the famous New York Giants. "Why, he isn't a bat boy! What gave you that idea?"

341

"Look at the size of him!" answered the other, a New York baseball writer. "I've a boy at home who is as tall as he is. And look at his baby's face. Bet he's never shaved. Don't tell me he's a ball player!"

McGraw chuckled. "Yes, he's a ball player. Sure he's short, but look at the size of his shoulders. He's young—only seventeen—but see how chunky he is. He's one of those old-young boys."

"What's his name?"

"Mel Ott, and he comes from some small town near New Orleans, across the river," said McGraw, rising to meet the newcomer.

"If he makes a ball player—a kid like him—I'll be the next president," muttered the writer. The other men laughed.

This happened many years ago, late in February of 1925. The Giants were then training at Sarasota, Florida, a small town on the West Coast. They had won the National League pennant the year before, but had been beaten in the World Series by Washington. They were a confident team, the Giants and their correspondents, when they convened at Sarasota to prepare for the 1925 campaign. A boy only seventeen years of age did not cut much ice in company like that, but the writer

who first ridiculed him before McGraw decided
to look into the youngster's background.

He found Ott a hard boy to talk to. "Trying to
get him to tell you anything about himself is like
getting blood from a stone," he complained one
day. "He's a nice kid, but he hates to talk. He's
too bashful, I guess."

But he did succeed in learning that Ott was
born in Gretna, Louisiana. Gretna, Ott had told
him, was a small town of about eight thousand
inhabitants just across the Mississippi River from
New Orleans. His father was Charles Ott, who
had been working for an oil refinery ever since he
was married. There were three children: Marguerite, the oldest; Melvin Thomas, and Charles,
the youngest.

"I haven't finished high school yet, sir," Ott
told the writer. "If I'd stayed in school, I would
have graduated in June, but I'd rather play baseball any day. I'll be able to finish school later if I
want to, but I might never get another chance to
play with the Giants."

Playing baseball was this lad's chief delight,
the writer discovered. In high school he had
played a little football and a lot of basketball, but
baseball was the sport he enjoyed most. He had

done some work around home, and he liked to fish and hunt, but most of the time when he was not in school, he was playing baseball.

"Where do you play?" he was asked.

"Oh, I'm a catcher," he replied.

"And what professional experience have you had?"

"None. You see, I only played a little semi-professional ball around home and in Patterson, which is just a little way off."

"Semi-pro? Well, how did the Giants ever hear of you?"

"It was my boss who got me the chance. His name is Harry P. Williams, the lumber man. He runs the ball team in Patterson, and he knows Mr. McGraw. Last fall he arranged for me to go to New York to see Mr. McGraw, and we made out a contract which I signed. That's how I got here."

"Well, you might be only seventeen years old like you say, but you sure have good connections," concluded the New Yorker. "Are you sure you're only seventeen? You look older than that, you know, and you act older."

"I'm only seventeen, sir," answered Ott, without batting an eyelash.

Two years later the truth came out, and it was

Mel Ott himself who revealed that he was born March 2, 1909, not 1908. Instead of being older than seventeen, he was a year younger. Why had he lied about his age to McGraw? "Because I was afraid he wouldn't have given me a chance if he had known I was only sixteen years old," said Ott, with a grin.

"Humph! I wouldn't have either," admitted McGraw, when he heard that he had taken a sixteen-year-old boy to Sarasota. Indeed, Ott celebrated his sixteenth birthday in training camp, so that he was only fifteen years old when he left Gretna for Sarasota. There is no record that there ever was a younger big league ball player than Mel Ott, who developed into the Mighty Mite.

When Ott reported to Sarasota, he weighed one hundred and sixty pounds and stood five feet seven inches. As he matured, he grew and added weight, and when he was in his prime, he stood five feet nine inches tall and weighed one hundred and seventy-two pounds. Not so tiny, you say? No, as men go, but exceptionally small as big league sluggers go. Indeed, Ott not only was the youngest breaking in, but he is the smallest fence buster the game has known. Babe Ruth, Jimmy Foxx, Hank Greenberg, Rudy York, Lou Gehrig, and Johnny Mize are inches taller and pounds heavier.

Ott reported to the Giants as a catcher, but it was not long before he was practicing in the out-field. Asked why he had made such a shift, Mc-Graw replied, "His legs are thick and heavy, and if he keeps on catching he is going to be slowed down to a walk from the steady crouching. What's more, I don't think Ott's ever going to be a real big man, and I like big catchers. They are better targets for the pitchers, and they can stand the work better than small men. Nope, he's going to be an outfielder, and a good one, too."

A few weeks after training camp opened, Harry Cross sent this story to the *New York Times*. The headline read: MANAGER McGRAW CONSIDERS YOUNG OTT A "FIND." The story:

"Sarasota, Fla., March 14, 1926—Manager McGraw has made a remarkable discovery. He has found a young ball player in the Giants' camp who, he says, is as rare a baseball possibility at the age of seventeen as his experienced eyes ever rested upon. The lad is Melvin Ott, a high school catcher from Gretna, La.

"He has been watching him, especially at bat, for a week, and he says that he has never seen a youth of his age and experience with such a perfect stance at the plate. As Ott is a bit too small to measure up to McGraw's proportions for a catcher, the young find will be developed into an outfielder. . .

"His attention has centered on Ott, and when during the past week Ott began to smash hits to left, center, and right fields, he concluded that this youthful bit of bric-a-brac was a great outfielder in the making. So hereafter Ott will put away his catcher's mitt and will be seen roaming the out-gardens."

John J. McGraw is one of the two greatest managers baseball has known, the other being Connie Mack. For thirty-three years he led a big league club on the field, first at Baltimore, where he was also a leading third baseman, and then, for thirty years, in New York, where he became the living symbol of the Giants. Ten times he drove the Giants to National League pennants, and three times went on to win the World Series.

A hard competitor, a man who demanded the utmost from his players, and a bitter loser, McGraw had another managerial requirement; the ability to recognize talent when he saw it. Many great players, still famous although some have long been dead, owed their careers to McGraw, among them Christy Mathewson, George Wiltse, Artie Devlin, Rube Marquard, Jack Bentley, Hal Schumacher, Frank Frisch, Casey Stengel, Charles Herzog, Ross Young, Fred Merkle, Fred Lindstrom and Bill Terry. McGraw saw their talent, and he capitalized on it.

So it was that Mel Ott never had to play minor league baseball; so it was that he was given a chance from the start; so it was that he became a big leaguer when only sixteen years old. John McGraw needed only a few weeks of spring training to make his appraisal of this boy from Gretna: "Ott is the most natural hitter I ever saw. His style at the plate is perfect."

"Are you going to send him out to get experience?" he was asked.

"Send him out? No. I'll keep him with me. He'll learn more up here than he will in any minor league. That boy is going to be a great batter some day."

McGraw superintended Ott's development as though the boy were his own son. "It was almost as though McGraw were playing baseball again in the person of the husky youngster," reports Rud Rennie of the *New York Herald Tribune*.

Every batting trick, every fine point in base running, every knack of outfielding was put at Ott's command. He was tutored not only by McGraw, but by the experienced stars McGraw always used as a nucleus for his teams.

And Ott was a willing learner. He did not finish high school, but it was not because he was weak in studies. He talked little, but it was not because he lacked imagination. He stayed with the Giants in 1925 and watched them fall short of the pennant, finishing second to the Pittsburgh Pirates. Watched is the word, for in that first season, Ott did not get into a single game, not even to pinch hit. He learned first by watching, and he had a brilliant outfield performing before him every day, Ross Young in right, Billy Southworth in center, and Emil Meusel in left. McGraw did not make the mistake of rushing his embryonic star, and his technique of developing Ott was completely successful, as is borne out by the player's long record of consistent and remarkable performance.

In 1926, when the Giants finished fifth after ten successive years of occupying a place in the first division, Ott was allowed to test his knowledge and skill against National League standards. He played in thirty-five games, and McGraw smiled his satisfaction with his pupil, who batted .383.

"I didn't get up to the plate much that year, but when I did, it was usually as a pinch hitter or in a game we'd lost," recalls Ott, "and I know I didn't hit a single home run. But still, I had a lot of power. I always could hit a ball a long distance, even when I was a boy. It was great experience for me, getting into those games. I was only seventeen years old, but everyone thought I was eighteen. Hitting .383 gave me a lot of confidence in myself."

The Giants trained at Hot Springs, Arkansas, in 1927. On his way from Havana where he had spent the winter, to camp, McGraw stopped at New Orleans to see his prodigy.

"Come along with me now, and you'll get a head start on the boys," said the manager. "The outfielders aren't supposed to report for a couple of weeks, but why don't you come along now? I want to try a little experiment with you."

Ott needed no persuasion. The six-months season was not so long that the chance to play a couple of extra weeks in spring failed to lure him. Besides, he wondered what kind of an experiment McGraw had in mind. Was he going to be converted into a catcher? Was there something about his batting that should be changed? Ott went to Hot Springs eagerly. He was in excellent condition from a winter of tramping around Louisiana, fishing and hunting.

When Ott reached Hot Springs, he discovered that he was the only player in camp who was not a pitcher or a catcher. He did not have to wait long to find out why McGraw had brought him there so early: He was going to learn to play second base.

"I'd fooled around some in the infield," Ott recalls, "but had never played it seriously. I liked it well enough, but there certainly was a lot more to playing second base than I had ever thought."

The Giants had a weakness at second base, because Rogers Hornsby had been traded to the Boston Braves and they were now relying on Andy Cohen, a minor leaguer of only moderate promise. If Cohen fell down, McGraw wanted to have someone to call in, and the best man he could think of was his young outfielder, Mel Ott, a steady, smart, nervy little fellow who seemed to be able to do everything pretty well.

Throughout spring training in 1927, Ott practiced at second base. There was no intention of making him the regular second baseman, but when the period of preparation was finished, McGraw proudly announced that Ott was being carried as a reserve infielder.

In Cincinnati, several weeks after the season opened, Ott had a chance to play second base. Andy Cohen became ill with influenza, and Ott was put into the lineup in his place. Until Cohen could resume playing, Ott performed creditably at the keystone sack. His fielding was steady, although not sensational. He was not quite agile enough, his legs were too big and strong, it seemed, for a star second baseman. When Cohen was well, he was given back his job, but McGraw said: "They thought I was crazy when I said Ott could play the infield. He's just a natural and can play anywhere. He might even be able to pitch. I think he's the most valuable player in the league."

Ott hit very well while he played second base, and he was fortunate in being able to step into an outfield position as soon as Cohen was ready to play. Frank O'Doul had sprained an ankle, so Ott found himself back again in an outfield sector. Then, a few days later in Pittsburgh, McGraw traded one of his veteran outfielders, George Harper, for Bob O'Farrell, a catcher.

"We need a catcher," explained the Giants manager, "and are able to sacrifice an outfielder, because we have Ott. We can't keep him on the bench. From now on, he plays when right-handed pitchers are working against us."

Ott was made. He had caught McGraw's eye at the start, and he had gradually justified the manager's confidence in him. After this there was no question of Ott's major league qualifications. The only doubt was just how far the quiet, unassuming, modest youth would go. Certainly he had the skill, the ambition and the courage; his lack, it seemed, was color, or glamour. There seemed little likelihood of him being a headline winner through anything more than his exploits on the field.

Ott failed to set the league on fire for the rest of the 1927 season, and he batted only .282, his lowest big league average, but McGraw was not discouraged in the slightest by this slump of the boy he discovered.

"Ott's going to be a regular outfielder for us in 1928, and he'll hit better, because then he'll have some experience in back of him and he'll know what most of these pitchers have on the ball,''·said McGraw.

The young outfielder, successor in right field to the great Ross Young, lived up to the rosy forecast. In 124 games in 1928 he batted .322 and drove home 77 runs. In addition, he hit 18 home runs, whereas he had hit only one homer in 1927. As he became older (he was still only eighteen years old), Ott became stronger.

Ask him which was his best season of all, and Ott will tell you: ''My 1929 season when I hit 42 home runs, my record total, and drove in 151 runs, also my best. We only finished third that season, and I wish we could have won the pennant, but it often happens that a man has his best season when his team does not finish first. I also scored more runs, and hit for more bases in 1929 than I did in any other season.''

If you pointed out to Ott that he batted for .349 in 1930, whereas he batted for only .328 in 1929, he would say: ''Yes, but batting average doesn't mean as much to a hitter as his runs batted in, and his homers. The most important thing of all is driving in the runs, for they are what win games. I'd rather be a good hitter in the pinch than a high average hitter.''

Consistency has been Ott's finest attribute. He fell under the significant .300 figure in 1931, 1933 and 1937, but for eight consecutive years, 1929-1936, he batted in over one hundred runs for the Giants, and in 1937 he fell short only by five. When Bill Terry succeeded McGraw as manager of the Giants, because of the ill health of the latter in 1932, Ott kept right on pounding the ball. As this is written, Ott has the unusual record of having played for only one team, the Giants, in fifteen years of professional baseball, and for only two managers, John McGraw and Bill Terry.

"Don't ask me to compare them," he says. "They both rate aces with me, and although they differ, both have proven themselves smart baseball men."

Mel Ott has had many big thrills in his career, but the greatest, he thinks, came in the 1933 World Series. He had batted only .283 during the season and knocked in only one hundred and three runs, a small number for him, and it was his poorest season since becoming a star. Curiously enough, the Giants won the pennant after a nip-and-tuck fight with the Pittsburgh Pirates. That was the season when Blondy Ryan, the team's shortstop, sent his famous telegram from a sick bed in New

York, as the Giants started to sag in the West: "They can't beat us. En route. J. C. Ryan."

Ryan joined the Giants, took his position at shortstop, and the team rallied to win the flag. Ryan, Hubbell, Fitzsimmons and Terry were the headline names as the Giants went into the World Series against the Washington Senators. Ott? He was a good player, all right, they said, but he seemed to have slipped. The fellows to watch were Blondy Ryan, Bill Terry, and Carl Hubbell.

The experts had reason to rue their advice. On his first time at bat, Ott exploded a 400-foot home run into the right-center field stands at the Polo Grounds with a teammate on base to send the Giants away to a 2-0 lead in the first inning. The Giants never trailed during the series after that wallop.

"I'll never forget that home run as long as I live," said Joe Cronin, then manager of the Senators. "Walter Stewart threw a slow ball to Ott and he teed off. That homer was worth a lot more than two runs to the Giants. It gave them a lot of confidence and it put us back on our heels. That homer probably won the Series for the Giants."

If it didn't, the second one he hit did. Entering

the fifth game of the Series, played at Griffith
Stadium in Washington, the Giants led three
games to one. One more victory would give them
the championship of the world. The Giants held a
3-0 lead behind Dolph Luque, but a three-run sixth
inning by the Senators tied the score. Ott was having his troubles that afternoon. He was hitless his
first four times at bat; twice General Al Crowder
had struck him out.

But that was all water over the dam for the little
man from Louisiana when he came up to the plate
in the tenth inning with two men out. Jack Russell was now pitching for the Senators, and he was
the best relief pitcher in baseball. Washington
fans were quite certain that their side would win
this fifth game and send the Series back to the
Polo Grounds.

They did not think so for long, however, because
Mr. Ott goose-stepped on Russell's second pitch
to him and sent a long, line drive towards the temporary stands in left-center field. Frank Schulte,
Washington centerfielder, raced over desperately
from his position, gave a last lunge to catch the
ball, and saw the ball glance off his glove into the
stands for a home run. Luque held the 4-3 lead

through the last of the tenth inning and the Giants, after eleven barren years, were again world champions.

"Yes, that was my biggest thrill all right," admits Ott. "I hit homers on my first and last times at bat in the 1933 World Series, and the second one won the Series for us. I'll never forget how happy we all were when the ball dropped into the stands and we were champions. It was my first World Series and none of the others ever gave me as much fun, maybe because I couldn't hit home runs that meant so much."

Two years elapsed, during which he hit steadily and batted in 135 runs in 1934 to lead the National League, and then the Giants were pennant winners again. For two years the World Series was waged exclusively in New York, for as the Giants won in their league, the mighty Yankees won in the American League. The series of 1936 and 1937 were unhappy ones for Ott, although he hit a home run in each, for the Giants were overwhelmed by their rivals.

In 1936 a striking display of the versatility John McGraw had so well marked in Ott was a principal reason for the success of the Giants in reaching the World Series. Lou Chiozza, who was expected to play third base for the Giants, proved a disappointment. Eddie Mayo was given a chance and he, too, was unsatisfactory. Travis Jackson, a veteran who had the skill to play the position where grounders are torrid and throws are long, was susceptible to injury. In desperation Bill Terry turned to Mel Ott, his rightfielder. Terry remembered that Series in Cincinnati, in 1927, when Ott had played second base. Indeed, Terry had been the first baseman then.

Ott played sixty games at third base in 1936, and his ten errors brought his fielding average for the position down to .940. He was consistent enough, but not sufficiently nimble and agile to be an outstanding third baseman. And yet, when All-Star teams were being selected at the close of the season, Ott was named by many experts, for his hard hitting placed him high even in the ranks of infielders.

In 1937, the Giants were still more desperately off for a third baseman. Travis Jackson, who had played the position when physically well in 1936, was released and made manager at Jersey City. Ott had to play 113 games at the hot corner and he brought his fielding average up to .971, second only to Joe Stripp's and better than the marks of such third basemen as Stanley Hack, Lee Handley, Lew Riggs, and Harry Lavagetto. The Giants tried George Myatt and Mickey Haslin at third base, but it was Ott who played there for the Giants in the 1937 World Series, which the Yankees won in five games. In 1938, Ott was able to return to the outfield again and he welcomed the shift.

Many thrills came to Mel Ott besides those of playing in World Series games. "Among them," he recalls with a laugh, "was training in Los Angeles in 1933, with earthquakes and tremors scaring us every day. It wasn't fun and we didn't go back."

Running through his career, Ott picks out such random highlights as these:

Hitting for the cycle (single, double, triple, and homer) in Boston against the Braves, May 16, 1929, one of baseball's rarer feats.

Hitting three home runs in a game against the Boston Braves at the Polo Grounds, New York, August 31, 1930, another unusual stunt.

Scoring six runs in a game, August 4, 1934.

Being chosen on every National League All-Star team except that of 1933, and playing against the American League representatives.

Drawing five bases on balls in a game on two

different occasions, in Philadelphia, October 5, 1929, and in Boston, September 1, 1933.

Setting a National League record for double plays by an outfielder (twelve) in 1929.

"And don't forget to include the record I tied in 1938 when I was hit three times by a pitched ball," advises Ott, smiling wryly. "That was a painful afternoon for me. Jim Tobin was the Pittsburgh pitcher who kept hitting me that day."

Ott has a batting style of his own. He stands as close to the plate as the rules allow, or only six inches away. This puts him so much over the target that pitchers find him capable of pulling a ball thrown over the outside of the rubber into the right field bleachers at the Polo Grounds, which is a short drive. Thus, many pitchers try to throw the ball inside to Ott, thus forcing him to hit the ball on the handle of his bat. Tobin probably threw the ball too far inside the day he hit Ott three times quite by accident, although frequently pitchers try to frighten hitters by throwing at them.

A peculiar hitch, a sort of goose step, is another characteristic of Ott's style. He is a left-handed batsman, and when he steps to meet the pitch, he lifts his right foot stiffly. Strangely, Ott does not know when he acquired this trick. "I didn't have it when I started playing," he says; "but I picked it up early in my career with the Giants. I think it gives me more power than I could get stepping like other hitters. It's a wind-up."

Ott is the greatest home-run hitter the National League has ever had. The only three men who have hit more homers in the big leagues than he are Babe Ruth, Lou Gehrig and Jimmy Foxx, all American League players. At the close of the 1939 season, Ott had a total of 369 homers, as compared with the 714 for Ruth, the 494 for Gehrig, and the 464 for Foxx.

It was late in the 1937 campaign that the Mighty Mite passed Rogers Hornsby as the leading National League home-run hitter. In nineteen seasons in the older circuit, the great Rajah hit 299 balls out of the playing fields. Veteran though he is, Ott should approach the records of Gehrig and Foxx before he slips over the major league horizon, for he should be playing in the upper flight until 1945, possibly later.

Because he keeps himself in splendid physical condition the year around, Ott puts on little excess weight in the off season. He is short and stocky and has the bulging muscles one would expect to find on a light-heavyweight wrestler, but during the sunny winter days of the South, Ott generally can be found on the golf links in the vicinity of New Orleans. He shoots between eighty and ninety, and when he gets under the eighty mark for a hard eighteen-hole course, he is as pleased with himself as you and I are when we score far under our average.

"Golf is great exercise for the legs," says Ott. "I have heavy legs and must keep them in condition during the winter, or suffer when spring comes and I start running. Golf also helps keep the arms, shoulders, and wrists loose and limber. The swing used in golf differs from that used in baseball, but in general the same muscles are called on."

Look through the baseball record books, and you will come often on the name of Melvin T. Ott. At the close of the 1939 season, his fifteenth campaign with the Giants since he joined them at Sarasota in 1925, he held such marks as these:

Most home runs hit in a lifetime by a National League player (369).

Most years 100 or more runs batted in (9).

Most consecutive years leading in runs batted in (8).

Most years hitting 30 or more home runs (7).

Most consecutive years leading league in home runs (4).

Most years leading in bases on balls (5).

First World Series outfielder to have three put-outs in one inning (1933).

Some hitting and playing honors failed to come Ott's way in his first fifteen seasons, among them the batting crown, the striking-out championship, and the most valuable player award. His highest average, .349 in 1930, was far behind the .401 average which won Bill Terry the National League title that year. The striking-out championship, of course, nobody seeks, but usually the free swingers like Foxx, Greenberg, Ruth, and Vince DiMaggio set the pace in whiffs at some time or other during their career.

Stranger by far is the fact that Ott has never been named the most valuable player in the National League. Ernie Lombardi, Joe Medwick, Carl Hubbell, Dizzy Dean, Chuck Klein, Bill Terry, Rogers Hornsby, Arky Vaughan, Jim Bottomley and Paul Waner have all been thus honored, but the quiet rightfielder for the Giants, one of the most inconspicuous great players the game has had, has never been better than an also-ran in this respect.

If Ott talked as much as Dizzy Dean, or if he had Joe Medwick's crackling personality, or if he paced a team to a brilliant season as Ernie Lombardi did the Reds in 1938, he might have been voted this most prized award by the nation's baseball writers, but it is the fate of certain leaders in all walks of life, all fields of endeavor, to receive less than is their due. The moral must be that recognition is not essential to greatness: genius is neither established nor withheld by the donation of prizes.

Ott has been good to baseball, and baseball has been good to Ott. He has been well paid, sometimes receiving as much as $20,000 a season. In 1930 he married Mildred Wattigney, a New Orleans girl. They have two daughters, Lyn and Barbara Anne, who help make life a joy and a delight, despite batting slumps, team collapses, and the inevitable injuries which are common in every baseball player's life.

Disposition has helped Mel Ott attain his preeminent place among National League sluggers. Mention, too, a fine competitive spirit, a stability of character, and an inherent versatility. He loves the game, he loves to win, but he is the kind who keeps plugging when he loses. In victory this

brown-eyed Southerner with the square jaw and
uptilted nose is no braggart. In defeat he is no
coward, no sulker. Year after year the Giants have
been built around him, and when he is gone his
worth and value will become more clearly defined.
They will speak often of Mel Ott, the Mighty Mite
who hit more balls over the fences than any other
National Leaguer.

MELVIN THOMAS OTT

Born, Gretna, Louisiana, March 2, 1909.
Bats Left. Throws Right. Height, 5 feet, 9 inches.
Weight, 160 pounds.

YEAR	CLUB	LEA.	POS.	G.	R.	H.	R.B.I.	S.B.	AVG.
1925	New York	N. L.	C	...	...	...	...	...	...
1926	New York	N. L.	OF	35	7	23	4	1	.383
1927	New York	N. L.	OF	82	23	46	19	2	.282
1928	New York	N. L.	OF	124	69	140	77	3	.322
1929	New York	N. L.	OF	150	138	179	151	6	.328
1930	New York	N. L.	OF	148	122	182	119	9	.349
1931	New York	N. L.	OF	138	104	145	115	10	.292
1932	New York	N. L.	OF	154	119	180	123	6	.318
1933	New York	N. L.	OF	152	98	164	103	1	.283
1934	New York	N. L.	OF	153	119	190	*135	0	.326
1935	New York	N. L.	OF	152	113	191	114	7	.322
1936	New York	N. L.	3B-OF	150	120	175	135	6	.328
1937	New York	N. L.	3B-OF	151	99	160	95	7	.294
1938	New York	N. L.	3B-OF	150	*116	164	116	2	.311
1939	New York	N. L.	3B-OF	125	85	122	80	2	.308

	YRS.	G.	R.	H.	R.B.I.	S.B.	AVG.
Major League Totals	14	1864	1332	2061	1386	62	.314

World's Series Record

YEAR	CLUB	LEA.	POS.	G.	R.	H.	R.B.I.	S.B.	AVG.
1933	New York	N. L.	OF	5	3	7	4	0	.389
1936	New York	N. L.	OF	6	4	7	3	0	.304
1937	New York	N. L.	OF	5	1	4	3	0	.200
World's Series Totals				16	8	18	10	0	.295

* League Leader.

ROBERT L. RIGGS: CROWN PRINCE OF COURT

ROBERT L. "BOBBY" RIGGS

CHAPTER XII

ROBERT L. RIGGS: CROWN PRINCE OF COURT

By Jerry Nason, Sports Writer, *Boston Globe*

As one scans the career of Robert L. (Bobby) Riggs, the irrepressible American tennis player, one is singularly impressed by the black-haired Californian's devoutness of purpose and the manner in which Riggs has adhered strictly to that old saw about the shortest distance between two points.

Young Mr. Riggs has been in a great hurry for four years. He will cast his first vote this year, and will cast it with the distinction of having achieved the pinnacle of American tennis before reaching his majority, of having twice played the role of a Davis Cupper while most young gentlemen of his own age were still university freshmen.

In 1936 this dynamic young product of California's unparalleled tennis "mills" plotted a five-year program which was designed to project him

371

above the racquet-wielding mob on America's clay and grass courts.

But Robert was in a hurry. He cut a great many corners on the way. In fact, he lopped a whole year off his program, cutting a wide swath through his domestic opposition in four seasons of devastating, often unpredictable, shot-making.

So today, with the incomparable Donald Budge having long since diverted his talents to the lucrative professional field, the sunny Californian with the carefree grin holds the destiny of American tennis in the palm of his hand. Riggs spearheads the charge of young America toward the Davis Cup where it stands behind grimly fortified bulwarks in Australia.

But since haste and the minister's son stroll hand in hand (he won his national men's singles championship in exactly fifty-eight minutes at Forest Hills last year) the fathers of lawn tennis are occasionally harassed by disturbing dreams.

Suppose Riggs, at twenty-one, with the world of lawn tennis apparently at his feet, should suddenly desert the swelling ranks of the amateurs, as Tilden, Vines, Stoefen and Budge before him? What price, then, Davis Cup challenge? This is something the United States Lawn Tennis Association reluctantly contemplates, but it is a bridge not yet encountered by the effervescent young Californian.

There can be little doubt but what the professional tennis promoters are already gazing with longing eyes on the comparatively diminutive monarch of American amateur tennis, incubator of the play-for-pay court circuit. Already Budge, the indomitable redhead, rules the professionals with an iron hand and a singing racquet.

Riggs met Budge while on the way up. Budge, then dominating amateur tennis around the globe, personally retrieved the historic Davis Cup from England, and assisted in its defense. Riggs was a new arrival in the top flight, confident and competent, but no match for Budge.

Of course the day will arrive when Riggs' ability and strategy will increase with his playing experience. Perhaps he, too, will rule the entire world of lawn tennis by extending his monarchy over the several seas. And then our smiling boy of tennis will be literally besieged by the representatives of professional tennis. It will be the familiar theme of old: Could Vines beat Tilden? Could Budge stand up before Vines?—Can Riggs stop Budge?

Just now Bobby is too busy in his dual role of a young Chicago business man and American tennis champion to be more than casually interested in professional tennis. It would not be entirely unlikely that he proceeded along lines similar to those of Don Budge, who burned up the courts for three seasons with his objective being the regaining of the Davis Cup and one successful defense of that trophy. Then, and not until then, did Budge turn professional, and with the Heaven-bless-yous of the lawn tennis fathers.

Well, enough speculation of the future. This piece is supposed to be concerned with the past of Bobby Riggs and a fact or two at this point appears to be appropriate:

Riggs was born at Los Angeles, California, on February 25, 1918. He stands only five feet, eight inches, weighs scarcely more than 140 pounds. His physique alone is enough to distinguish him in American lawn tennis, for he is in stature one of the smallest champions in the history of the game. Finesse rather than force is the backbone of his game, but Bobby can really dust the back court when the occasion demands, and smash and deliver a fire-ball service. In a prolonged duel from the baselines he is master of most all he surveys, and can be a hard hitter in every sense of the word.

On the occasion of his annexing his national singles title at Forest Hills, Long Island on September 17, 1939, the California-born Chicagoan extracted all the fire from his final opponent's game by raking the championship court with a hot service and even hotter baseline strokes.

Basically, Bobby is a "retriever"; that is to say, his game is constructed around an almost indefatigable ability to cover court, but he also has the shots to support such strategy. Riggs has the ideal tennis temperament. He is able to enjoy himself even in the midst of a tight-lipped Davis Cup match, and even as a stripling fresh out of California his imperturbable play caused a flutter among the critics.

Perhaps no better example exists of Bobby's nerveless approach to tennis than that oft-told incident just before the first Davis Cup performance of his young and fruitful years at Germantown Cricket Club, Philadelphia, in 1938.

United States was lacking just fifty minutes of launching its first defense of the Davis Cup, returned the year before from England. The team was built around the indomitable J. Donald Budge, and Riggs, the neophyte, was the one-man supporting cast. California Bobby was to test Australia's strength in the challenge round by meeting the erudite and brilliant Adrian Quist. Only Bobby could not be found. They hunted high and they hunted low. Lawn tennis officials of normal calm and reserve were positively frantic when a meticulous search of the veranda, the dining room, the lounge and the locker rooms failed to uncover the spectacular No. 2 man of the American forces.

Then a ball boy announced a monumental discovery, equal at that tense moment to the hour Columbus first detected land on his westward voyage. Mr. Riggs could be found in the basement of the club house shooting pool, gentlemen!

And he was. Unmindful of the packed and expectant stadium outside, completely engrossed in the spinning balls on the emerald green surface, Bobby was nonchalantly chalking a cue when the harassed tennis officials swarmed breathlessly down the basement staircase. Even then he didn't share the anxiety of the elders. Bobby calmly called his shot, sent the last ball curling into the side pocket, then sallied forth to smother Quist in four sets: 4-6, 6-0, 8-6, 6-1.

That, then, was Bobby's introduction to Davis Cup tennis. He carved the first notch against the challenging Australians, contributed a victory that was greatly instrumental in retaining the trophy, and was about as flustered as an engineer on a local run during the entire proceedings.

Cocky. That's a word often mouthed in conversations revolving about the subject of Bobby Riggs. Preposterous! Self-confidence would be more like it. He has a great deal of faith in his own ability, and that faith has not been misplaced, for Riggs reached tennis' dizzy heights the hard way and was not long in learning that confidence, next to shot control, is the greatest asset of them all.

Yes, bouncing Bobby was no pampered, tutored, tennis prodigy of some swank country club, carefully schooled in the ethics and the shots of tennis by the best instructors money could hire. He was, instead, a product of California's public courts and he made a single-handed climb up the ladder to success.

In this FAMOUS AMERICAN ATHLETES SERIES we have written of Glenn Cunningham and Donald Lash, the great runners, and the influence older brothers had upon their ultimate careers.

Bobby Riggs, too, owes to an older brother much of the success that has been, and will be, his. Only where Glenn and Don were led by admiration of older brothers to perfect themselves as runners, it was Bobby's original disdain for a game his brother loved that set the wheels of fate in motion.

The game was tennis. Bobby was then a dozen years old, engrossed in the fascinating game of baseball, which was natural enough. An eighteen-year-old brother, however, was a tennis addict of the type that is never reformed; a very fortunate thing for the Lawn Tennis Association.

One thing led to another, one supposes. The younger Riggs no doubt made disparaging remarks about the game the older brother so devoutly played, and rebuttal probably resulted in Bobby's initial appearance on a near-by Los Angeles tennis court in an effort to substantiate his forthright opinions.

Actually this happened, and Bobby, possibly to his great amazement, found that it was a he-man's game after all, and far from the sissy sport the fellows on the ball grounds so stoutly believed. Well, from then on, Bobby was a "goner." Less and less frequently did "the fellers" have the opportunity to select Bobby Riggs in choosing up sides for a ball game. More and more often did he find his way to the tennis courts.

Tennis and Bobby made a natural combination. He seemed to know the answers to the riddle that is tennis almost by instinct. The fourth occasion upon which the twelve-year-old played the brother who inveigled him onto the courts, it was the younger Riggs who prevailed. The boy was in a great hurry even then, you see.

Great oaks from little acorns, etc. A month from the day he first jested before swinging at a tennis ball for the first time, Bobby entered a tournament: The championship of Southern California, for boys of thirteen years and under.

The neophyte from Los Angeles didn't perform in quite the true Horatio Alger style by whaling the daylights out of all the other very young men in his first tournament appearance. But he did conform to that literary pattern right through to the final round, which he lost. Naturally there was considerable oohing and aahing over Bobby's performance, because the vast majority of the youngsters seeking the title had from one to five years start on him in learning the game.

Perry Jones was the early Riggs tutor, a Californian who has been extremely instrumental in developing many superb young players from that state. At subsequent intervals Riggs picked up valuable pointers from Dr. Esther Bartosh and Eleanor Tennant, the woman who coached Alice Marble in that player's comeback in 1939.

Three seasons later Bobby was one of a bevy of fine young tennis prospects California shipped East to Indiana to compete for the national junior championship at Culver Military Academy.

It was then and there that Bobby Riggs first projected himself into the national tennis picture. He journeyed many miles to meet in the final match an old rival and doubles partner from Los Angeles—young Joe Hunt. Bobby won the match, 6-3, 1-6, 4-6, 6-0, 6-4, a stormy final between two of the most promising young players in the nation. Incidentally, they combined their prowess to annex the junior doubles title an hour later in five bristling sets, 4-6, 4-6, 6-3, 6-4, 6-2. Their final opponents were Lawrence Nelson and Bob Underwood of Los Angeles, which indicates the manner in which that sun-kissed West Coast community virtually monopolized the junior championships of 1935.

The rivalry between Riggs and Hunt, now attending the Naval Academy at Annapolis, extends far back to those knee-breeches days in Los Angeles when each was learning the rudiments of the game. Their meeting in the final of the junior championship at Culver in '35 was their twenty-third formal match in various small sectional and stepping-stone tournaments en route to their respective goal: Davis Cup play, and Bobby registered his twenty-first victory in that tense, if friendly rivalry at Culver that afternoon in Indiana.

Hunt, a year younger than Riggs, was claimed at that time by several Coast critics to be the more promising of the two, however, and many felt he would make the greatest volleying player since the immortal Vinnie Richards. Indeed, the estimates of the Hunt supporters appeared to be bearing fruit a year later when in his first four matches with Riggs he divided the victories. Yet Hunt had been playing tennis since his fifth birthday at San Francisco's Golden Gate Park, where "Little Bill" Johnston made his start. That gave Hunt a total of twelve years of tennis to Riggs' six, but eventually it was Riggs who shone the brighter in the tennis constellation.

Riggs had dominated the younger California set for three years, starting with the boys-under-thirteen division and progressing to the boys-under-fifteen class. Then he took over the national

juniors at Culver and sought new worlds to con-
quer in 1936. He was now sixteen, and still eligible
to compete in defense of his junior championship,
but within Bobby's breast burned ambition. The
green grass carpets of the Eastern summer circuit of which he had so breathlessly read, held a
tremendous lure for him. In one sudden decision,
typical of the young man from California, Riggs
decided to abandon his junior title and strike out
for himself against the top-flight players in the
Eastern campaign.

Confident that he was prepared to meet and beat
many of the elite, Bobby even announced that it
was his fondest expectation to be playing No. 1
on the American Davis Cup squad within five
years. Of course there were several audible snick-
ers heard at the time.

Disaster at the start almost capsized Bobby's
well-laid plans to invade the East. It was not to
be expected that the crown princes of the court—
the Lawn Tennis Association—would take kindly
to Bobby's decision to abandon his defense of the
junior championship. And they didn't. Their dis-
pleasure was first felt when they refused to finance
his trip East. The Riggs family, of moderate circumstances, could not well afford to send a son

off across the continent on what might have been a wild goose chase, not that they lacked faith in Bobby's ability. The result was Bobby's annexation of a car of questionable antecedents and obvious antiquity, and it was within the groaning carcass of this veteran of the thoroughfares that Riggs sallied East to the wars.

It is not very difficult to picture the scene as the young Riggs boy, that inimitable grin curling the corners of his mouth, waved a cheery goodbye and proceeded toward the outskirts of Los Angeles in his gasping vehicle. A brave start, like the cavaliers of yore, but it was also the start of a very discouraging era in the life of young Robert Riggs of Los Angeles, California.

When Bobby ultimately reached the Atlantic he possessed practically nothing but that indomitable grin, an intense desire to make a good showing in the tournaments, the clothes he wore upon his back, and one tennis racquet.

In a tourist encampment, a few days en route, a shadowy form stealthily sought out Bobby's ancient gas buggy during the night, rifled it of his clothes, leaving Bobby with nothing in the line of wearing apparel save the sweater and slacks he wore. Nothing daunted, Bobby made a tentative, glum inspection of his raiment, hopped aboard his mechanized steed, and was soon engrossed in the pleasant contemplation of his impending Eastern debut.

Not long after his wardrobe had been misappropriated Bobby's financial means were almost completely liquidated under similar circumstances. This time the Riggs boy paused in his flight across the country to investigate the quality of cooking done at a roadside lunch room. The implication is that he judged the cooking excellent, for it was when he returned to the counter to order a second helping of some culinary delicacy that his well-worn wallet was snipped from his sweater pocket.

This, as the Bard wrote, was the unkindest cut of all. His finances now failed to extend beyond the few coins that jingled disconsolately in his trouser pocket. But Bobby is made of stern stuff, and he also has a claim to ingenuity. So he converted into cash one of his two fine tennis racquets, and both of his precious spare tires, and continued Eastward undaunted by fate's pranks.

Stern stuff. That's Riggs. Fate wasn't finished toying with that young man who pursued a dream through thick and thin. Somewhere at mid-continent fate chose to disperse this tenacious young

man once and for all. So Fate and Bobby Riggs
came to the cross-roads, and this time it was the
groaning, but faithful car that came off second
best. With a tired moan it figuratively turned
over on its side, emitted some smoke, and expired
on the spot. All of which left Master Riggs several hundred miles from his destination with no
means of conveyance; his only possessions a tennis racquet, a few coins, and a wealth of courage.

Still undefeated, Bobby became an amateur
knight of the road and by means of a very agile
thumb he eventually gained the site of the annual
Seabright tournament in New Jersey. He arrived
with his sense of humor intact, but with his attire
in slight need of repair, which caused no little
comment on the veranda of the very smart Seabright club. Nobody was aware that the young
man from California had no clothes other than
those on his back.

Riggs was eliminated in the second round, a result which probably was gratifying to those who
felt the youngster was "getting too big for his
boots" in jumping out of the junior ranks a year
ahead of schedule, but when Bobby finally got his
game organized after his eventful journey across
the continent, the picture immediately underwent

several changes. Among other spectacular performances during his first season in the East was the annexation of the clay-court title at Jackson Heights Club, New York; the winning of the Newport Casino singles in a blazing final match with Frankie Parker, and the winning of the Nassau Country Club tournament in an equally spirited final with Gregory Mangin. Bobby was runner-up to the competent and experienced Parker in the final of the Longwood singles at Chestnut Hill, Massachusetts, a match which he dropped 2-6, 6-2, 3-6, 5-7, but which definitely established him as the find of the season. He topped off the final round of the Eastern grass-court championship at Rye, New York, by meeting the incomparable Budge. Bobby won the first set, a protracted and fiercely fought 8-6 encounter, before bowing out in the last three sets, 2-6, 4-6, 3-6.

Bobby had arrived with an audible explosion, winning forty-two of forty-nine matches. His spectacular exploits that first season of big-time campaigning earned him fourth spot in the national amateur rankings for that season, an almost unprecedented climb in the short space of twelve months.

Let us mention at this point the fact that some

of the most grueling matches Bobby Riggs played
in his climb to the pinnacle of amateur tennis were
with that master strategist—Frankie Parker.

In 1937 Bobby was primed to challenge the rule
of Budge, his fellow Californian. While it was
true that Bobby didn't have the game to destroy
Budge as ruling power at that time, there was reason to suspect that the younger and smaller of the
two Californians could and would provide the
elder with the fiercest sort of competition.

At Newport young Riggs was pretty close to the
top of his game. He had won ten out of the dozen
tournaments in which he had competed to that
point. Presumably he was ready to explode a barrage of shots when he met Budge that would extend the then unbeatable redhead. But it was
Bobby's misfortune to run into the tenacious
Parker in the semi-final round, and this match
just about killed any hope Bobby and the spectators might have harbored of seeing Budge extended. For it took three hours, thirty minutes
of stubborn, grueling tennis before Riggs finally
swept the brilliant Parker from his path to the
final in a wild five-set encounter. This was a pun-
ishing match, and a leg-weary Riggs was unable
to hold the hard-hitting Budge in the final. Bobby

made it interesting while his legs held up, splitting
the first two sets, 4-6, 8-6. He attempted to hold
Budge beyond the baseline in order to conserve his
own stamina, and so long as he succeeded in main-
taining a long-range game, he held his own, but
when Budge stormed the net in his own spectacular
style, Bobby was doomed, losing the last two sets,
1-6, 2-6.

At this time Riggs was playing tennis with a
sort of careless abandon that made students of the
game shudder and filled the lawn tennis moguls
with irritation. Both on and off the court he
seemed to ignore any sense of responsibility that
may have been his. He was a young man of considerable importance in the tennis world, but he
appeared to be completely carefree. He had the
annoying habit (to the officials) of allowing some
mediocre player to win a set or two at his expense
and then bearing down to defeat that unfortunate
individual under a torrent of brilliant shots, sav-
ing himself right on the brink of elimination. On
the occasion of shoddy shots he would dramatically
appeal to some higher power. When he scored with
a good one he was a laughing, irresponsible court
jester. Naturally, Bobby was a favorite with the
gentlemen of the press. He possessed in his dram-

atizations of grief and joy that peculiar quality known as "color." Bobby made good copy, and consequently, in no time at all, was the most widely-discussed tennis player of the year.

Meanwhile, Don Budge and Gene Mako and Frankie Parker, et al, had retrieved the long-lost Davis Cup from England. The tennis fathers were planning ahead for the defense of that trophy. They felt Budge would soon be unavailable, since he might at any moment yield to the constant pressure of professional promoters. When Budge abdicated, Bobby Riggs was his natural successor, and for this reason, the officials were disapproving and irritated by the immature tactics of this particular young man who was, after all, only a schoolboy. The persistence with which he threw away points to inferior players was their chief concern, and it was the verdict of all and sundry that some day Bobby would get himself humiliated in an important tourney by his "have two sets, I'll take the rest" tactics. In fact, it wasn't good tennis, and probably the tennis officials had reason to be disturbed by it, for some day they might have to entrust the defense of the Davis Cup to this irresponsible player.

But one bright afternoon Bobby learned his lesson from Gilbert Hunt. In nine matches out of ten Riggs could probably defeat the collegian, but this was the tenth occasion. Hunt was at the top of his game, stroking the ball crisply and threading a needle with his shots. Bobby clowned around as was his custom, employing with Hunt the tactics he used when toying with an inferior opponent. Came the awakening, and an important one for Bobby. Hunt took over an early lead as Riggs played carelessly, but when Bobby came to the usual place in the script where he was to rally on the verge of defeat and drive his opponent off the court, he found that Hunt was playing a brand of tennis which would not permit it. So Bobby left the court a victim of his own tactics, and it wasn't long after this lesson that he adopted a more serious approach to the game, without losing the keen sense of humor that has ever stood him in good stead.

In 1938 Riggs drove relentlessly ahead in his quest of tennis glory, and through the agency of fifteen victories in nineteen tournaments he achieved No. 2 national ranking behind Budge.

On September 3, at Germantown Cricket Club, Riggs drove the first spike in the big gun that Australia had moved into position for an assault upon the Davis Cup defenses, and come what may, that afternoon will stand out in red letters in the career of Bobby Riggs.

Adrian Quist and Jack Bromwich were the Anzac key men and brilliant players they were. Quist was a young veteran of international play, an amazing shotmaker and a crafty court tactician. Bromwich was a powerful hitter who had devised a unique, yet very effective, two-handed backhand shot. Kingpin of the American defense was Budge, of course. He was scheduled to play two singles matches and share the doubles burden with Gene Mako. But there was reason to believe that the Australians could beat the Budge-Mako doubles combine. The Aussies, in fact, were counting on it. Thus, if the Aussies each fell in singles to Budge, they could still win the three necessary matches by winning the doubles and downing young Bobby Riggs, the No. 2 American, in two matches.

That was a well-laid plot which Bobby Riggs, the American No. 2, knocked galley west on the occasion of the very first match of the three-day battle, and it was on the day he abruptly nicked the last pool ball into the side pocket, then nonchalantly strolled out to scuttle the Australian ship by trimming Quist, second-ranking player in the world, 4-6, 6-0, 8-6, 6-1.

The Australians were fifteen thousand miles from home and twice that far from the Davis Cup, appropriately wrote the Associated Press reporter that day. Indeed, the cause was lost when Bobby blew the vastly more experienced Quist off the spike-nicked grass courts at Germantown, for Australia was faced with the impossible assignment of beating Budge, the No. 1 player of the world, in two singles matches and winning the doubles as well. Thanks to Riggs, the Cup freshman, Australia's bid was smashed at the very outset. Budge shook Bobby's hand warmly and himself took over the court to beat Bromwich and remove all but the formality of playing out the string in the trophy's defense.

Steady and strong, Riggs completely routed Quist after dropping the first set. The Australian's forehand collapsed and although he is considered one of the great net players in the game the inspired California youngster even mastered him in that department. That was one of the most important matches Riggs will ever play. He couldn't duplicate it at Merion Cricket Club a year later, although for a matter of more than two hours and through five brilliant, pulsating sets he strove to stop Quist and prevent the loss of the Cup he assisted in defending in 1938.

Many claimed that the 1938 Australian team was badly over-tennised. To some extent that was probably so, for when Quist and Bromwich returned in 1939 they employed entirely different tactics. This time they played a minimum amount of preparatory tennis, concentrating almost entirely on the Davis Cup zone eliminations, etc.

Meantime, Don Budge, with the Cup safely stored away in this hemisphere, finally turned professional. Bobby Riggs was his logical successor as kingpin of the defense, and Bobby was filled with a sense of responsibility. The careless boy of yore was no more. He hearkened to advice from non-playing Captain Walter L. Pate, and the elder man cautioned Bobby about playing himself out in the innumerable winter tournaments in California and elsewhere in the warmer climates. Instead, he suggested a retreat to the gymnasium, and plenty of road work to keep those important legs in shape. Bobby's legs, incidentally, are very sturdy and they are his salvation in many important matches. High school basketball and track have developed them to the point where they stand him in good stead in the retrieving type of tennis he plays.

Although the Riggs-led American team lost the Davis Cup to Australia in 1939 let there be no mistake about the intensity with which Bobby prepared for that meeting, or the determination of the young Californian to successfully defend the trophy.

"I think we have an even chance of defending that cup even with Budge gone," he remarked months before. "I haven't any ideas about pro tennis at all. All I'm interested in right now is keeping in trim to help keep that Davis Cup right here in this country!"

Bobby prepared diligently for the big day. He curtailed his winter tennis and worked in the gymnasium. Finally he made his first trip abroad to compete in the French and Wimbledon championships. His ventures abroad were not completely crowned with success. In London he ran into a quite unexpected two-set, 0-6, 1-6 defeat from the veteran German net wizard, Baron Gottfried von Cramm, whom Bobby had literally brushed off the court two years before in the Pacific Coast championships. The defeat at the hands of the German Baron caused Bobby to make one of the most widely-quoted retorts in tennis ranks at Wimbledon, England, that summer.

Asked if he felt the presence of the King and Queen would upset his game, Riggs made this historic reply: "Nope, kings and queens don't upset me—only barons!"

Riggs accomplished a rather remarkable feat in winning the All-English championship in his first trip across the Atlantic, but returned to America only to be the victim of a colossal third-round upset at Seabright. Frank Guernsey of Orlando, Florida, performed this operation, and Bobby was tremendously disappointed. He was after his third straight Seabright victory. However, he inflicted defeat upon his old antagonist—Frankie Parker—which was that worthy's first grass-court defeat of the summer at the Eastern championships, the scores being 1-6, 6-4, 6-4, 7-5. Bobby also won a straight-sets final at Meadowbrook to take permanent possession of the $1000 President's cup.

He was well tuned up for the Davis Cup defense at Merion Cricket Club on September 1, and he and Frankie Parker instigated the defense in a highly promising manner. Bobby was at the very top of his game in routing Jack Bromwich in straight sets, 6-4, 6-0, 7-5. Parker out-finessed Adrian Quist in a five-set match.

Again the Australians appeared doomed at the outset, but they won the doubles the following day, a victory that had long been conceded their No. 1 world-ranking combine of Quist and Bromwich, and on the third day, Bromwich, who had been helpless against the deadly placements of Riggs, caught on fire to smother Parker.

But the cup was really lost when Quist stood off Bobby Riggs previously in one of the fiercest Davis Cup matches of all time. The scores were 6-1, 6-4, 3-6, 3-6, 6-4 for Quist and the Australian was on the verge of a collapse when the deciding point went in his favor and with it the Davis Cup.

At the finish, he lauded Riggs in no uncertain terms. "This was the best tennis I've ever played in the United States," he panted. "I couldn't let Australia down today. I couldn't let Bromwich down. I knew he'd beat Parker. I just had to win. But Riggs is one of the hardest men to beat I've ever faced on a tennis court. He not only is a fine tennis player, but he never quits. I beat him ten straight games at the start of that match and still he came back!"

No greater tribute to the tennis played by Bobby

Riggs in the cause of the Davis Cup can be inscribed on these pages. He went on from Merion to blaze through the national singles championship tournament at Forest Hills, L. I., with the loss of only two sets in the process, and won his final match in the flying time of fifty-eight minutes from young Welby Van Horn, also of California, 6-4, 6-2, 6-4.

As we mentioned previously—Bobby is always in a hurry. His goal is now the world's No. 1 ranking, and it would be typical of Bobby if he wasted little time getting there.

ROBERT L. RIGGS

Born Los Angeles, California, February 25, 1918.

1935

National Junior Singles—Riggs defeated Joe Hunt, Los Angeles, 6-3, 1-6, 4-6, 6-0, 6-4.

National Junior Doubles—Riggs and Hunt defeated Nelson and Underwood, Los Angeles, 4-6, 4-6, 6-3, 6-4, 6-2.

1936

Eastern Clay Court Championship—Riggs defeated John Law, Pasadena, California, 6-3, 6-0, 6-4. Final Round.

Nassau C. C. Tournament—Riggs defeated Gregory Mangin, New York, 9-7, 6-2, 5-7, 6-3. Final Round.

Longwood Bowl Tournament—Riggs lost to Frank Parker, Spring Lake, New Jersey, 2-6, 6-2, 3-6, 5-7. Final Round.

Newport Casino Tournament—Riggs defeated Frank Parker, 8-6, 10-8, 3-6, 6-1. Final Round.

Eastern Grass Court Championship—Riggs lost to J. Donald Budge, California, 8-6, 2-6, 4-6, 3-6. Final Round.

National Singles—Riggs lost to John Van Ryn, 2-6, 3-6, 6-3, 3-6. Third Round.

National Clay Court Championship—Riggs beat Frank Parker, 6-1, 6-4, 6-4. Final Round.

Southampton Invitation Tournament—Riggs lost to Frank Parker, 7-9, 8-6. Third Round.

Pacific Coast Doubles—Riggs and Wayne Sabin defeated Culley and Hunt, 12-10, 6-4, 7-5. Final Round.

National Doubles—Riggs and Sabin lost to Allison and Van Ryn, 5-7, 1-6, 3-6. Semi-final Round.

National Clay Court Doubles—Riggs and Sabin defeated McDiarmid and McCauliff, 4-6, 6-2, 6-4, 7-5. Final Round.

1937

Eastern Grass Court Championship—Riggs defeated Frank Parker, Spring Lake, New Jersey, 6-3, 7-5, 7-5. Final Round.

Newport Casino Tournament—Riggs lost to J. Donald Budge, 4-6, 8-6, 1-6, 2-6. Final Round.

Pacific Coast Championship—Riggs lost to J. Donald Budge, 6-4, 3-6, 2-6, 4-6. Final Round.

National Singles—Riggs lost to Baron von Cramm, Germany, 6-0, 8-6, 3-6, 3-6, 2-6. Semi-Final Round.

National Doubles—Riggs and Bernard Coghlan lost to Budge and Mako, 5-7, 8-10, 2-6. Third Round.

National Clay Court Championship—Riggs defeated Joe Hunt, 6-3, 4-6, 6-3, 6-4. Final Round.

Southampton, Invitation—Riggs defeated Jiro Yamagishi, Japan, 6-4, 6-3, default. Final Round.

Atlanta Invitation—Riggs defeated David Jones, 6-3, 2-6, 6-4, 8-6. Final Round.

Dixie Tournament—Riggs defeated Wayne Sabin, 6-3, 6-0, 7-5. Final Round.

Surf Club, Florida, Tournament—Riggs defeated Frank Kovacs, 3-6, 6-3, 6-4, 6-2. Final Round.

Sugar Bowl Tournament—Riggs defeated Joe Hunt, 6-4, 6-4, 6-8, 6-4. Final Round.

Miami-Biltmore Tournament—Riggs lost to Byron Grant, 6-3, 2-6, 9-7, 6-8, 3-6. Final Round.

Surf Club Doubles—Riggs and Wayne Sabin lost to Kovacs and Cooke, 7-5, 6-4, 5-7, 1-6, 3-6. Final Round.

1938

Coral Gables (Florida) Singles—Riggs lost to Byran Grant, Atlanta, 6-3, 2-6, 9-7, 6-8, 3-6. Final Round.

Seabright (New Jersey) Tournament—Riggs defeated Elwood T. Cooke, Portland, Oregon, 6-1, 6-3, 6-1. Final Round.

Meadow Club Tournament—Riggs defeated Sidney B. Wood, New York, 6-0, 6-3, 7-5. Final Round.

Eastern Grass Court Championship—Riggs defeated Joe Hunt, Los Angeles, 6-4, 6-3, 3-6, 10-8. Final Round.

Pacific Coast Championship—Riggs lost to Jack Tidball, 4-6, 4-6, 6-2, 3-6. Semi-final Round.

National Singles—Riggs lost to Joe Hunt, 2-6, 6-0, 7-9, 6-0, 4-6. Fifth Round.

National Clay Court Championship—Riggs defeated Gardner Mulloy, 6-4, 5-7, 4-6, 6-1, 7-5. Final Round.

Longwood Bowl Singles—Riggs defeated Frank Kovacs, 6-4, 6-0, 6-4. Final Round.

Longwood Bowl Doubles—Riggs and Charles Hare, England, defeated Kovacs and Harmon, 6-1, 6-2. Final Round.

National Doubles—Riggs and Byran Grant lost to Allison and Van Ryn, 1-6, 6-8, 2-6. Third Round.

Davis Cup Matches

1938—Riggs defeated Adrian Quist, Australia, 4-6, 6-0, 8-6, 6-1.

1938—Riggs lost to John Bromwich, Australian, 4-6, 6-4, 0-6, 2-6.

1939

Bermuda Tournament—Riggs defeated Elwood T. Cooke, 6-3, 1-6, 1-6, 6-2, 6-4. Final Round.

Meadow Club Tournament—Riggs defeated Sidney B. Wood, New York, 10-8, 6-4, 6-4. Final Round.

Eastern Grass Court Championship—Riggs defeated Frank Parker, 1-6, 6-4, 6-4, 7-5. Final Round.

National Singles Championship—Riggs defeated Welby Van Horn, Los Angeles, 6-4, 6-2, 6-4. Final Round.

National Doubles Championship—Riggs and

Elwood T. Cooke lost to Adrian Quist and Jack Bromwich, Australia, 1-6, 4-6, 0-6. Semi-final Round.

Seabright (New Jersey) Tournament—Riggs lost to Frank Guernsey, Jr., Orlando, Florida, 5-7, 4-6. Third Round.

French Hard Court Championship—Riggs lost to Don McNeil, Oklahoma City, 5-7, 0-6, 3-6. Final Round.

Wimbledon, All-English Singles—Riggs defeated Elwood T. Cooke, 2-6, 8-6, 3-6, 6-3, 6-2. Final Round.

Wimbledon, All-English Doubles—Riggs and Cooke defeated Wilde and Hare, England, 6-3, 3-6, 6-3, 9-7. Final Round.

Queen's Club Singles—Riggs lost to Baron Gottfried von Cramm, Germany, 0-6, 1-6. Second Round.

Davis Cup Matches

1939—Riggs defeated John Bromwich, Australia, 6-4, 6-0, 7-5.

1939—Riggs lost to Adrian Quist, Australia, 1-6, 4-6, 6-3, 6-3, 4-6.

TWO NEW YEAR'S RESOLUTIONS:
THE SUGAR BOWL AND THE ORANGE BOWL

TULANE STADIUM, "SUGAR BOWL", NEW ORLEANS, LOUISIANA

CHAPTER XIII

TWO NEW YEAR'S RESOLUTIONS:

THE SUGAR BOWL AND THE ORANGE BOWL

By Jerry Nason, Sports Writer, *Boston Globe*

In the sixth volume of FAMOUS AMERICAN ATH-
LETES OF TODAY we discussed the famous Rose
Bowl at Pasadena, California; its history and
origin, and described to the best of our ability the
numerous games of football played there annually
between the outstanding college teams of the country. The Rose Bowl is, of course, the granddaddy
of all the Bowls and while space in this particular
edition of the series forbids a complete résumé of
them all, this chapter aspires to present the story
of two eminent prototypes of the Pasadena struc-
ture: the Sugar Bowl at New Orleans, Louisiana,
and the Orange Bowl at Miami, Florida.

The growth of each in a comparatively short
space of time is almost unparalleled. The Rose
Bowl game was first staged in 1902, and resumed

after a fourteen-year lapse in 1916. On the other hand, the Orange Bowl at Miami did not come into being until 1933 and the Sugar Bowl two years later. But each of these Johnny-come-latelies has become such an important annual football fixture that no longer does the celebrated Rose Bowl game dominate the extra-curricular football of our country. As this edition goes to press the controlling committees of New Orleans and Miami have just held their 1940 contests on New Year's Day and have enjoyed successes surpassing any in the brief, but colorful history of each Bowl game. If this, then, will suffice as an introduction let us examine first the Sugar Bowl annual:

Sugar Bowl, New Orleans, Louisiana.

The New Year's Day sponsors of the Sugar Bowl organized in March, 1934, with several bright ideas and a vast amount of initiative. They called themselves the New Orleans Mid-Winter Sports Association and at that time they had no particular name in mind for the annual football game they proposed to sponsor. So the public was given only a general idea of what the Association planned in the way of a replica of the Rose Bowl and its accompanying and equally famous Tournament of Roses. The citizens were asked to select an appropriate name for the bowl and the overwhelming recommendation for a "Sugar Bowl" was adopted without further ado by the association.

The name was a natural. It not only suggested itself to the football fans all over the country right on their home or restaurant tables every day, but was more than appropriate on account of southern Louisiana's vast sugar production, which is so large that New Orleans and vicinity have often been referred to as the nation's "sugar bowl".

The association had a name for its game, but it was still a long way from completion and consisted chiefly of a mere handful of young, enthusiastic and civic-minded men who shared a bright idea. The next step was to interest men of business and official prominence in that idea. With this in mind the original group issued invitations to all civic organizations, luncheon and social clubs, and individuals of high standing in the State of Louisiana, to form an association. The membership fee was a nominal ten dollars for organizations and five dollars for individuals. They pointed out that the project was one of civic worth, since the general idea was not only to promote amateur sports but to encourage tourist trade.

But Louisiana's innumerable clubs and organizations lacked vision, and only thirty-nine individuals and organizations responded to the invitation to join the Mid-Winter Sports Association.

Undaunted and still ablaze with enthusiasm the progenitors of the Sugar Bowl progressed doggedly on their collective ways. They solicited guarantees of one hundred dollars each from three hundred residents of the State of Louisiana. That was a total of $30,000, and on the strength of those guarantees they went ahead. The visiting team could be guaranteed $15,000, the Southern team $12,000, and the remainder would be directed toward the actual promotional expenses of the game.

It really wasn't much of a stake, but it was enough. So with high courage and the press in a receptive mood and eager to inject a publicity stimulant, our bright young men of New Orleans got the consent of the Tulane University officials for their team to play; invited Temple University of Philadelphia to come South, and thereby launched a mighty important annual game.

It was a tremendous competitive and financial success. Tulane won the game, which was pleasing to Louisianans, for Tulane is located in New

Orleans. The Mid-Winter Sports Association won a great victory, financially and otherwise, for the guarantee money for this initial contest had been placed in banks in escrow and refunded to the guarantors without so much as a dollar being actually used in the promotion of the contest. Since then, of course, the Sugar Bowl has grown and grown, and the last word we had heard from the Mid-Winter Sports Association was that the seating capacity of the Sugar Bowl, *nee* Tulane Stadium, was being increased to 70,000. There was every reason to believe a capacity throng would witness the 1940 contest.

Since the third year of its birth the Sugar Bowl game has been presented without call upon guarantors. The surplus has reached and passed the $30,000 required to assure a successful promotion. Incidentally, the Tulane Stadium, scene of the game, is a rent-free contribution to the Mid-Winter Sports Association. Originally, its seating capacity was 50,000, and there the largest football crowd in the history of Southern football watched Texas Christian's national champions in action on January 1, 1939.

The winning team of the annual Sugar Bowl game is awarded a handsome, solid silver bowl, made in England during the reign of King George IV one hundred and ten years ago. This trophy is retained by the victorious team for a period of a year, when it is returned to the Association to be put up for competition once more. However, for permanent possession, that team is awarded an equally beautiful silver plaque, bearing a replica of the bowl.

The Mid-Winter Sports Association is not exclusively concerned with football, strangely enough. It promotes a vast and varied program of sports, not by any means the least of which is the track and field meet which annually brings many of the nation's great stars to New Orleans. Bobby Riggs and numerous other tennis stars have played in the Sugar Bowl tournament, and outstanding college basketball teams have met there.

The Association has a unique arrangement with Tulane University. The university from the very outset donated the use of its stadium for the game, and it will always be available to the Association free of charge. But lately the stadium has proved insufficient in size to accommodate the thousands wishing to see the game. In 1937 a total of 15,000 seats were added. Tulane loaned the Association

$160,000 for that addition which is being repaid at a rate of $20,000 a year from the revenue of the Sugar Bowl game. Two such payments have already been made.

Now, however, the Association has planned to extend the seating capacity to 70,000, and it will require a half-million dollars to enlarge the stadium. It adopted what it felt was the only practical way to finance such a vast proposition, which was by bond issue. The bonds will be retired out of revenue from future Sugar Bowl games, and the entire enlargement will become the property of Tulane University which, in turn, will assume the maintenance of the additions at its own expense.

Well, this more or less briefly outlines the rise of the Sugar Bowl game from an idea to an astonishing actuality. There is no reason to feel that this contest has reached the peak of its greatness yet. Its self-confessed goal is the Number One spot now held by the Rose Bowl in matters of post-season football. The Sugar Bowl is a splendid monument to the enterprise and courage of a handful of Louisianans, at present presided over by Herbert A. Benson, president; A. N. Goldberg, vice-president; Clarence H. Strauss, secretary, and R. H. Fleming, treasurer. An executive committee makes the final selections of the teams to play in the annual bowl game, and preparatory to the momentous decision, twenty-five football writers and commentators in various sections of the nation are asked to wire the committee their first, second and third choices of teams from the Southeastern, Southwestern, and Southern conferences, plus their first, second and third selections elsewhere in the country. These selections are used as guides, representing the consensus of opinion from many sections, a valuable source of knowledge in the promotion of an inter-sectional game, for the Sugar Bowl games are definitely that.

In five years of play, Louisiana State University at Baton Rouge has the singular distinction of having thrice played in the Bowl. Texas Christian University of Dallas has appeared twice, as has Santa Clara University of California.

Only two Northern football elevens have played at the Bowl, those being Temple University of Philadelphia and Carnegie Tech of Pittsburgh. But this very definite control of the competitive roles in the Sugar Bowl is accountable as much as anything to the comparative youth of the affair.

At the outset and for a period of four years it was in the various stages of construction. Interest in the Sugar Bowl in sectors far away was slow in forming. The Rose Bowl had the prestige and the background, and any fine teams shopping around for a trip would wait to hear from Pasadena before they would commit themselves. Gradually this has changed. In 1939 the Sugar Bowl unveiled the first and fourth best teams in the entire nation, in the opinion of the press associations. They were Texas Christian University, one of the finest football teams of all time, and a hard-hitting, fundamentally terrific Carnegie Tech team from Pittsburgh.

As mentioned before, near-by Tulane was selected to represent Dixie in the first Bowl game. Temple University was the choice for an opponent. That was in 1935 when Tulane's vaunted "Green Wave" was a great Southern football power. Temple was climbing the glory road under that able and venerable double-wingback magician —Glenn Scobey (Pop) Warner.

A thrilling offensive game was the prediction, and the prophets were right. Ted Cox of Tulane had a well-devised offense built around the irrefutable prowess of "Little Monk" Simons, one of the best Dixie backs of the decade. Warner's offense demanded a pulverizing fullback to operate on spins and power bucks and he had one in the 215-pound Dave Smuckler. Tulane prevailed, 20-14. Or rather, Simons prevailed over Smuckler. They were the outstanding football players of that day, or any day, for that matter.

The emphasis on scoring in the first bowl game was not repeated in 1936. The renewal, in fact, produced the most unique score ever recorded in a contest of this nature. It was reminiscent of a mighty pitchers' battle in the World Series. Louisiana State's power house of the Southeastern Conference lost to Texas Christian University of the Southwestern Conference and the score was 3-2. This score was a tremendous surprise to one and all. Texas had in the immortal Sammy Baugh, one of the most accurate and brainy forward passers in the history of football, and Louisiana had two remarkable pass receivers in Jeff Barrett and Gaynell Tinsley. But a field goal for Texas and a safety for Louisiana were the scoring efforts of a titanic struggle.

The scoring tempo in 1937 reverted back to the original bowl contest. Louisiana State was back again to defend the prestige of Southern football.

The opponent chosen to play the Tigers of Baton Rouge was without question capable of beating any football team of the 1936 season proper. And they were capable of beating a remarkably good Louisiana team on January 1, 1937. They were the redoubtable Broncos of Santa Clara, California.

Buck Shaw had been developing mighty gridiron units at Santa Clara for some time. They'd played hard schedules, defeated several leaders of the Pacific Coast Conference of which they were not members, and this was their best team of all to date.

Louisiana had several left-overs from the previous season, including the incomparable Tinsley at end, and he was one of the greatest flankmen in a section renowned for its ends.

Santa Clara, thanks to the indomitable play of Nello Falaschi in the backfield, won the game by a score of 21-14. It was a pulsating offensive struggle, as the score suggests. Tinsley played superb football for Louisiana, and while he had for two years been selected All-American he was never more brilliant.

Louisiana established a mark for Coach Bernie Moore that has never been matched in any bowl.

They played for the third consecutive season in the Sugar Bowl on January 1, 1938 and again their opponent was the high-striding Bronco of Santa Clara.

Scoring was at a premium this time. Two brilliant sets of forwards struggled up and down the field in a memorable battle, with thrills being paraded throughout the sixty minutes of play, so that the great crowd was limp with emotional exhaustion when the whistle found Santa Clara a 6-0 victor.

Thus the Californians were the first to score twin victories in the Sugar Bowl, a noteworthy feat. Back home they were not considered eligible to compete in the Rose Bowl because of their lack of Pacific Conference affiliation. So they journeyed across the great desert and conclusively proved two years running that they were the uncrowned kings of football on the Pacific slope.

Young Bussey, a sophomore tailback, and Ken Kavanaugh, a sophomore end from Arkansas, were the Louisiana standouts. Kavanaugh was later to be called a greater pass receiver than Tinsley. He led all the Southern ends in scoring during the 1937 season, and in the first four contests of 1939 (at which juncture this story was written) he had scored seven of his team's nine touchdowns.

The biggest and perhaps the most savagely contested game of football played in the Sugar Bowl was that between Texas Christian and Carnegie Tech on January 1, 1939.

The Texans, who had pulverized eleven opponents and led the nation in scoring, represented one of the truly great teams of modern times. Their rushline was brawny and competent and their ends were glue-fingered pass receivers and grim guardians of the flanks. Their backs were fast and sure-footed, and they had Dynamite Davey O'Brien in their backfield.

At 152 pounds O'Brien was the most diminutive player ever to compete in the Sugar Bowl. He was also one of the best. He was well established as the Number One passer in the nation, he was an astute signal caller, and a great offensive "spark."

Carnegie Tech was powerful and a typical product of the "Pittsburgh System." Their blocking and tackling were ferocious, and though less adept at forward passing than Texas Christian, they ran the ball behind furious blocking. They had beaten Pittsburgh and almost stopped Notre Dame. The result was a pulse-lifting struggle in which O'Brien threw the football with amazing accuracy and kicked an important field goal in a 15-7 victory, the hardest game the Texans had played. Carnegie Tech showed in George Muha, a 191-pound halfback, one of the hardest runners in Sugar Bowl history, but Carnegie's smashing ball carrying was not enough on this particular occasion. This contest virtually established the Sugar Bowl on a "major league" pedestal. It had presented, for the first time, the best team in the nation, which was Texas Christian. And Carnegie Tech was, without question, the top ranking team in the North. The throng of fifty thousand people who saw this game, constituted the greatest crowd ever to witness a football game in the Southland. The Mid-Winter Sports Association had good reason to stick a thumb in its collective vest.

Here are the men who had faith in an idea and the courage to develop one of the most important sporting annuals of this era: The Mid-Winter Sports Association:

Ralph J. Barry, Herbert Benson, J. H. Bodenheimer, Dr. M. P. Boebinger, George Butler, J. R. Conniff, Sam Corenswet, Joe M. Cousins, Joseph B. David, Paul De Blank, Louis diBenedetto, Fred

ORANGE BOWL STADIUM, MIAMI, FLORIDA

Digby, Joseph Dresner, P. K. Ewing, R. H. Fleming, Harry Fletcher, A. N. Goldberg, B. J. Grenrood, H. Jumonville, Warren V. Miller; A. B. Nicholas, J. M. Niehaus, Herbert A. Pailet, Irwin Poche, F. D. Reilly, W. P. Rovira, Frank V. Schaub, George Schneider, Dr. Leo J. Schoeny, Raleigh Schwarz, W. A. Simpson, Jr., Allan Smuck, Walter Snider, Clarence H. Strauss, Albert Wachenheim, Jr., Douglas S. Watters, P. B. Williamson, Dr. Fred J. Wolfe, C. C. Zatarain.

Scores of the Sugar Bowl games:

Jan. 1, 1935—Tulane (New Orleans) 20, Temple (Philadelphia) 14

Jan. 1, 1936—Texas Christian (Dallas) 3, Louisiana State (Baton Rouge) 2

Jan. 1, 1937—Santa Clara (California) 21, Louisiana State (Baton Rouge) 14

Jan. 1, 1938—Santa Clara (California) 6, Louisiana State (Baton Rouge) 0

Jan. 1, 1939—Texas Christian (Dallas) 15, Carnegie Tech (Pittsburgh) 7

Jan. 1, 1940—Texas A and M (College Park) 14, Tulane (New Orleans) 13

Orange Bowl, Miami, Florida.

Let us now take a figurative flight from New Orleans, across the sparkling waters of the Gulf of Mexico, over the tangled Everglades on Florida's east coast to that gem of Southern communities—Miami.

Here we find, or will find on any January 1, a stupendous festival which for breathless scope and beauty is difficult to rival. And the crown of that festival, the center piece, the hub of it all, is the Orange Bowl game.

The State of Florida has never, naturally, been reluctant to advertise its unlimited charms or capitalize upon them in the interests of the commonwealth. And the Orange Bowl game is one of its biggest sales talks, even as the Sugar Bowl contest at New Orleans serves in a salesman's capacity. It was estimated that in 1939 more than twelve thousand out-of-State visitors flocked to Miami for the purpose of witnessing the fourth annual, and promotionally the best, Orange Bowl game. This was enough to make any business man sit up and take notice because the visitors were all spending money.

Just now the entire state of Florida is solidly behind the Orange Bowl game, and although this idea was a trifle late off the mark, as we track scribes have a habit of saying, the day is undoubtedly on its way when the Miami extravaganza will

be pushing and shoving for the national spotlight
with the Rose and Sugar promotions. At any rate,
present figures strongly intimate that such will be
the case, though the first Orange Bowl game was
by no means a howling financial success. Less than
four thousand persons witnessed it. Here in Massachusetts interscholastic rivals of long standing
more than triple that figure, and we know that is
also true of school games elsewhere in the nation.

But the Orange Bowl committee had its chin
up. To begin with, its national press notices had
been slim, and the Rose Bowl game had dominated
the sports pages. It was a somewhat obscure beginning, but hope springs eternal and all that sort
of thing, and Miami determined to do something
about it, so they rolled up their collective sleeves
and pitched into a three-year job. In 1937 a crowd
of 9,210 attended; not exactly the desired result,
but a decided improvement. Miami went to work
again, and was rather grim about it this time. It
had been stymied in the past because the Rose and
Sugar people had been snatching up all the top
teams, leaving Miami good, but lesser publicized
elevens. So it matched Auburn and Michigan State
on New Year's Day in 1938 and more than doubled
its attendance record. A throng of 18,972 persons

witnessed that struggle and the sun commenced to pour through the gloom.

Last year, 1939, the Miami game came into its own with a tremendous bang when Tennessee and Oklahoma played to almost thirty thousand fans in a picturesque setting and on a perfect, sun-kissed Florida afternoon.

Now Miami has both feet dug in, like an aggressive lineman, and prepared for months ahead to make the 1940 contest the greatest of all. Under the impetus of that grand football game played by Tennessee and Oklahoma, the Orange Bowl was furnished a lift that promises a pageant of color and thrills in the future. All of Florida has rallied around the Orange Bowl game, and the merchants have whole-heartedly endorsed it, because it is a medium of greater business.

Perhaps the most typical cooperation the Bowl committee has received so far is that move by the racing moguls at the famous Tropical Park and the Florida State Racing Commission to arrange their program of horse-running events to take place in the morning, rather than to run in competition with Miami's latest "brain child."

Like the Sugar Bowl at New Orleans, the Miami

contest came into existence in the form of an idea, born in 1931 or thereabouts. A group of Miami businessmen were contemplating, over their cigars, business in general, Florida as a whole, and the game of football particularly. Vision was present, enthusiasm soon developed, and before long a contest of the nature of the Rose Bowl was being seriously considered. One presumes that much ridicule was encountered at first, but the gentlemen from Miami were not easily discouraged. They went ahead and promoted a game between the local eleven—the Hurricanes of Miami University—and Manhattan College of New York City.

That was in 1933, and was not a significant encounter for the most part. In the first place, the game had little to recommend itself to tourists, for Miami University was strictly of local appeal and visiting Manhattan was not a really outstanding football team. This first venture was part of what was called the Palm Festival, and that was where Miami "missed the boat" right at the start. Palms certainly were suggestive of Miami, but nobody has ever yet retired on the proceeds of selling palm trees to visitors, so it wasn't until the committee retired temporarily and revamped the entire project that it commenced to function as was originally intended.

In 1936, the game was promoted as the Orange Bowl Festival, and Floridans immediately got the general idea. At the mention of the Orange Bowl, the average citizen of the nation immediately conjures of a picture of a crate of oranges and more often than not he thinks of Florida, for which State the orange is indeed a juicy symbol. This rechristening, then, was greatly instrumental in the ultimate success of the Orange Bowl; successes which are sure to exceed those to date as time rolls on. The entire State has gradually assumed a paternal interest in this event so that, at the present moment, Miami has to share its lusty young offspring with Daytona, Pensacola and St. Petersburg, etc.

Floridans think of it this way: the greater the support given the Orange Bowl, the greater proportions the game will assume; the more publicity it receives over the nation, the greater the number of people who will be orange-conscious, and the more people who come to Florida to spend their winter vacation money, means greater benefits, not only for Miami, but for all Florida as well.

Floridans control and promote the game, the city of Miami underwrites it, and it is very rapidly becoming the biggest thing in Florida since the land boom.

In 1936 a government loan was obtained, and the lovely Roddey Burdine Stadium constructed in Miami to house the annual game. The seating capacity up to that time was in the vicinity of thirty thousand. Obviously, it wasn't enough, for it was conservatively estimated that in excess of ten thousand football fans were unable to gain admittance to the game between Tennessee and Oklahoma, so the stadium will shortly be mushrooming.

As Jack Bell of the *Miami Daily News* so lucidly put it: "This year (1940), with the help of the gods, the people, and the PWA, we hope to have ten thousand additional seats at the stadium. Possibly, quite probably, that won't be enough."

This gives you a general idea of how the Orange Bowl has grown out of the short-pants stage. Just now, it and the weather are the two things that the folks from all over Florida are unanimously agreed upon.

Also, the festival within which the football game sparkles so brilliantly has itself blossomed out.

The 1940 affair was only in its first stages of preparation when this was written, but read like a stroll through wonderland.

Seven days were given over to the last festival, which included not only the inevitable parade of spectacular floats, but the selection of a pretty maiden as Miss Orange Bowl, the converging of innumerable bands from all sections of the State, window-display contests, concerts, carnivals, street dancing, aerial maneuvers, horse racing, and a variety of other attractions.

Incidentally, we mentioned at one juncture how the racing officials at Tropical Park, eager to assist the Orange Bowl venture even if at a sacrifice to themselves, scheduled their program for the morning of the game. So what happened? Why, instead of being recipient of a financial licking it had prepared itself to take, the racing people were figuratively stormed by one of the greatest crowds in the history of Tropical Park.

Here's a brief résumé of the games played at Miami during the development of the Orange Bowl:

In 1933, as mentioned previously, Manhattan College traveled South to play Miami University and much to the amazement of all and sundry the local lads beat the well-regarded Northerners, 7-0. Actually, amazement was not registered very audibly, for less than four thousand people watched the game; a tremendous disappointment. The next year, the local university made an incredible showing, and against teams of unquestionable strength, they piled up an undefeated record. Naturally they again moved in as one of the competing forces on New Year's Day, 1934. They played Duquesne University of Pittsburgh and lost, because Duquesne had a powerful team, one of the best in the North.

Duquesne, by the way, was coached by Elmer Layden, who since has moved to his alma mater at Notre Dame and been eminently successful.

Miami appeared for the third time in 1935, the first game under the "Orange Bowl" standard. This time they lost to Bucknell, and the next year marked the gradual upward trend of the bowl away from a national angle. Miami was a small university, and while it produced, off and on, excellent teams in its own class, it was not a nationally prominent football force. So in 1936 the committee invited Catholic University of Washington, D. C., coached by Dutch Bergman of Notre Dame fame, and the Rebels of University of Mississippi. These two powers put on a devastating brand of offensive football which attracted national attention to the Orange Bowl, and in a game replete with long and dazzling runs, the Bergman eleven won out, 20-10.

It is unlikely any back yet to appear at Miami in a New Year's Day game ever thrilled the crowd as did Ray Mapes, a marvelous Mississippi back. Catholic University produced a big lead at the outset, but Mapes gave them chill after chill in the closing moments of the game as he desperately sought to catch them.

The contending units in 1937 were Mississippi State University, coached by Major Ralph Sasse, formerly of West Point, and again Duquesne, first Northern team to reappear in the bowl.

Duquesne was still a power back home. It had engineered the stunning upset of mighty Pittsburgh, its town rival, and it beat the Mississippians, 13-12, through the agency of the longest pass play in the history of any bowl contest. It was a seventy-yard throw by Carl Brumbach, a truly great football player, and was contributed at the very end of the rugged game. Another astounding feature of the game was the tackle play of Buster Kinnard, Mississippi.

The 1938 game was played between Alabama Polytechnical Institute of Auburn, or the Auburn Plainsmen, if you will, and Michigan State College of East Lansing.

Michigan State, the first team from its section to appear in a bowl contest in Dixie, was a team skilled in the Notre Dame style of attack, and had in Johnny Pingel an outstanding left halfback, who was perhaps the best kicker in the country that season.

Auburn's dynamic Plainsmen, paced by Fenton and Russell, shut off the Notre Dame attack and registered a 6-0 victory. Nearly twenty thousand people witnessed the game, the first occasion upon which the Orange Bowl intimated its potentialities as an annual fixture. And, of course, the 1939 contest between Tennessee's vigorous Vols and the power-laden giants from Oklahoma, projected the bowl into the national limelight. For the first time, the Orange Bowl committee frightened its promotional rivals. Both of these teams were undefeated and both were ranked among the first five in the nation for the regular season of 1938. Tennessee was generally ranked even with Texas Christian as the national standout, and Oklahoma, a smashing team that had crushed all the opponents on its schedule, was ranked between third and fifth by every commentator of significance.

The Orange Bowl folks really scored high this time. The Rose Bowl game was being played between Southern California, which had been beaten, and Duke University, which hadn't been beaten or scored upon, but had an inferior offensive record. At New Orleans the Sugar Bowl game had Texas Christian as an unbeaten presentation, but Carnegie Tech had lost to Notre Dame, however unluckily. Naturally, the Floridans were elated. For the first time their game was prominently displayed beforehand in the nation's sporting pages. It was the only bowl contest between two major unbeaten and untied teams. It promised to be a thriller and it was. Bone-bending blockings, teeth-chipping tackles, thrilling runs, and flashing forward passes came in rapid succession, and were but a few of the outstanding features of the game in which Tennessee's indomitable running attack was responsible for a stunning 17-0 defeat of a big Oklahoma team that everyone felt could not be held scoreless. But Tennessee's defense achieved that goal and Waddy Young, All-American end from Oklahoma, and a dangerous pass receiver, was unable to snare the ball across the goal.

This game had the further distinction of being the only bowl contest of that year in which three bonafide All-American players demonstrated the various reasons for their almost-unanimous selections. Those players were Young, the big, aggressive Oklahoma end; Bowden Wyatt, end, who played sensationally for Tennessee, and George Cafego, the Tennessee halfback. Cafego has been called by veteran and competent Southern football critics one of the greatest football players ever developed in Dixie. Nearly thirty thousand fans were ready to support that verdict when the final whistle blew on January 1, 1939, in the Orange Bowl at Miami, and the supposedly invincible Sooners of Oklahoma had bowed to the Vols of Tennessee as a new era dawned on the Miami bowl.

One presumes all Florida should share in the prominence which has lately come to the Orange Bowl. The bowl committee itself is headed by Charles F. Baldwin, Van C. Kussrow is the first, A. A. Ungar the second, and Oscar Dooly, Jr., the third vice-president, John G. Thompson the secretary, and H. Blake Oliver the treasurer. Ernest E. Seiler is the business manager. To them and their associates the world of football can throw the pro-

verbial bouquet of orchids, for they tackled a difficult job and saw it through to the finish. They are
still going strong and the Orange Bowl is booming
on the national football market.

Scores of the Orange Bowl Games

1933—Miami University (Florida) 7, Manhattan College (New York) 0

1934—Duquesne University (Pittsburgh) 32,
Miami University (Florida) 7

1935—Bucknell University (Lewisburg, Pennsylvania) 26, Miami University (Florida) 0

1936—Catholic University (Washington, District of Columbia) 20, University of Mississippi (Oxford) 10

1937—Duquesne University (Pittsburgh) 13,
Mississippi State College 12

1938—Alabama Polytechnical Institute (Auburn) 6, Michigan State College (East Lansing) 0

1939—University of Tennessee (Knoxville) 17,
University of Oklahoma (Norman) 0

1940—Georgia Tech (Atlanta) 21, University of
Missouri (Columbia) 7

RECAPITULATION

CHAPTER XIV

THIS volume is the seventh in the series, FA-MOUS AMERICAN ATHLETES OF TODAY. The seven books, taken together, form an athletic Who's Who for those leaders who have been important in the sport world during the past fifteen years. For the information and assistance of the reader there is given below a list of the athletes whose biographical sketches are included in the first six volumes, as well as the general articles on sporting subjects. As other stars appear in the sports firmament, they will be included in future volumes of the series, which will mean that this set of books will serve as a complete reference library for all those whose names have been important to the world of sport.

ADAMS, CHARLES FRANCIS: Ex-Secretary of the Navy and Expert Yachtsman, Second Series.

ALLISON, WILMER: Mighty Marvel of the Tennis Racquet, Fifth Series.

BAER, MAX ADELBERT: Dramatic Pugilist and Heavyweight Champion of the World, Fourth Series.

435

BOROTRA, JEAN: One of the Four Tennis Musketeers, Second Series.

BRADDOCK, JAMES JAY: Who Staged the Most Remarkable Comeback in Pugilism, Fifth Series.

BRUGNON, JACQUES: One of the Four Tennis Musketeers, Second Series.

BUDGE, DONALD: Champion of the Tennis Courts, Fifth Series.

BYRD, RICHARD EVELYN: First Aviator to Circle the North and South Poles, Second Series.

COCHET, HENRI: One of the Four Tennis Musketeers, Second Series.

CUNNINGHAM, GLENN: Master of Miles. Maker and Breaker of World Records, Sixth Series.

DAVIS CUP VICTORY OF 1937: Includes the achievements of Donald Budge in that game, Sixth Series.

DEAN, JEROME HERMAN (DIZZY): The Wizard of the Pitching Box, Fifth Series.

DE MAR, CLARENCE: Victorious Marathon Runner, First Series.

DIDRIKSON, MILDRED BABE: The World's Greatest Girl Athlete, Third Series.

DI MAGGIO, JOSEPH THOMAS: At Twenty-one a Master of Baseball, Fifth Series.

EARHART, AMELIA: First Woman to Fly Across the Atlantic, Second Series.

EDERLE, GERTRUDE ("TRUDY"): Champion Woman Swimmer, First Series.

FOXX, JAMES EMORY: New Sultan of Swat and Rival of Babe Ruth for the Glories of Clout, Fourth Series.

FRANK, CLINTON (CLINT): All-American Football Star, Fifth Series.

GEHRIG, HENRY LOUIS ("LOU"): "Larruping Lou"—Manufacturer of Home-runs, Third Series.

GEHRINGER, CHARLES LEONARD: Baseball's Mechanical Man, Sixth Series.

GOODMAN, JOHNNY: The Omaha Insurance Broker Who Surprised the Golfing World, Fourth Series.

GOWDY, HENRY M. ("HANK"): Sterling Catcher and First Professional Ball Player to Enlist in the Great World War, First Series.

GREEK GAMES: The Beginning of Organized Sport, and a Comparison with Our Own Athletics, First Series.

HARTNETT, CHARLES LEO (GABBY): One of the Greatest Catchers of all Times, Fifth Series.

HAVE A HEART: A Plea for the Preservation of That Vital Organ, First Series.

8 FAMOUS AMERICAN ATHLETES

8 FAMOUS AMERICAN ATHLETES

"HEADS UP": Athletics Is Not Everything, Second Series.

HICKS, HELEN: Queen of the Golf Links, Third Series.

HITCHCOCK, THOMAS, JUNIOR: Daring World War Aviator and Able Poloist, First Series.

HUBBELL, CARL OWEN: Wizard of the Diamond and Worthy Successor of the Great Walter Johnson, Fourth Series.

INDOOR RACQUET GAMES: The Story of Lawn and Table Tennis, Squash and Badminton, Sixth Series.

JACOBS, HELEN HULL: Fiery Wielder of a Tennis Racquet and Premier American Player, Fourth Series.

JARRETT, ELEANOR HOLM: Olympic Back-Stroke Champion, Fourth Series.

JOHNSON, WALTER PERRY: The "Big Train," Greatest of All Pitchers, Second Series.

JONES, ROBERT TYRE ("BOBBY"), JUNIOR: Golf Star from Childhood, and Persistent Winner, First Series.

KELLY, LAWRENCE M. (LARRY): All-American Football Star, Fifth Series.

LA COSTE, JEAN-RENE: One of the Four Tennis Musketeers, Second Series.

LINDBERGH, COLONEL CHARLES A. ("LINDY"): The Lone Eagle, First Series.

LITTLE, WILLIAM LAWSON, JUNIOR: The Greatest Athlete of 1935, Fifth Series.

LOUIS, JOSEPH ("JOE"): The Brown Bomber, Sixth Series.

MADISON, HELENE: Record-Holder of Free-style Swimming, Fourth Series.

MARTIN, JOHN L. ("PEPPER"): A World Series Hero, Third Series.

MEADOWS, EARLE, and BILL SEFTON: The Vaulting Twins of Troy, Sixth Series.

MEDWICK, JOSEPH MICHAEL: Winner of National League Honors, Sixth Series.

METCALFE, RALPH: The Black "Flash" from Marquette, Fourth Series.

MILESTONES ON THE ROAD TO CHAM-PIONS, Third Series.

MOODY, HELEN WILLS ("LITTLE POKER FACE"): Former Women's Tennis Cham-pion of the World, First Series.

OUIMET, FRANCIS: The Story of a Remarkable Golfer, Third Series.

OWEN, GEORGE, JUNIOR: Ace of Hockey Players, Second Series.

OWENS, JAMES CLEVELAND (JESSE): The Black Buckeye Bullet, Fifth Series.

SKI JUMPING: Most Spectacular of Sports, Fifth Series.

SMITH, CECIL: The Hard-Riding Texan, Sixth Series.

SONNENBERG, GUS: King of Wrestlers, Second Series.

STEPHENS, HELEN: America's Speed Queen, Fifth Series.

STRIBLING, WILLIAM LAWRENCE ("YOUNG" STRIBLING): Pathetic Figure in Contemporary Pugilism, Fourth Series.

TERRY, "BILL": Able First-Baseman of the New York Giants and Scintillating Manager, Fourth Series.

THORPE, JAMES: Magnificent All-round Athlete, Second Series.

TILDEN, WILLIAM T. ("BILL"), 2ND: Wizard of the Tennis Courts, First Series.

TOLAN, EDDIE: The Black "Flash" from Michigan, Fourth Series.

TOWNS, FORREST G.: Mr. Towns Goes to Town, Sixth Series.

TRUE SPORTSMANSHIP, Third Series.

TUNNEY, JAMES JOSEPH ("GENE"): Ex-Champion Heavyweight Boxer of the World, First Series.

VANDERBILT, HAROLD STIRLING: Internationally Famous Yachtsman, Third Series.

VAN WIE, VIRGINIA: Champion Woman Golfer and Persistent Climber to Athletic Supremacy, Fourth Series.

VARE, GLENNA COLLETT: Ex-Champion Woman Golfer, Second Series.

VINES, HENRY ELLSWORTH, JUNIOR: Ruler of the Grass Courts, Third Series.

WARBURTON, IRVIN: All-American Quarter-Back and Mainstay of the Southern California Football Team, Fourth Series.

WIGHTMAN, HELEN HOTCHKISS: Maker of Champions, Fifth Series.

WILSON, HARRY E. ("LIGHT HORSE HARRY"): Captain of West Point Football Team for 1927 and Brilliant Performer on the Gridiron, First Series.

WOOD, WILLIAM BARRY, JUNIOR: All-American Quarterback, Gentleman and Scholar, Third Series.

WYKOFF, FRANK CLIFFORD: The World's Fastest Sprinter, Third Series.

YORK, RUDOLPH PRESTON ("RUDY"): Challenger of Ruth's Records, Sixth Series.

INDEX